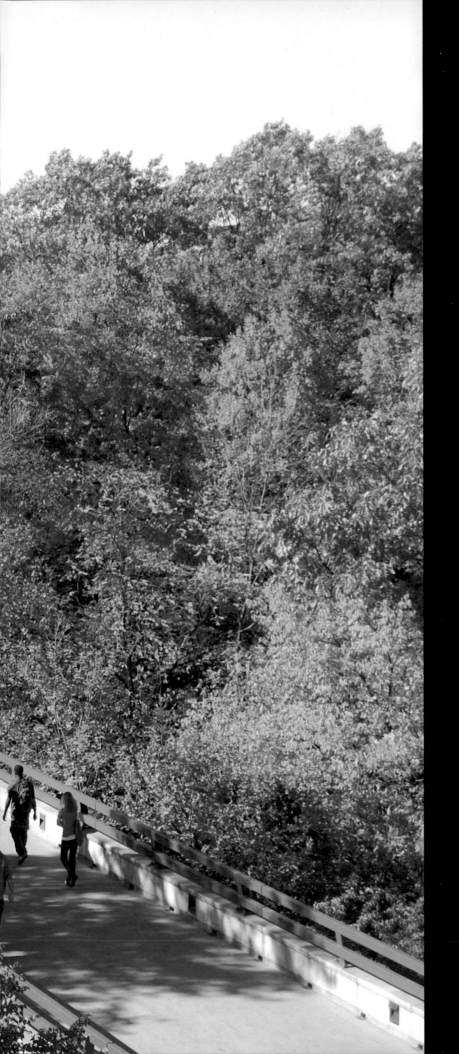

ONONDAGA
COMMUNITY COLLEGE

Celebrates 50 Years
1961-2011

Explore.

Discover.

Transform.

Text is based on the research and writing of Barbara S. Rivette.

Edited By:
Kathleen L. Eisele, D.A.
Timothy D. Stedman
Debbie L. Sydow, Ph.D.

Photo Sources:
OCC Archives, Sidney Coulter Library
OCC Office of Public Affairs
OCC Foundation
Onondaga Historical Association Museum & Research Center
Town of Onondaga Historical Society
The Post-Standard
Institute for Resource Information Sciences, Cornell University
OCC Alumni, Employees, and Retirees

Cover Photo by Skip Frost, Copyright © Syracuse Poster Project, Inc.

Published by Data Key Communications, Inc.
Printed by Quartier Printing

ISBN 978-0-615-57556-8

Table of Contents

1961
Onondaga County
Board of Supervisors
undertakes sponsorship
of a community college
(May 1)

State University of New
York Board of Trustees
approves creation of a
community college for
Onondaga County
(May 12)

Onondaga County
Board of Supervisors
and Governor Nelson
Rockefeller name initial
College Trustees
(July & September)

First Board of Trustees
meeting held; Ransom G.
MacKenzie elected Chair
(September 28)

1967
College Master
Development
Plan for new
campus unveiled
(November 27)

1957
Various
community
groups formally
request
Onondaga
County Board
of Supervisors
to investigate
establishing
a community
college

1964
College graduates first
class at Onondaga
County War Memorial
(June 7)

OCC Alumni Association
established

1957

1964

1968

1958
Onondaga County
Board of Supervisors
appoints
Community College
Study Committee

1962
Francis Almstead
becomes first
College President
(April 1)

First classes begin at
Midtown Plaza with
enrollment of
1,294 students
(September 24)

Evening and extension
classes begin
(October 8)

1966
Permanent campus site
dedicated on former
County Farm
(November 15)

1968
OCCFT recognized
by Onondaga
County as the
bargaining agent
for OCC Faculty
(February 24)

First contract
ratified by the
County Legislature
(August 5)

Construction
begins for new
campus
(October 25)

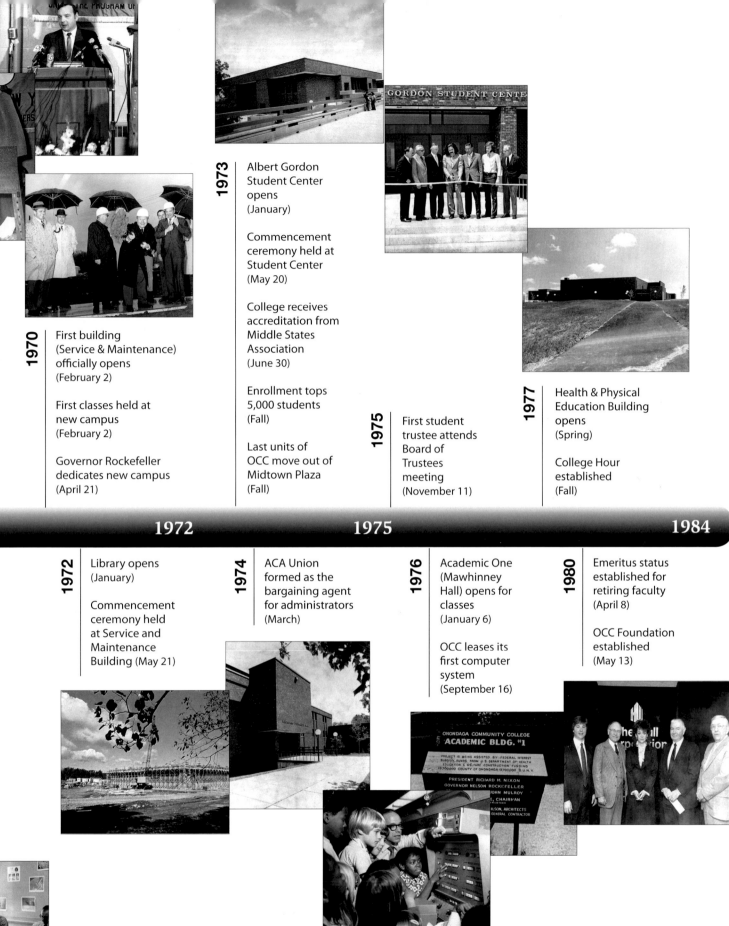

1970
First building
(Service & Maintenance)
officially opens
(February 2)

First classes held at
new campus
(February 2)

Governor Rockefeller
dedicates new campus
(April 21)

1973
Albert Gordon
Student Center
opens
(January)

Commencement
ceremony held at
Student Center
(May 20)

College receives
accreditation from
Middle States
Association
(June 30)

Enrollment tops
5,000 students
(Fall)

Last units of
OCC move out of
Midtown Plaza
(Fall)

1975
First student
trustee attends
Board of
Trustees
meeting
(November 11)

1977
Health & Physical
Education Building
opens
(Spring)

College Hour
established
(Fall)

1972   1975   1984

1972
Library opens
(January)

Commencement
ceremony held
at Service and
Maintenance
Building (May 21)

1974
ACA Union
formed as the
bargaining agent
for administrators
(March)

1976
Academic One
(Mawhinney
Hall) opens for
classes
(January 6)

OCC leases its
first computer
system
(September 16)

1980
Emeritus status
established for
retiring faculty
(April 8)

OCC Foundation
established
(May 13)

7

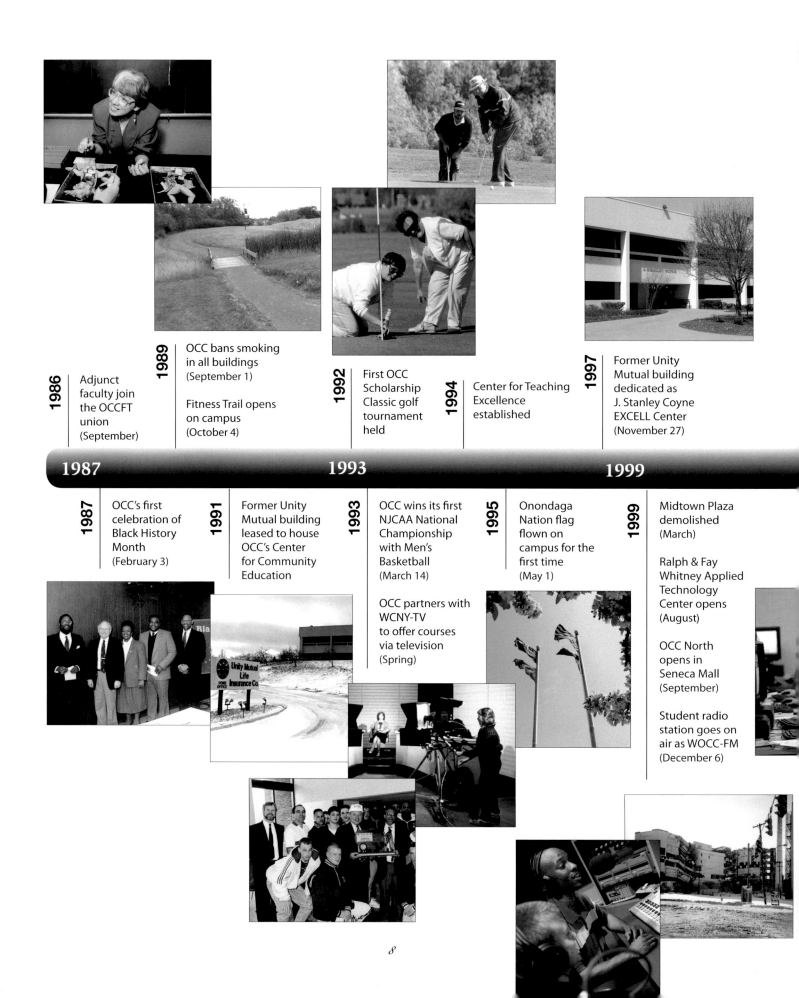

1986 Adjunct faculty join the OCCFT union (September)

1989 OCC bans smoking in all buildings (September 1)

Fitness Trail opens on campus (October 4)

1992 First OCC Scholarship Classic golf tournament held

1994 Center for Teaching Excellence established

1997 Former Unity Mutual building dedicated as J. Stanley Coyne EXCELL Center (November 27)

1987   **1993**   **1999**

1987 OCC's first celebration of Black History Month (February 3)

1991 Former Unity Mutual building leased to house OCC's Center for Community Education

1993 OCC wins its first NJCAA National Championship with Men's Basketball (March 14)

OCC partners with WCNY-TV to offer courses via television (Spring)

1995 Onondaga Nation flag flown on campus for the first time (May 1)

1999 Midtown Plaza demolished (March)

Ralph & Fay Whitney Applied Technology Center opens (August)

OCC North opens in Seneca Mall (September)

Student radio station goes on air as WOCC-FM (December 6)

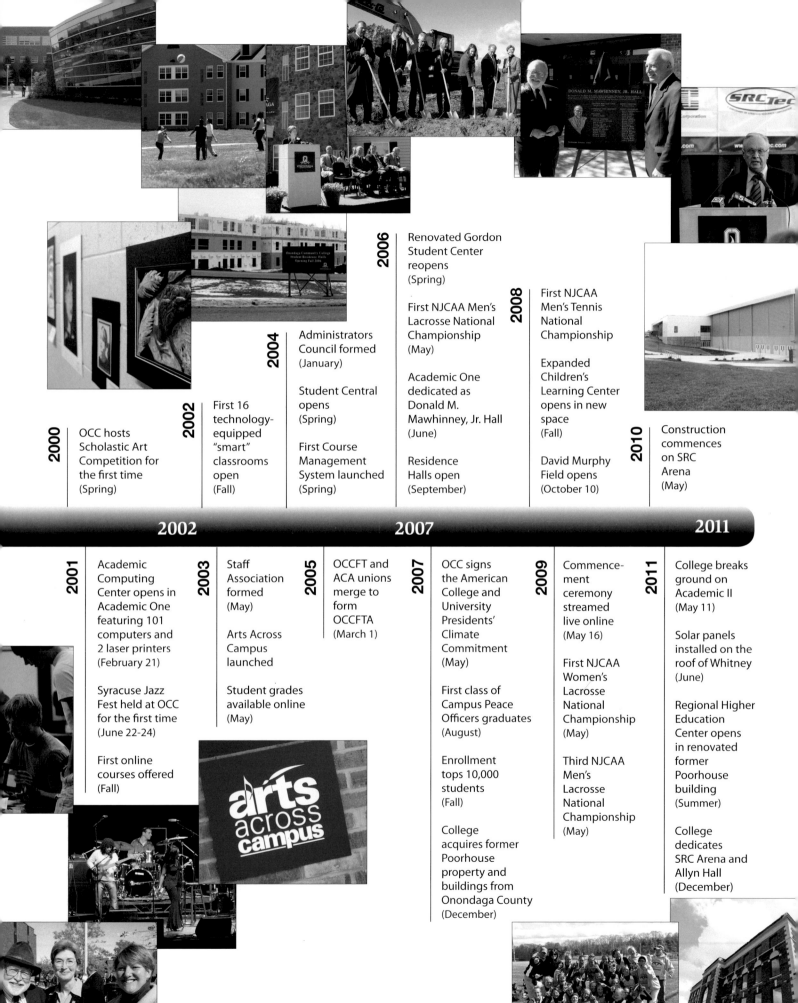

2000 — OCC hosts Scholastic Art Competition for the first time (Spring)

2002 — First 16 technology-equipped "smart" classrooms open (Fall)

2004
- Administrators Council formed (January)
- Student Central opens (Spring)
- First Course Management System launched (Spring)

2006
- Renovated Gordon Student Center reopens (Spring)
- First NJCAA Men's Lacrosse National Championship (May)
- Academic One dedicated as Donald M. Mawhinney, Jr. Hall (June)
- Residence Halls open (September)

2008
- First NJCAA Men's Tennis National Championship
- Expanded Children's Learning Center opens in new space (Fall)
- David Murphy Field opens (October 10)

2010 — Construction commences on SRC Arena (May)

2002   2007   2011

2001
- Academic Computing Center opens in Academic One featuring 101 computers and 2 laser printers (February 21)
- Syracuse Jazz Fest held at OCC for the first time (June 22-24)
- First online courses offered (Fall)

2003
- Staff Association formed (May)
- Arts Across Campus launched
- Student grades available online (May)

2005 — OCCFT and ACA unions merge to form OCCFTA (March 1)

2007
- OCC signs the American College and University Presidents' Climate Commitment (May)
- First class of Campus Peace Officers graduates (August)
- Enrollment tops 10,000 students (Fall)
- College acquires former Poorhouse property and buildings from Onondaga County (December)

2009
- Commencement ceremony streamed live online (May 16)
- First NJCAA Women's Lacrosse National Championship (May)
- Third NJCAA Men's Lacrosse National Championship (May)

2011
- College breaks ground on Academic II (May 11)
- Solar panels installed on the roof of Whitney (June)
- Regional Higher Education Center opens in renovated former Poorhouse building (Summer)
- College dedicates SRC Arena and Allyn Hall (December)

Preface

By Donna J. Gilberti DeSiato, Ed.D.
Class of 1969

As a proud graduate of 1969 and one of the students who attended during the College's first decade, I am honored to write this preface in celebration of the 50-year history of Onondaga Community College.

Onondaga Community College opened its doors 50 years ago, creating a pathway of opportunity, preparation and hope for Central New York's high school graduates. The idea of a college supported by the community with greater accessibility and affordability was ignited in the same year as the Sputnik launch, a time period in which America recognized that education is essential to the success of our country in a global environment. Preparing to write this preface brought back memories of my transition into college and my decision to attend OCC. From the voice of a former student, I would like to share with you what that choice has meant for my life and why I so strongly believe that OCC was the best choice.

I grew up in an Italian-American family during the 1950s and '60s and remember that the importance of education and pursuing life goals were main topics at our family dinner table. The oldest of three siblings, as I prepared to graduate from high school I wasn't sure about what I wanted to do next or what career opportunities to pursue. The thought of going to college was somewhat intimidating and also intriguing. In those days, women were not necessarily encouraged to further their education. However, both of my parents were sure they wanted me to go to college. My father and mother wanted all of their children to have opportunities in life that they had not been able to take advantage of, and college was at the top of their list. I would be the first in my family to take this important step.

As I contemplated my options, my mother encouraged me to consider Onondaga Community College. At that time, OCC was not the campus on the hill as we know it today. In the '60s, OCC occupied two floors of Midtown Plaza in downtown Syracuse, where I attended classes. Yet, what I experienced at OCC was an environment that focused on student success in learning. It wasn't about the building or the fixtures or the furnishings; it was about the people. OCC for me was about faculty members who were committed to facilitating student learning, building on student strengths and providing a foundation and formula for success.

I believe it is quite fitting as we celebrate the golden anniversary of OCC that its original location is now home of the Syracuse Center for Excellence. Excellence has been at the core of OCC since its inception.

Attending OCC enriched my life experiences. I valued the diversity of the students and the broad array of opportunities for student engagement in learning and extracurricular activities. Through those experiences I learned the value of attending a college where faculty members cared about my learning. I was fortunate to experience firsthand the difference that one individual can make in the life of a student. For me, that person was Marjorie (Midge) Mitchell, a very special guidance counselor. Ms. Mitchell helped me to recognize my intellectual capabilities, identify my interests and talents, and realize the importance of organizing my time to achieve my goals. Through her guidance, I set my sights on fulfilling my dreams and ambitions by investing my energy in my education and preparing for my future. I now realize that it was during those early years at OCC that I experienced the motivation that comes from learning to love learning, and from learning that I could succeed at anything I put my mind to by applying what I was learning to my life goals.

After receiving my Associate of Arts Degree in Humanities, I applied and was accepted to the University of Miami in the field of education. My continuing education has led to a fulfilling career as a teacher and educational leader in the Syracuse City School District and, most recently, seven years as Superintendent of the East Syracuse Minoa Central School District.

As I reflect on what OCC means to me in celebrating this moment in its history, I realize that I am truly blessed to be one of many thousands of lives whom this institution has touched throughout the Central New York area. As a matter of fact, my family has been triply blessed because my two younger siblings, who are both successful attorneys, also attended OCC as the

Dr. Donna J. Gilberti DeSiato

launching pad for their future endeavors. Onondaga Community College provided a strong foundation for each of us. At OCC I can truthfully say that I experienced the ability to *explore*, *discover* and *transform*.

In the decades that followed, OCC evolved as it moved to a new campus setting on the hill, expanded its course offerings, added certificate and degree programs, and increased student enrollment. Changes in the world, and our region's transition from an industrial age to an information-technology and innovation age, have guided the development of Onondaga Community College throughout these first five decades. OCC responded to the challenges and changes of the latter half of the 20th century and emerged as a state and national model for community colleges under the leadership of Dr. Debbie Sydow. OCC is a beacon of light perched on Onondaga Hill, recognized by many for outstanding accomplishments, successful alumni and ongoing commitment to the education of the students it serves.

Today, the campus encompasses an array of well-equipped academic buildings, state-of-the-art residence halls, Student Central, Coulter Library, excellent dining services, athletic facilities, a fitness center operated by the YMCA, and the new SRC Arena and Events Center. As Superintendent, I have the privilege of providing the leadership in preparing thousands of students for future success in college and career.

Shortly after becoming Superintendent at ESM, I was at our high school one day when one of the seniors came around the corner walking very proudly with a radiating smile that lit up the hallway. The young lady was holding a piece of paper in her right hand while raising and waving her right arm above her head. I approached her and said, "That must be something very special in your hand by the look on your face." Without hesitation she turned to me with the most enthusiastic expression as she proudly announced, "Yes, it's a letter from Dr. Sydow telling me that I've been accepted to OCC!" She then exclaimed, "I'll be the first female in my family going to college," her face beaming with pride! This moment touched my heart, ignited wonderful memories and signified to me that OCC continues to be the place of hope for a promising future.

The founding Board of Trustees for Onondaga Community College served as pioneers of a new frontier. They charted a course that guided the development of OCC and its pathway to great heights in national and international recognition for student success, faculty engagement and tremendous leadership as one of our country's premier community colleges. Most recently, I have been given the honor to serve as one of the ten-member Board of Trustees for Onondaga Community College, preserving its enduring principles while providing leadership and support in addressing the challenges and the opportunities of the 21st century.

As we celebrate the half-century point of the institution that catapulted the education and careers of many of us who call Onondaga Community College our alma mater, let's take a moment to reflect on the history of challenge, change, transformation and success of these first 50 years, and with unified commitment and determination, embrace the promise of its future.

O.C.C. Press

VOL. I, NO. 1   SYRACUSE, NEW YORK   NOVEMBER 6

NEW COLLEGE IN ONONDAGA COUNTY

Onondaga Community College opened its doors at Midtown Plaza, Sept. 24. The college is the first of its kind for Onondaga County.

In 1960, plans for the college were accepted and approved by the Onondaga County Board of Supervisors and the Board of Trustees in Albany. Five trustees were to be appointed by the Board of Supervisors and four by the Governor. The following year Francis E. Almstead was named as President and shortly thereafter the present location was picked.

A survey of students and parents throughout the community was taken to determine the need for such a college. Questions were asked regarding what courses would be of most interest and how many students would attend. Response indicated that a two-year college with technical and liberal arts couses would fill the need.

The need for a community college was first felt in 1945 so this is not a new idea. Little actual work was forthcoming, however, until 1959, when the Onondaga County Research and Development Group gave a cost report to John H. Mulroy, chairman of the Board of Supervisors. From then on work went quickly.

The thought and research invol-

'PRESS' TO PUBLISH

The presses rolled Tuesday morning to produce the first newspaper for the first community college of Onondaga County.

Thirty-eight students held organization meetings of the OCC Press last week.

The newspaper will be published on the first and fifteenth of each month. Temporary staff positions for the first issue are; Richard Hendrickson: editor in chief; Phil Noyes, administrative assistant; Lise Frostad, editor; Ronald Schweikert, Production Manager.

The office is located in the southeast cornor of the building housing the college, Midtown Plaza, 700 East Water Street.

Plans are in the making for a school journalism club in connection with the newspaper.

DANCE SET

"Autumn Nocturne", the first social event for students of the new Onondaga Community College, is set for Nov. 7 at the Jefferson Street Armory.

College students will dance to the music of the Tommy Dorsey orchestra directed by Sam Donahue,

Prelude
1957-1962

Who could have imagined 50 years ago that empty farmland atop Onondaga Hill would become a thriving college campus, one of the largest in the SUNY system, serving nearly 12,000 students? On its 50th Anniversary (1961-2011), today's Onondaga Community College (OCC) is an unmistakable Central New York landmark centered in the heart of the County. With 15 buildings situated on 280 acres overlooking Syracuse, the expansive, meticulously maintained campus of today is a far cry from the College's first days in a former factory building in downtown Syracuse. As part of the maturation process, there were growing pains in the early years of Onondaga's development, but throughout its history the College has been steadfast in its dedication to academic excellence and student success.

MAKING A NEW IDEA A REALITY

The whole concept of a public community college was new in 1961. No one could foresee exactly what was ahead, certainly not Onondaga County's Board of Supervisors, the sponsoring governmental unit. Those supervisors from all over the County were struggling with new ideas, new responsibilities and, most of all, new costs for the taxpayers. No one was quite sure how a community college would fit into the existing educational system.

For over 150 years, local elected officials had been dealing with concrete issues: maintaining law and order, building better roads and providing limited social services. Spending local tax dollars to support a two-year college was a totally new prospect for County government. The Board of Supervisors was composed of the Town Supervisors, the chief elected officials from each of the 19 towns in Onondaga County, and the Ward Supervisors, the elected representatives from each of the 19 wards in the City of Syracuse. The Board approved all County spending, supported at the time primarily by a tax on real property with very limited state assistance. A 1965 publication, *Decisions in Syracuse* by Roscoe C. Martin, characterized Onondaga County government as "cautious" in dealing with its responsibilities.

However, the city's Research Bureau had compiled several reports about the new two-year post-secondary educational trend. As early as 1946, the local Manufacturers Association stressed the need for improved technical education, and in 1953, the North Syracuse School District met with County officials to discuss the idea of a two-year community college. In 1957, after months of meetings and discussions among the Manufacturers Association, local school districts, Syracuse University and Le Moyne College leaders, the Board of Supervisors was formally asked to study the creation of a two-year community college. The City of Syracuse and its Board of Education asked to participate in planning, emphasizing the need for technical education. The County's School Boards Association wanted action as soon as possible.

On March 3, 1958, Chair of the Board of Supervisors Gerald Ladd appointed 16th Ward Supervisor Donald H. Miller to lead a Special Community College Study Committee. Chairman Ladd also appointed Tully Supervisor Fay L. Cummings, along with Onondaga Supervisor George Savage, 15th Ward Supervisor Ephraim E. Shapero and Marcellus Supervisor John H. Mulroy, who later headed the Study Committee.

RANSOM G. MACKENZIE

Ransom G. MacKenzie was one of four individuals appointed by New York State Governor Nelson Rockefeller as a founding trustee of Onondaga Community College. When trustees convened for the first time in September 1961, they immediately elected him Chair, a post he held for the next 12 years. He continued to serve as a trustee until 1977 for a total of 16 years and then became the Chair of the committee to create the OCC Foundation.

Mr. MacKenzie graduated from Syracuse University in 1929 and started work at Syracuse Trust Company, a forerunner of the Marine Midland Bank (now HSBC). There, he was a business development officer, senior trust officer and then CEO. He also served on many community boards, as well as on the boards of several local business corporations.

In recognition of his work for OCC, the perimeter road on the main campus was named in his honor in 1978. After his death in 1982, his widow gave an electric organ to the Music Department; in 1983 a rehearsal and performance room in the Gordon Student Center was given and dedicated in his memory.

NATIONAL AND STATE TRENDS

When the concept was developed at the University of Chicago in the early 1900s, the two-year community college was viewed as preparation for completing a four-year (baccalaureate) program. However, when Joliet Junior College (Illinois) opened in 1901 as the first recognized public community college, it was for a general education with no further degree anticipated. California led in the development nationally, advocating both general and vocational education beyond high school and setting up independent junior college districts beginning in 1912. The 1920s and 1930s saw many technical and commercial schools becoming two-year or junior colleges. A Carnegie Foundation report on education emphasized the basic need for general knowledge, and the nation's broader adult education movement gained strength between the World Wars.

However, in New York State, no substantive change in education could be advanced without the approval of the state's Board of Regents, the nation's oldest, continuous state educational policymaker (established by the New York State Legislature on May 1, 1784). The Regents maintained its support of the state's private two-year colleges already in operation and opposed the establishment of two-year public colleges.

When federal funds for two-year advanced education became available in 1934 from the Federal Emergency Relief Administration (FERA), approximately 30 junior colleges started across the country as extensions of public high schools. The end of these federal funds, plus the fear of federal intrusion into education policy, closed all of these colleges by 1936. During these Depression years, the age of work force entry shifted from 16, 17 and 18 to the 18, 19 and 20-year-old age group. Without money to go on to college and without job prospects, many high school seniors remained in their own high schools to take post-graduate classes.

In 1946, the New York State Legislature established, on a five-year experimental basis, five Institutes of Applied Arts and Sciences, featuring two-year programs of technical training (Brooklyn, Buffalo, Binghamton, Utica and White Plains). The Regents were also facing considerable pressure to set up an overall state university system as every other state had done. In 1948, the State University of New York (SUNY) system was established; the agreement included provisions to convert the five state technical institutes into locally sponsored public community colleges with more to follow.

In 1950, two community colleges were created under the 1948 SUNY legislation: Orange County Community College in Middletown sponsored by the Board of Supervisors and Jamestown Community College sponsored by the City of Jamestown. Nearby, Auburn (City) Community College, which evolved into Cayuga (County) Community College, began in 1953. That same year, New York City Community College (Brooklyn), Broome (Binghamton), Erie (Williamsville), Mohawk Valley (Utica) and Westchester (White Plains, later Valhalla) were all converted from technical institutes into community colleges. A rapid increase in the number of high school graduates, plus action by the State Legislature in 1957 to allow liberal arts programs in community colleges, accelerated the trend. In 1957, the state had 18 community colleges; by 1962, there were 31.

There were several nearby examples of two-year, post-high school educational institutions. Morrisville Technical Institute in Madison County was a state-affiliated institution with a vocational and agricultural slant. Founded by Methodists in 1824 as a co-ed seminary, Cazenovia College drew enrollment from Onondaga County and was chartered by the state in 1934 as a two-year college.

By 1960, two-year public colleges were the fastest growing segment of higher education in the nation, with a total of 405 institutions, compared to 250 in 1940.

IN ONONDAGA COUNTY

At the outset, Onondaga County officials emphasized that the county-operated community college would not compete with the privately operated one- and two-year, for-profit business schools that had a long tradition in Syracuse of providing clerical and accounting training. Also, careful discussions with leaders of Syracuse University and Le Moyne College had two goals: to make sure everyone understood that the County would not try to compete with the larger institutions and, in the long term, to pave the way for full acceptance of local community college credits so that OCC graduates could pass seamlessly into third and fourth year studies. The endorsement by Chancellor William P. Tolley, then in his eighteenth year at SU and a well-respected education leader, was especially important.

The final decision about starting a community college fell to men whose formal academic experiences were long past. After a favorable recommendation from John H. Mulroy of Marcellus, Chair of the County's Special Community College Study Committee, the full Board of Supervisors voted unanimously on May 1, 1961, to create Onondaga Community College. Technically, the resolution asked permission from the State University of New York to sponsor a community college.

When he became Chair of the Board of Supervisors in June 1961 and then became the first County Executive six months later, Mr. Mulroy carried with him the community college dream that he had nurtured so carefully since the idea's first inception during the late 1950s. Obtaining approval to launch the community college from the Board of Supervisors was a shrewd tactical strategy on Mr. Mulroy's part. Looking back, fellow supervisors believed the new idea would have faced much more resistance later when the form of County government was converted in 1968 from the Board of Supervisors to a County Legisla-

ture, which gave less voting power to individual towns.

It was an era when the County's issues received detailed coverage in the two local daily and two Sunday newspapers, whose response to the community college concept ranged from lukewarm to outright hostile. In addition to often abrasive headlines, there were the riptides and cross currents of party politics that always face elected officials.

The early OCC administrative staff was quickly filled from the County's Board of Supervisors' staff, the County Research and Planning agencies and other County offices. They were mostly men, used to dealing with other men in County offices and used to dealing with bureaucracy. All salaries, work rules, individual expenses and even magazine subscriptions were voted on item by item. Most County officials clearly believed that OCC was an arm of County government and should be operated—and should behave—accordingly. That viewpoint, so contrary to the academic ideal of shared governance, likely contributed to many of the ensuing conflicts with the faculty.

THE FIRST BOARD OF TRUSTEES

MEMBERSHIP

By New York State Education Department regulations, governance of the community college would rest with a nine-member Board of Trustees: four appointed by the Governor and five by the local sponsor, in this case Onondaga County. Trustees served without pay. Terms of the initial Board members ranged from one to nine years to establish continuity, until staggered full nine-year terms were established.

The County appointments were made in July 1961. Two were lawyers: Sidney B. Coulter and Donald M. Mawhinney, Jr., who was also a member of the Board of Supervisors. Other County appointees were the Rev. Dr. Alexander Carmichel, Jr., long-time pastor of DeWitt Community Church, and Albert Gordon, President of Penfield Manufacturing Co., Founding President of the Hiawatha Boy Scout Council, Manlius Town Justice and Manlius Town Republican Chair. The only woman on the Board was appointed also by the County. Carolyn Hopkins, always referred to in the style of the day as Mrs. Peter A. Hopkins, was a founder and first Board President of the Syracuse Symphony, similarly just getting underway.

FIRST OFFICIAL SEAL 1961-1969

This first College seal was designed by Edward S. Jay, an inaugural member of the OCC English faculty, and accepted by the Board of Trustees in July 1961. Prof. Jay had been a teacher at local public and private schools until he joined the OCC English Department faculty. He was a graduate of the University of Alabama and the Syracuse University College of Law. The seal includes an outer circle (Onondaga County); a central Long House with five spokes (the Onondaga Nation as one of the original five nations of the Iroquois Confederacy); a peace pipe and wampum (the price paid by the Onondagas to make the Confederacy a reality); fire (the sacred fire of the Iroquois Confederacy); a space satellite (the scientific era); a graduation cap, diploma and slide rule (academic achievement); and a salt vat (Syracuse's historic industry). Prof. Jay died August 18, 1962, barely a month prior to the commencement of the first OCC classes. His wife, Gertrude Jay (Eiler), served as the first OCC Registrar until 1964.

Appointments were made by Governor Nelson A. Rockefeller and included Tracy H. Ferguson, an attorney; Nicholas Ferrante, Executive Secretary of the Greater Syracuse Labor Council, AFL-CIO; Ransom G. MacKenzie, CEO and Executive Vice President of Marine Midland Trust Co.; and Allen W. Sherman, a lawyer and the Vice President for Personnel of Carrier Corporation.

These nine people were all known to each other, and most had worked together previously as volunteers on other civic projects. The trustees also had links to local colleges. Mr. Ferrante was President of Le Moyne College's Industrial Relations Council. Mr. Gordon was on the Advisory Board of the Youth Development Project of Syracuse University. In addition, they had state and national connections. The Rev. Dr. Carmichel was a member of the State Committee on Probation and the Governor's Committee on Children and Youth. Mr. Gordon was the New York State representative to the 1960 White House Conference on Children and Youth. Mrs. Hopkins, a professional harpist, was Chair of the State Performing Arts Association and a local golf champion. Mr. Mawhinney was a former State Assembly staff member and a member of the Onondaga County Board of Supervisors.

Advertisement published May 9, 1962, in the *Syracuse Post-Standard*. (Courtesy of *The Post-Standard*)

FIRST MEETINGS

The first Board of Trustees faced uncharted territory. Yes, they were aware of a few other government-sponsored two-year community colleges, but whatever educational ideas might be favored had to be tempered by the fact that even though they were overseers of the College, the trustees simply did not have control of the money. The Onondaga County Board of Supervisors, which held the purse strings, were fierce guardians of the dollars, constantly aware of the resistance from taxpayers. The state, although lending moral support for the community college idea, would only supply one-third of the operational costs (revised to 40 percent in 1970). Another third would come from the County, and the remaining third from tuition and other college income.

The trustees met for the first time on September 28, 1961, and discussed what was ahead. Their first action was to elect Ransom MacKenzie as Chair and ask the Board of Supervisors to share one of its staff assistants. They identified the criteria for choosing a college president, a dean and a finance officer and agreed to aim at opening for classes in the fall of 1962. They needed to find a location for the classrooms and staff offices, to negotiate with the Onondaga County Board of Supervisors for money and to find faculty members.

There was even some confusion about the College name. The County name is permanent recognition of the first residents, members of the Onondáge'gah (Onondaga) Nation of the Haudenosaunee (Iroquois) Confederacy, whose villages, which moved from time to time, were located primarily in the County's southern hills with seasonal fishing camps on the rivers and lakes. Should the college be Community College of Onondaga County? Onondaga County Community College? Or could it be just Onondaga Community College?

The serious decision about whether the new community college would be for liberal arts or technical education or both was left for another day. Several potential locations for classes were discussed. In addition, there was the looming question about a permanent location for OCC.

These challenges were an ambitious agenda for Board members, especially when they reminded each other that no money would be available until the County's next fiscal year started on January 1, 1962. Nonetheless, they agreed to try to meet every two weeks. The meetings usually started at 4 p.m., to avoid interfering with the regular workday, and continued for at least an hour and a half. Meetings were often held at the County's new office building at 600 State Street, or, in the case of a lunch-time meeting, at the University Club overlooking Fayette Park. E. Norbert Zahm, Jr. became the first official staff member when the supervisors loaned him on a part-time basis to assist in the new venture. He was Research Assistant in the County Office of Research & Development; for the College he served as Financial Secretary (1962-1964). In November, the trustees hired Seymour Eskow, Dean of Mohawk Valley Technical College, to be a consultant on admissions policies.

INITIAL DECISIONS

Exactly where the classes would be held was under intense scrutiny. Committee members, along with John Mulroy, who had become Chair of the Board of Supervisors, visited 16 locations and reported that none were completely suitable either because of location, physical facilities or cost. One of the State Fair buildings was considered, but the entire OCC operation, including all the furniture, would have to be moved to completely empty the space for two weeks at the end of each summer. Syracuse's former Central High School, then operating as a technical school, was not affordable. Other locations given consideration included the upper floors of the Onondaga Hotel on the corner of Warren and Jefferson Streets (the bar on the main floor was objectionable); the Delavan Building on West Fayette Street (needed too much renovation); and Syracuse University's downtown University College at Fayette and McBride Streets (too expensive). Several Syracuse grade school buildings were also surveyed, as well as the land and buildings at the former Syracuse Municipal Airport at Amboy in the Town of Camillus.

One of the buildings discussed was the Midtown Plaza building owned by Anthony Bersani and Bruno Low at 700 East Water Street.

No less important than the location was the choice of a president to guide the new College. In the context of the early 1960s, trustees assumed it would be a man. Francis E. Almstead, a consultant on educational television for the State University at Albany, was hired for start-up advice. By February, the Board had interviewed two candidates for President. On February 7, 1962, the Board decided to offer the position to Mr. Almstead. He possessed experience with community colleges from his background with the State Education Department.

The first *College Catalog* (1964-1966) replaced brochures that the College previously prepared detailing the programs of study. From the Board of Trustees' minutes of March 9, 1962, "Mr. Almstead presented a rough draft of a folding brochure he would like to have printed. Two thousand could be available for $300. It would contain a list of courses and present facts concerning the College. Mr. Almstead reminded [the Trustees] that all courses must be approved by the State University before presentation to the public." By April 9, he also had prepared an application folder describing the new College to send to all of the County's high school seniors. Following his advice, trustees agreed to schedule registration on September 19 with classes starting the week of September 24, 1962.

The work now turned to determining the type of education the College would offer. Should OCC provide a technical education, leaving the more academic fields to Syracuse University and Le Moyne College? Should OCC have both technical training and a general education program? Any decision needed the approval of the State Education Department in Albany. In the end, the trustees reasoned that if Albany approved a wide range of courses, then the actual choice of classroom offerings could

be decided later. The Board sent both the liberal arts and technical curricula to Albany. Thus, the new College received official state permission to offer major programs in Mechanical Technology, Electrical Technology, Dental Hygiene, Liberal Arts & Sciences: Humanities & Social Sciences, and Liberal Arts & Sciences: Mathematics & Science.

Beginning with their first meeting, the Board considered buildings that might be used temporarily for classrooms. Now a decision was needed. In April 1962, trustees unanimously agreed to lease parts of the second and third floors in Midtown Plaza, the former Smith Corona typewriter factory close to Syracuse's downtown. This large brick building had eight floors, plus a basement level, and was being renovated for offices. One important factor was that more space could be made available to accommodate growth. In addition to the office and classroom space, the lease included parking spaces, heat and lights. The availability of a cafeteria was one of the factors that finally led to the selection of Midtown Plaza. By April 26, a skeleton College staff was moving into the building. Even as renovations proceeded all around them, they processed applications for the initial class.

PREPARING TO OPEN

By June, trustees were hiring faculty and staff. Each individual hired was considered and approved by the Board of Trustees. To help gain community acceptance for OCC programs, advisory committees of professionals were established for the Dental Hygiene, Electrical Technology and Mechanical Technology programs. This practice set the pattern for establishing advisory panels to guide the curricula of the technical programs as new majors were added.

On July 25, trustees approved plans for an entering class of 450 students.

The trustees recognized that living at home might not be possible for everyone, but they firmly resisted any thought of providing residential space. An unofficial dormitory was reserved for ten young women at the Mizpah Hotel, a women's residence at the corner of Montgomery Street and Jefferson Street in downtown Syracuse in the same building as the First Baptist Church sanctuary.

Prior to holding a single class or hiring a full staff, trustees were obligated to decide on a budget for the coming academic year (1962-1963) so that it could be reviewed and approved by the Board of Supervisors. The timing was essential to include funds for OCC in the full County budget, which was used to create the January tax bills sent to property owners. The lack of any financial history for the College made the immediate task all the more difficult.

The final September days before classes were to begin became a "do-it-yourself" frenzy. Faculty members rounded up furniture and used their own trucks and muscles to bring desks and chairs in from various County storerooms. Shelves for the library were bought at the Salvation Army store, and faculty hammered nails to build more. The Library was all in one room with the stacks "very close, maybe 20 inches apart," remembered Prof. Dan Rizzo, Librarian. Directions to classrooms and offices were taped on the floor to help everyone with way-finding during these first momentous days.

MIDTOWN PLAZA

The first home of Onondaga Community College was Midtown Plaza, a downtown Syracuse office building which was once the home of L.C. Smith & Bros. Typewriter Company. The company and its original factory dated back to 1903. In 1910, the company undertook a major expansion of its facilities. The structures that would later become Midtown Plaza were sited on the city block defined by East Water Street to the north, East Washington Street to the south, Almond Street to the west and Lemon Street (Forman Avenue) to the east. The architect who oversaw the factory expansion was Carl W. Clark, Sr., father of Robert T. Clark (lead architect for the construction of the College's Onondaga Hill campus).

In 1926, L.C. Smith & Bros. merged with the Corona Typewriter Company of Groton, New York, to form Smith Corona. During World War II, Smith Corona temporarily suspended typewriter manufacturing to produce rifles and other small arms for the U.S. armed forces. The company left Syracuse in 1960 for a new facility located just outside of Cortland, New York.

The following year, developers Anthony Bersani and Bruno Low acquired the property and announced their plans to create a commercial center with space for offices, retail and light manufacturing. While the smaller buildings of the fomer Smith Corona complex were demolished, the eight-story buildings were retained, forming a U-shaped plaza. The entire red brick exterior was refaced with permaglaze cement.

The OCC Board of Trustees selected the Midtown Plaza as the first campus site in April 1962. Initially, OCC occupied only parts of two floors of Midtown Plaza, while the rest of the building was filled with other tenants, which was a cross-section of commercial and business life in the 1960s. A beauty parlor and barber shop, absolutely separate in those days, were permanent fixtures in the basement, along with a dry cleaner and Bill Allen, a commercial photographer. The lobby contained a newsstand and a ticket office for the New York Central Railroad, as well as a cafeteria. Real estate and insurance firms, lawyers, accountants, architects, engineers,

L.C. Smith & Corona Typewriters, circa 1937. After Smith Corona left Syracuse, this building became the central portion of Midtown Plaza. (Courtesy of *Onondaga Historical Association Museum & Research Center*)

Advertisement for Midtown Plaza from the January 7, 1962, Post-Standard. (Courtesy of *The Post-Standard*)

doctors and dentists—even the Pinkerton Detective Agency and a gift shop—were on other floors. The American Red Cross, American Heart Association and other health-related groups had offices at Midtown. Offices on two floors were occupied by the federal Department of Agriculture with its soil and dairy testing divisions. The State and County veterans agencies, the County's Board of Elections and the Syracuse Press Club were also neighbors. A fountain and a landscaped driveway marked Midtown Plaza's entrance on East Water Street, but most students found the doors directly on East Washington Street more convenient.

Classrooms were stark factory floors with huge pillars at inconvenient locations. Each classroom had students hidden behind the pillars, especially in the classes of 40 or 50. Some rooms still had opaque industrial windows. The physical equipment was reminiscent of high school—blackboards, fluorescent lights, uncomfortable chairs and desks, but that was no different from the equipment in any other college of those days. Slides, filmstrips and movies were the visual aids, and the large factory windows were covered with cardboard when darkness was needed. Heavy printed textbooks, pencils and notebooks were the standard learning tools of the day. Students jostled each other as they moved in the narrow halls, running in the stairways from floor to floor to be on time. Both faculty and students used the stairs as smoking lounges, and the air is remembered as being blue with cigarette smoke. On the plus side were new carpets in some classrooms, new paint and sometimes air conditioning in season. These "luxuries" were under forceful attack by the local daily newspapers.

After the College moved the last of its operations to the Onondaga Hill campus in the fall of 1973, Midtown Plaza began a slow decline, losing its last tenant in 1981. The City of Syracuse finally had the building demolished in March 1999 after it sat vacant for 18 years.

In 2005, Syracuse University began a brownfield remediation project on the site and commenced construction of the Syracuse Center of Excellence in Environmental and Energy Systems, which opened in 2010.

The main entrance to Midtown Plaza, on East Water Street, featured a courtyard and a fountain, circa late 1960s.

In March 1999, Midtown Plaza was demolished by Bianchi Industrial Services.

Midtown Plaza

The Midtown Plaza Years
1962-1973

OCC students loved their College at Midtown Plaza from the beginning and welcomed the new experiences. Many were part-time, some attended day classes, and some were in classes at night. Almost everyone lived at home, and most also held jobs. Determined mothers and fathers stood behind most of the early students. For some families, OCC was viewed as the steppingstone to a four-year degree. For others, OCC satisfied a yearning for some academic or technical training before the younger generation stepped into the family business. For all, the new College was the opportunity of a lifetime. These students, along with the faculty and staff who supported their learning, gave life to those first days.

BOARD OF TRUSTEES

OPENING THE NEW COLLEGE

As classes began on September 24, 1962, amidst the euphoria of launching a brand-new enterprise, trustees were plunged into the give and take of College operations. They initially had authorized acceptance of 450 students and were overwhelmed by the unexpected demand. The first class included 583 full-time and 711 part-time students. Two counselors were needed immediately, one male and one female, to help students. Suddenly there was a need for policies, including guidelines about who should be allowed to speak at OCC events. More classroom space was required. Differences with some of the faculty arose. Board meetings began to take three hours or more as trustees tried to balance the needs of the College against the financial resources allowed by the County. The trustees keenly felt the weight of their responsibilities, and they examined and discussed each aspect of student conduct before granting approval to everything from club activities to official designs for sweatshirts and jackets. The level of detail that was assumed by the trustees is indicated by a resolution that gave the head librarian permission to keep her job after she married the College's Dean of Admissions.

Trustees Gordon and MacKenzie together gave the College its official flag in November 1962.

The all-volunteer, unpaid trustees were setting salaries, evaluating faculty and dealing with labor issues for the educational enterprise, just as the full Board of Supervisors was doing on a county-wide level. Trustees also faced the ever-present attention of the Syracuse newspapers. In the *Herald-Journal*, the evening newspaper, Executive Editor Alexander "Casey" Jones used his front-page signed editorials to critically examine all facets of the new College operation and to constantly remind everyone that OCC was "a public institution" that required great scrutiny. "Education or Country Club" was his steady theme.

The new College opened for the second year with more than 2,500 students (1,079 full-time and 1,443 part-time). Space on two more floors at Midtown Plaza was leased, and more parking was sought as car use increased for both the students and the staff. Students marched in protest about the lack of parking, a difficulty that seemed beyond solution.

The trustees used their local contacts to entice potential employers, as well as business and industrial leaders, to become involved with OCC. The Allied Chemical Corporation of Solvay was enlisted to offer a science award and to give books to the library. The new Community General Hospital agreed to cooperate in clinical training for Nursing students and for Medical Technicians. (In 1964, Community Hospital merged with the 69-year-old Syracuse General Hospital, resulting in Communty General Hospital of Greater Syracuse, and in 2011 merged with SUNY Upstate, becoming Upstate University at Community General.)

Professor Robert Malek instructing his biology class on the College's opening day at Midtown Plaza, September 24, 1962.

Students quickly set about establishing their own traditions, including a freshman beanie and a "Frosh Squash," circa early 1960s.

EARLY CONTROVERSIES

Trustees were plunged into a series of highly publicized controversies that, from their viewpoint, were sometimes as unjustified as they were unexpected.

To the newspaper readers of the day, OCC seemed embedded in controversy. Often trustees and County supervisors could not agree. Trustees and the administration were frequently at odds. The faculty had disputes with County officials, the administration and trustees, sometimes all at once, over different issues. It seemed that every argument was spread out publicly in glaring detail with each side vying for a reporter's ear and the resulting headline. The conflicts came

Students at Midtown reading the student newspaper, *The Blue Banner*, September 26, 1968.

Registration for classes at Midtown, circa early 1960s.

Students studying in the College Library at Midtown.

in the midst of contentious deliberations regarding a permanent location for the College. Trustees shifted from one issue to the other during their lengthy meetings. Also under consideration were hiring policies, personnel policies and the Faculty Association Bylaws. In 1964, a special committee was appointed by the Board with authority to "resolve the faculty problem," a problem that would remain largely unresolved for many years to come. Several times, trustees met twice a day as they tried to deal with OCC issues and maintain their own personal workload.

While these were turbulent times for the trustees, administration and faculty, the students remained intent on their own classes and activities, for the most part oblivious to the surrounding controversies.

> "I'm not sure I would have gone to college without OCC. It truly provided a life-changing experience for me. We had teachers who truly cared about us. Our success in school and in life was a shared goal."
>
> — *Suzanne Speach Rubino (Dental Hygiene, 1965)*

A NEW PRESIDENT

In December 1965, President Francis Almstead submitted his resignation, and trustees immediately chose Dr. Karl D. Larsen, OCC's Dean of Faculty, as Interim President. In June 1966, after interviewing four candidates, the trustees chose Dr. Marvin A. Rapp, Vice President and Executive Dean for five years at Nassau Community College at Mitchell Field on Long Island, to become the College's second President. He was also named Professor of History in recognition of his background in researching and publishing local history books.

President Rapp set about enhancing the public image of OCC and tried to move trustees into a more collegial mode. There were luncheon meetings in his office to familiarize them with "basic questions related to policy, procedure and further considerations relating to college operations," according to the minutes. In addition, a Board Room was set up at Midtown Plaza.

CONTINUING GROWING PAINS

In spite of these efforts, significant challenges remained. There was the unrelenting financial pressure from County officials. The $10.5 million initial estimate outlined for construction of a permanent campus met with fiery opposition and more daily newspaper headlines about "out-of-town country club" luxuries.

Students working on an experiment in a laboratory at Midtown Plaza.

Trustees were also dealing with day-to-day decisions. They approved new degrees developed by faculty members, made tenure decisions and set policies for sabbatical leave. Part of their burden was relieved when labor negotiations were moved from trustees to the County Attorney and County Personnel Chair. At the same time, the faculty began to organize.

OCC's annual budget was climbing each year, which created continuous alarm among County officials. According to Board minutes, the operating budget for 1961-1962 was $198,828; by 1964-1965, it was $943,299 with $78,000 in capital equipment. Nationally, the economy was beginning a long, steady plunge into unemployment, recession and inflation. Throughout the next two years, Dr. Rapp and trustees struggled to improve communications with the County, especially about salaries.

Nationwide student unrest penetrated the OCC Trustees' meetings. In May 1970, Dr. Rapp went to Washington, D.C., to discuss student unrest with New York's two senators, Jacob Javits and Charles A. Goodell. State, national and local officials continued to be disturbed by the strident protests. In June 1970, trustees asked Dr. Rapp to study "procedural con-siderations" related to student protests "during the past month" that focused on civil rights and anti-war rallies dominating the national and local news.

A NEW KIND OF COLLEGE

THE FIRST STUDENTS

Students brought life to the vision of Onondaga Community College. In 1962, the idea of open admissions to college classes was unheard of in Onondaga County, where both Syracuse University and Le Moyne College chose freshmen on the basis of graduation class standing and test scores. Instead, almost all prospective OCC students were accepted, carrying out the open enrollment plan in the New York State Education Law that authorized community colleges.

"A real blessing" is how one of those first students looked at the chance to attend college. OCC was economical and close to home. Questionnaires had been sent to every public and parochial pupil in Onondaga County in January 1962, asking what type of instruction would be desirable. Specifics meant little. The lure of college was plainly sufficient. OCC offered a wide array of subjects with flexible scheduling so that many could attend class and still maintain full- or part-time jobs. Fall 1962 tuition at OCC was $150 a semester for state residents and double that for out-of-state students. This cost was much less than the Syracuse University tuition of $685 a semester and the Le Moyne College tuition of $450 a semester.

The first student officially accepted was a senior from Onondaga Valley Academy, Marie Arlene Marceau, who planned to study Humanities & Social Sciences. She was a trained soprano and classical violin player.

Faculty and students greeted each other with enthusiasm as OCC launched its first semester in September 1962. The ages in the classrooms were mixed. Students 22 and 23 years old were considered "older," and those between ages 30 and 40 were considered "mature learners" who had gone directly into the workforce after high school and now saw the potential of a more for-

Alumni Snapshot

David H. Bench, '64

- A.A.S., Mechanical Technology
- Worked in Telephone Business for Nearly 40 Years
- Founding President of OCC Alumni Association

David H. Bench and the inaugural class at Onondaga Community College built the Midtown Plaza campus from the ground up—literally.

"Our first assignment was to assemble our own desks," Bench shares. "The installers for the company that the College ordered them from were on strike. We walked into the classroom, and everything was in boxes—chairs, too. If we wanted to sit, we had to put it all together."

But desks and chairs wouldn't be the only legacy Bench and his class left. They formed the first Student Senate. The first yearbook. The first class ring. The first student clubs. The first freshman orientation. They even stocked the shelves of the library with its first books.

"We all built this camaraderie with one another, building everything from scratch," he says. "We became part of a family." Bench left a legacy of his own, forming and acting as president of the College's Alumni Association for nearly seven years. And though he's lived in North Carolina for the past two decades, he always talks proudly of the College that changed his life forever.

"Before coming to Onondaga, I was immature. I wasn't goal-oriented," Bench says. "I learned how to buckle down. I learned what it is to be part of a growing process—to be part of a community, a part of something greater. And I am what I am today because of OCC."

Students outside of Midtown Plaza in the late 1960s.

mal education. Some had found classes at a four-year college too overwhelming or else had let social activities consume their time. For those students, OCC was a second chance. Faculty members recall that students were all highly motivated to do well and very respectful of their professors.

The majority of the student body came from three distinct backgrounds: the first generation in the family to go to college, military veterans and older women. A few male students admittedly were taking at least 12 hours of credit to avoid the military draft. The classroom mix was recalled by Prof. Jim Dupree (History), who had three generations in one of his classes: daughter, mother and grandmother.

For both staff and students, getting to Midtown Plaza required careful planning. Many families had no car, or only one used by the main breadwinner. To get to OCC, those living outside downtown Syracuse rode with spouses or neighbors, or used the bus system that went by the East Washington Street door. Students walked the six blocks to the YMCA for their required Physical Education class.

The Allied Chemical Corporation, Solvay Process Division, donated books to the library. (from left) Driver Edward Compton unloaded the truck. Solvay Process Assistant Director of Research Dr. Alan Fallows, Solvay Process Librarian Mrs. Betty Emery and President Francis Almstead are pictured in July 1964.

OCC ALMA MATER

Words and Music by Philip G. Klein

OCC's Alma Mater was written in the spring of 1963 by Prof. Phil Klein (Music) before he was even hired by the College. After applying for a position in the Music Department, Prof. Klein was asked by Prof. Dick Rhodes, then the only member of the Department, to write an alma mater. Figuring that the College would not turn down the person who wrote their alma mater, Prof. Klein proceeded to author a piece with a traditional feel (befitting the early 1960s), writing the text and the music simultaneously, one line at a time, and matching the rhyming of each stanza.

Sing we now a song of praise
that everyone may hear,
A song of our own Alma Mater
to all hearts so dear.

-Refrain

All Hail, our Alma Mater,
most noble sight to see!
We gratefully acknowledge
our faith and trust in thee.

Happy hours at Onondaga
go too quickly by,
But words of truth and golden wisdom
will not ever die.

-Refrain

Though years may come and go
sweet mem'ries ever dwell,
Of friends and days at Onondaga
that we loved so well.

-Refrain

Trustee Donald Mawhinney with Librarian Grace MacDonald.

1965 Sciences Department Faculty. (standing from left) Ory Carbonero, Paul Bertan, Bob Malek. (seated from left) Margaret Tubbert, Carl Oney, Alan

The evening and extension classes started on October 8, 1962. Trustees decreed that these divisions had to be financially self-sustaining, so it was important to generate enough interest to keep these class offerings on the schedule. It was a long day, sometimes ending at 10 p.m. in order to accommodate people with jobs, but the night classes were packed with eager students of all ages. The College's night staff was a small, tight-knit community that worked from 1 p.m. to 9 p.m. Faculty members, staff and students often took coffee and meal breaks together in the cafeteria.

The first Annual Commencement was held on June 7, 1964, with 179 graduates. At 3:30 p.m. on that Sunday afternoon, Onondaga Community College's first graduating class walked across the stage at the Onondaga County War Memorial to receive their diplomas.

THE FIRST FACULTY

Many faculty members were young, some younger than their students. Most of the initial faculty were in the first five years of their teaching careers. Some faculty members had known each other before coming to OCC. A large number were Syracuse University graduates or graduate students. Graduates of the University of Delhi (India), the University of Belgrade (Yugoslavia) and the University of Toronto (Canada) brought an international flavor to the faculty. "We loved to teach" was one memory. Faculty members devoted their full attention to students who brought a wide range of abilities and experiences to each classroom. Because of the open enrollment policy, faculty found themselves providing basic study skills, in addition to providing course content. They were dealing with English as a Second Language when very few in the community knew the phrase. Student memories of these Midtown years almost always include the "great support" offered by faculty. As satisfied students and families shared their success stories, enrollment mounted (2,522 students in fall 1963). About half of the students were from the City of Syracuse.

The person many students saw most, some by choice and some by command, was Mrs. McCarthy—Helen Margaret McCarthy—who handled the phone and the steady stream of students in the third floor Counseling suite during the Midtown years. There, she helped, cajoled and chastised as she deemed appropriate and necessary.

The early students are remembered with fondness by their faculty, who in many cases kept track of their careers. "The car kids," Sam Dell, Steve Aloi and Pete Reynolds, were among the sons of West Genesee Street's automobile row. The Bernardi trio included Harold, Katherine and Roy, who eventually became Mayor of Syracuse and Assistant Secretary of Housing and Urban Development in Washington, D.C. Another Northside trio, the Gilbertis, also met with success: William and Carmel both became attorneys, and their sister, Donna DeSiato, serves as Superintendent of the East Syracuse Minoa School District and, at OCC, as a member of the Board of Trustees.

Prof. Bruce F. Haney (Mathematics) recalled that he came to teach at the College in 1967 because it seemed "more exciting and interesting" than other community colleges he knew. He taught for 37 years, going, as he said, from "slide rules to calculators, cell phones and computers." Haney recalls that despite the lack of space and other amenities, the faculty "put the interest of students and the College above our personal feelings."

Faculty members shared offices, sometimes so small that one had to leave in order to accommodate a guest. The quarters at Midtown were spare and crowded. Windows were an unfulfilled dream. Prof. Dorothy Harth (Modern Languages) remembered her desk among the mops and brooms. But the mops and brooms were handy because faculty shared janitorial responsibilities when needed.

Then there was the issue of babies. In the days when male faculty predominated throughout academia, OCC had a large proportion of female faculty. Those who were starting families suddenly found themselves swept up in the County's rigid administrative policies regarding maternity leave. In fact, some women faculty members admitted that they carefully planned their lives to be

Gammon, Norbert Faltyn, Burke Leon, Bob Weathers, Paul Cassedy.

Music staff, faculty and visitors from the New York State School Music Association. (from left) James Truscello (President of NYSSMA), Sheila Fenn (Department Secretary), Phil Klein (Faculty) Jim Mosher (Faculty) and Dr. Fay Swift (Historian of NYSSMA).

ready to teach every day, since there were no concessions for new mothers. As a result of policies and traditional County government attitudes, arguments ensued, especially in those days when working wives were still viewed with skepticism. Professors Barbara Davis (Modern Languages) and Gloria Battaglia (Counseling) appealed to the Human Rights Commission and eventually sued Onondaga County about its maternity policy. Their efforts won the right for County employees to use sick leave for maternity leave.

CURRICULAR INNOVATIONS

OCC had many firsts through the years. Prof. Jane Donegan began teaching History classes at Midtown Plaza, and soon after moving to the Onondaga Hill campus, she introduced Women's History classes in 1974 that were among the first in the state. She later developed the Women's Studies Concentration (now Minor). OCC already had African-American Studies courses when Prof. Jim Dupree arrived to teach History in 1970. Prof. Dupree had been studying American and East African History at Syracuse University since 1969. He further developed OCC's African-American courses, later including outreach programs at the Southwest Community Center.

The College offered the state's first community college Music Program with Prof. Richard Rhodes, recruited from the Fayetteville-Manlius School District, as the Chair. Some of the faculty, like Prof. Phil Klein, were involved in the local scene, playing in restaurants and on radio shows. Others, like Prof. William Harris, taught both at OCC and Syracuse University while playing with the Syracuse Symphony. With great support from the faculty as the department developed, Music graduates went on with full transfers to the nation's top music schools, such as Eastman School of Music in Rochester, the Juilliard School in New York City, the New England Conservatory of Music in Boston and the Crane School of Music in Potsdam.

The relatively new world of television was part of OCC's growing number of programs. Prof. Kathy Stampalia (Hawkins)

(Radio-Television), known locally for her *Romper Room* and other children's programs on local Channel 9, developed a strong television and radio broadcast program that she was able to connect directly to the local entertainment world.

> "Being able to attend OCC was a great opportunity for many of us. It was very affordable and convenient as we could live at home. Many of my classmates would not have been able to attend college had it not been for OCC. I have wonderful memories of being a part of the first class at OCC. It was small, intimate and everyone knew one another."
>
> – *Karen A. BeVard Tucker*
> *(General Studies, 1962-1964)*

FULFILLING A DREAM

These first years helped many families to fulfill a dream. Students found faculty members always approachable and willing to help them overcome difficulties. "We all were in about the same shape," recalled one of the first students. Everyone got to know everyone else because they were all crammed in together in the compact floors of Midtown Plaza. And almost all were on tight financial budgets. As sophomores, a few women students were hired by the Registrar's Office, first to sort admission applications and class schedules on paper, and later to wrestle with the early IBM punch cards that were OCC's first records management system. Other students helped in the library, and some found work at offices located in other parts of Midtown Plaza or in nearby Salina Street offices.

Even after the College expanded to occupy five floors, the closeness of the Midtown days is remembered with great affection by both employees and students alike. Although there were many other tenants in Midtown Plaza, the student numbers and the college atmosphere overwhelmed any formality.

Students remember the internal television system installed by President Almstead that "never worked"—probably because the concept was ahead of the technology available. To speak with a student or anyone else, one stepped into the hallway and shouted down the corridor toward the other office or classroom—or told someone to tell someone else. Closed circuit radio also was a limited success. Run by students, WSBC was on the air weekdays from 8 a.m. to 4 p.m., broadcasting from a second floor studio. It was characteristic of the "we're all in this together" style that marked the Midtown years.

BEYOND THE CLASSROOM

ESTABLISHING TRADITIONS

Once the College was underway, students quickly sought to establish extracurricular activities similar to those in four-year colleges and universities. They found both assistance and resis-

THE FACULTY ORGANIZES

Faculty Association

The general spirit of unrest throughout the nation was evident early within the OCC faculty, which was without its own traditions, such as those found in older colleges and universities. In the fall of 1963, the Faculty began meeting as a collective body and electing a Chair but without recognition from the Board of Trustees. The first chairs were Professors James Decker 1963 (Philosophy), George Dmohowski 1964 (Mathematics) and Nancy McCarty 1965 (History/Political Science). Committees formed to officially establish a Faculty Association that would embody faculty governance. The Constitution Committee included Professors George Dmohowski, Gary Esolen (English), Phil Klein (Music) and Nancy Mc-Carty. The Bylaws Committee (also known as the Purposes & Communications Committee) included Professors Joe Agonito (History), Gary Esolen, Norma Foody (Reading), Al Gammon (Physical Science), Phil Klein (Music), Bill Krall (Technologies), Carl Oney (Biology) and Janet Reust (Dental Hygiene and Dean of Women). In June 1965, the Faculty approved the Bylaws. Eventually, the Constitution and Bylaws became one document, the Faculty Bylaws.

Turmoil resulted when College President Almstead refused to take the document to the Board of Trustees. Instead, Faculty meetings were taken over by the Administration. Finally, at a meeting of the Faculty convened by President Almstead in November 1965, Prof. Esolen moved "that the Faculty express its willingness to meet with our Chief Administrative Officer at his pleasure at any time…but that we also insist that such meetings are no substitute for an official, elective and authoritative faculty organization, and cannot be construed to provide an adequate Faculty voice in policy making." Seconded by Prof. Agonito, the motion passed unanimously and, along with the minutes, was sent to the trustees.

The next meeting of the Faculty (December 1965) was called by Dr. Karl Larsen, Dean of the Faculty and Interim President, appointed because Dr. Almstead had resigned. Dr. Larsen was accompanied by three Board of Trustees members. Prof. Nancy McCarty conducted the meeting. By spring 1966, Prof. James Decker was elected as the first Faculty Chair acknowledged by the Board. The dispute was resolved nearly three years later (April 1968) when the Board finally approved the Bylaws document and officially establishing the Faculty Association.

Faculty Union

With trustees following the formal County-sanctioned methods of operation, there was great opportunity for dissention with the OCC faculty about working conditions. Under the County's system, each individual faculty member had a separate contract and salary agreement.

Then a new method of dealing with contracts and grievances appeared in September 1967 when the Taylor Law went into effect for public employees in New York State. For the first time, faculty at OCC, already in conflict with the administration and trustees about salary and governance issues, could be recognized as labor union members and use collective bargaining to obtain a contract package. Within three months, faculty had met with an organizer for the American Federation of Teachers (AFT). With the guidance of the organizer, Albert Shanker, who was also the AFT state president, a charter for Local 1845, OCC Federation of Teachers, with 80 members, was approved within two months. The first elected officers reflected the group who had made the first contact with the AFT: President Joe Agonito (History), Vice President William Krall (Technologies), Secretary Lorraine Desruisseaux (English) and Treasurer Dorothy Kelly (English, later Human Services). The union was affiliated with the national American Federation of Labor-Congress of Industrial Organization (AFL-CIO). At OCC, the Union and the Faculty Association were parallel organizations with overlapping membership. Prof. Agonito recalled that the Union focused on working conditions, while the Faculty Association dealt primarily with academic issues.

Even before the charter or election of officers, the Union leaders were embroiled in complex contract negotiations. Because they were unable to reach an agreement, a mediator was called in. The first contract, ratified in May 1968 for a one-year term (1968-1969 academic year), was in place within six months of the first contact with the AFT. OCC became the first Onondaga County agency to operate under the Taylor Law, and the OCC contract was the second in New York State to use collective bargaining to replace individual academic contracts. The contract dealt with a number of contentious issues. A statement of professional rights of faculty and provisions for tenure rights was included along with the pay, benefits and grievance package. As Prof. Agonito recalled, it allowed "faculty participation in academic life and decisions." Other faculty members viewed the grievance procedures as the most essential factor. This first contract also covered counselors and librarians; included individual pay raises of at least $1,000; and set the teaching load at an average of 13 credit hours when 15 was the norm for community colleges.

Because the contract carried no provision for handling grievances that occurred prior to the contract's formal approval, George J. Dmohowski, Professor of Mathematics and in 1966 acting Dean of Faculty, whose dismissal first galvanized the faculty, took his grievance to the American Association of University Professors (AAUP). "George D.," as he was known, had been notified by the trustees a year in advance that he would not be rehired. He moved to Utica College, where he taught until his retirement. Based on an investigation of his grievance, AAUP issued a censure against OCC in 1972, which was not rescinded until 19 years later (see The College Matures).

tance. Soapsuds in the fountain in front of Midtown were a rite of spring, along with jello in the same fountain on several occasions. Doctors and lawyers, fellow tenants at Midtown, called the president's office and County officials to complain about these and other student antics. "Having OCC in the building was an education for the other tenants," recalled Ralph Jones, one of the student leaders.

In the first semester, students voted to sponsor a basketball team, using Student Activity funds. Paul N. Seymour, a former professional basketball player with the Syracuse Nationals, agreed to coach the team for $1 a year. Seventy young men showed up in the Jefferson Street Armory for the early practice sessions, and games drew 150 in the bleachers. Students also began a Guys vs. Gals pick-up football game, played at Meacham Field on Seneca Turnpike in The Valley, a long bus ride south from Midtown Plaza. By November, a male chorus was ready to sing at a trustees' meeting and at the Open House for parents. Informal dances were underway. Before the end of the first semester, plans began for a yearbook, which was a paperback publication, *Onondaga Community College Presents the Plaza Programme*, issued in June 1963.

The first class immediately instituted College traditions: a beanie, an orientation and a beanie-removal ceremony. An aquamarine class ring with the "OCC" emblem was chosen.

By 1964, students assembled a more traditional, hardcover yearbook, the *Chieftain*. Faculty were remembered with individual photographs. Students in the Class of 1964, OCC's first, appeared in formal pictures taken in graduation gowns with white shirts and ties for men, white collars for women. Pages in the first *Chieftain* reflect the times. The Dental Hygiene Capping Ceremony shows the students (all women) in white uniforms, white stockings and white shoes. Club pictures have women in skirts, stockings, blouses and sweaters; while the men are in slacks, shirts and sweaters or blazers. Blue jeans were not visible in the classrooms or even in informal pictures. Long dresses and formal attire were worn at the dances during *Winter Weekend, Spring Weekend with a Sweetheart Queen*, and the *Senior Ball*. Clubs and organizations included in the 1964 yearbook were Senior Senate, Freshman Senate, Basketball, Cheerleading, Wrestling, Golf, the *Chieftain*, *The Blue Banner* (student newspaper), Social Studies Forum, Debate Club, College Choir, OCC Dance Band, Gentlemen of Note (men's choir) and Roscian Players (drama club).

A mimeographed student newspaper produced on an old manual typewriter originally appeared as *The OCC Press*. It grew into four press-printed pages in 1964, still being written on the same beat-up typewriter. Cartoons appeared regularly. The main themes were pleas for more student parking and elimination of the dress code as "outmoded and unenforceable." (The admonition "to dress appropriately" because of the other Midtown tenants was frequently voiced by College officials; the faculty decided that no one wearing shorts could take any final exam.) The student newspaper also fought a continuous battle with student apathy, once producing blank pages to demonstrate the lack of student interest. The paper folded several times, only to rebound, sometimes under a new name. During these years, the paper appeared under the mastheads of *The OCC Press*, *The Blue Banner*, and *The Other Paper*.

Orientation at Midtown Plaza, circa 1960s.

Cafeteria at Midtown Plaza.

FIRST INTERNATIONAL STUDENT

He got off the plane in Syracuse from Haifa, Israel, at 5 a.m. and was in an OCC classroom at 10 a.m. on October 1, 1962. "[I was] dead tired, but I had to go to school," remembered Nicolas Habayeb, OCC's first student from overseas. The advance paperwork had been done by local relatives, so Nicolas and later his wife, Hyam Habayeb, immediately started classes upon arrival and remembered everyone as being very helpful.

They overcame the new and different accents by tape recording the classes and then deciphering the words at home. Without a car, they walked downtown to attend the required volleyball and swimming at the YMCA, where swimming in a pool instead of the ocean was a new experience. And Syracuse's cold, cold winter was totally different from anything they had known along the Mediterranean.

Both juggled classes and work—Nicolas in the early morning at a bakery from 2:30 to 11 a.m. and Hyam at St. Joseph's as a medical technician. Eventually with a baby at home, they found that maintaining straight "A" averages became a challenge as mononucleosis, then chicken pox and mumps came along.

After Nicolas' graduation in 1965, they became U.S. citizens. Nicolas later taught French, first at Jamesville-DeWitt and then for 27 years in the East Syracuse Minoa School District. Hyam continued her career, becoming a microbiologist at St. Joseph's Hospital, where she worked for 35 years. He now

is President of Multilingual Translation Services.

Interview with Nicolas A. Habayeb, A.A. degree from OCC 1965; degrees from Le Moyne College and Syracuse University. Interview with Hyam Habayeb, A.A.S. degree from OCC 1968; attended Le Moyne College; degree from St. Joseph's Hospital – School of Medical Technology.

STUDENT GATHERING PLACES

Midtown's first-floor cafeteria, operated by Linda and Sol Kaplan for the Meltzer family, was as much a part of OCC as any classroom. "Most of the education was in the cafeteria," remembered one student. "It was our student lounge" is the universal memory. Because there were other offices in the building, the original idea was that the College people would stay on one side, leaving the other side for the usually older, more traditional occupants in the building. It was a plan that seldom worked. One plan that did work was to ask students to refrain from using the elevators, leaving them for visitors and other tenants. Most of the students ran up and down the stairs. "It was certainly faster anyway," students agreed.

Early in 1963, the official Student Lounge on the third floor was closed by the administration for being "messy and having a poor impact on visitors." So that it could be reopened strictly for study, the Canada Dry Beverage Corporation paid to have a student-monitor for three hours a day. Late in 1963, a snack bar was added, operating for both day and evening students. The Student Senate found it necessary to forbid card playing in the Lounge.

While the Midtown Plaza building dominated the block between East Water and East Washington Streets, small neighborhood bars, the Rescue Mission and several auto repair shops were nearby, along with Hendricks Camera Shop and industrial contractors. Students were admonished not to frequent the nearby 800 Club bar on East Washington Street at Forman Avenue, where male (and adventurous female) students were going for refreshment and the free bar meal that was offered. The bar rented parking spaces for a monthly fee, which increased its lure. Throughout the Midtown years, contention over parking was a constant. The Midtown lease offered 177 spaces, of which 87 were assigned to faculty and staff, leaving only 90 to be parceled out among more than 500 students. As more and more employees and students had cars, there was increasing agitation over parking.

Midtown Plaza Lobby. The lines in the photograph are crop lines from the 1964 yearbook.

Student social activity, circa 1971.

STUDENT ACTIVITIES

Student activities continued to develop. On stage, Prof. James DeBlasis (Drama) directed a regular succession of Broadway-style hits such as *See How They Run, Sabrina Fair* and *Blithe Spirit*. These productions were performed at local theaters, most often at the old Regent Theatre on Genesee Street near South Crouse. Props and costumes came from thrift stores. Music classes provided a number of performing groups, such as a choir, brass sinfonia, chamber band, jazz combos, and male and female singing groups.

The official OCC views about these student activities varied. Dean of Faculty and later Interim President Karl Larsen said, "Extracurricular activities are desirable but not essential." But President Marvin Rapp encouraged the start of a new literary magazine *Graffiti*, and he added his own poem, *The Young*, to the 1968 yearbook. Many of the faculty vigorously supported student activities. Prof. Carl Oney (Biology), who came to OCC in August 1962 from the State University College of Forestry at Syracuse University, now the State University of New York College of Environmental Science and Forestry, believed in the need to offer students a full range of music, drama and sports to supplement their classroom experiences. He began making coffee in his lab and bringing in donut holes to encourage students to pause and talk about their futures. This practice evolved into lunchtime discussions and then *Flick and Snack,* a chance to comment on the films they watched together.

Rod Serling, Odgen Nash, Julian Bond, Shirley Chisholm, Alex Haley, Roger Mudd and Bella Abzug, all young and rising to national prominence, were guest speakers at the College. In the newspapers, local citizens and public officials questioned whether certain speakers should be allowed to appear under the auspices of OCC and whether certain authors should be studied in class.

Alumni Snapshot

Maureen F. Moon, '66

- A.A., General Studies
- Administrative Assistant, United Parcel Service

Independence. Responsibility. Enlightenment.

These are just a few of the qualities Maureen Moon gained during her time at Onondaga Community College. Coming from a strict family, Moon describes herself as "sheltered" before stepping into the world of higher education.

"I was an only child. My father was very protective," she shares. "But going to Onondaga helped me grow up. Going to an affordable college and learning to involve myself sounded like a good idea."

Like her husband, alumnus Floyd Moon, Mrs. Moon discovered more than just academics at the College. She found a bustling environment, caring professors and a new sense of self identity. She explored topics that she never would have before while learning how to become a more autonomous person.

"It makes me feel really good inside that I went to college and got an associate's degree," Moon explains. "It got me into things that I never would have done before, like archaeology class or orientation committee, things that made me want to help people."

And she's held that desire to help people close throughout the years. She worked as an administrative assistant at C&S Companies in Syracuse, New York, for more than a decade—the very same company that played a key role in developing the new SRC Arena and Events Center and the Academic II building at Onondaga.

"The fact that they're building at the College tugs at the heart. It makes me proud that they're there," Moon says. "And it makes me proud that I was a part of it."

On October 24 1970, student protesters marched in Downtown Syracuse in reaction to the Kent State shootings that occured on May 4, 1970 in a confrontation between students and National Guardsmen.

ACTIVISM AND PROTESTS

It was a time when very committed individuals believed their own actions could change the world, or at least solve the immediate crisis. OCC faculty and students became part of that movement. Students increasingly became involved in protests about national issues such as the fighting in Vietnam and racial segregation. The Newman Club of Roman Catholic students, formed at OCC in 1966, worked with inner city school students, in addition to holding symposiums on race-related issues. Minority students continued to organize. Prof. Jim Martin (Counseling) recalled that the Black Collegians became JAMAA in 1969, a name which the organizers attributed to the Swahili word for family. JAMAA held numerous events, including Black Awareness Weekend.

Several groups of Civil Rights workers were welcomed to the campus, brought from the South by the Rev. Adam Vermilye (Social Sciences), an adjunct faculty member. For the first Earth Day (April 1970), Prof. Nancy McCarty (History and Political Science) led her Social Science students in a Dirty Picture Contest to document the worst evidences of local pollution. Signs in

the halls urged everyone to boycott grapes and lettuce to bring about better working conditions in the California growing fields. Prof. Jerry Berrigan (English), already well known as an anti-war protester, had two brothers in the national news leading civil rights and anti-war demonstrations all over the country to protest injustices, such as Freedom Riders being jailed in maximum security prisons, tortured and killed.

The assassination of President John F. Kennedy in November 1963; the escalation of the fighting and the rising death toll in Vietnam; civil rights turmoil in Selma, Alabama, and other Southern cities; the Civil Rights March on Washington, D.C.; and the assassinations of Senator Robert F. Kennedy and the Rev. Dr. Martin Luther King, Jr. in 1968, and the ensuing riots, were all flashpoints.

The military draft for 19-year-old men that began in December 1969 brought the war in Vietnam closer to home. Students carrying at least 12 credit hours of classes were exempt from the military. Keeping draft boards informed about a student's academic status became another paperwork challenge for staff. Two faculty members, Professors Dorothy Harth (Modern Langua-

SECOND OFFICIAL SEAL 1969 – 2005

On June 28, 1967, Public Information Director George Allen presented the Board of Trustees with a new seal, designed by Steve Meltzer, Art Director for WCNY-TV, for the inauguration of President Marvin Rapp. For the next two years, this seal was used periodically on updates and publicity releases, alternating with the original one designed by Edward Jay. On April 23, 1969, the Board of Trustees adopted the new design as the official seal for the College.

In an October 1969 interview with the student newspaper, *The Blue Banner*, Mr. Meltzer explained that the seal, a medallion bearing a three-point flame, was a symbol of the three major divisions of the College: Liberal Arts, Technical Arts, and Creative and Performing Arts. The three-point flame was a modification of the traditional three-point leaf used in many seals and insignias. Meltzer said that the traditional leaves still remained in the seal as a laurel border, symbolizing success.

Students in Syracuse marched when the courts indicted the Kent State student protestors, but refused to indict the National Guardsmen.

ges) and the Rev. John Wagner (Counseling), stood beside the dry fountain at Midtown's entrance to read each week's list of names of United States soldiers killed in Vietnam. "No speeches, just the names," Prof. Harth recalled.

Was OCC a "controversial place"? Some, both inside and outside the College, seemed to think so. Despite strong opposition from their administration, SU students and a few faculty members were in the local headlines as a result of their rallies and marches focusing on human and civil rights issues. After the Kent State shootings in May 1970, the SU bookstore was firebombed, windows all over campus were smashed and campus roads were blockaded by students. OCC students also reacted sharply to sending troops to Cambodia and the killing of students at Kent State by National Guard soldiers. A convocation in the auditorium and a sit-in at Midtown Plaza were held with Ralph Jones, Student Senate President, and Dr. Mary Savage, Dean of Student Personnel Services, protecting the elevators from rebellious students so Midtown Plaza's regular tenants would not be kept from their offices. The next day, OCC faculty and students joined those from Syracuse University in a silent march that shut down all traffic and filled Salina Street with protestors from Fayette to Harrison Streets. On the SU campus, with one more week of the semester to go, the administration cancelled classes for two days and handled bomb scares. At OCC, students voted for a two-day suspension of classes, 476 yes to 339 no. On the issue of closing for the rest of the semester, students voted 235 yes and 366 no.

Looking back on the 1970 and 1971 period as "very eventful," Student Senate President Ralph Jones remembered the OCC actions as both "creative and constructive." The presence of military veterans as students kept protests focused, he believed. The Black Collegians and the Veterans' Association had a strong and vocal presence on campus. However, only a fraction of OCC and SU students became involved in the protesting. The agitation at both places was intense, but unlike at SU, at OCC no actual incidents of student violence or arrests occurred.

Alumni Snapshot

Dolores A. Speach, '67
- A.A., Humanities/Liberal Arts
- B.A., Biology and Psychology – Syracuse University
- M.S., Science Education – Syracuse University
- Educator For More Than 30 Years

Dolores Speach stepped onto the Midtown Plaza campus nearly 50 years ago with only one thing in mind: academics.

"I was married with two children, and I was completely focused on getting my education," she says. "We made a lot of sacrifices. I wanted so much to improve myself. Onondaga gave me the confidence and reassurance to know I could."

Thanks to Onondaga's evening programs and courses, Speach was able to balance her personal and academic commitments while exploring new opportunities. She immersed herself in the sciences, discovered the beauty of the arts and learned what it took to succeed in the classroom.

"I wanted to do something for me. I wanted to be able to stand next to my husband—to be educated, have an education, and make something of myself," Speach says. "The fact that Onondaga offered a flexible schedule made it a perfect match."

And it didn't take her long to launch a career after Onondaga. She taught biology at Sacred Heart High School in Syracuse, New York, right after earning her associate's degree—at a time when teaching jobs were scarce. Since then, Speach has gained a number of additional degrees and credentials, working in science, counseling and special education for the last 30 years.

"Onondaga Community College opened up a whole new world for me. It opened doors and allowed me to enjoy a rich, fulfilling and beautiful life," Speach says. "It was truly a blessing."

THE EARLY STUDENT DAYS: BEING INVOLVED

"Coming out of high school, I had no clue what I wanted to do, so I came to OCC, and then I got involved. I was on Student Senate my first year, and the person in charge of the newspaper said, 'We need help. Would you want to take a shot at it?'" remembered Lou Tripoli, class of 1968. That initial involvement led to his becoming editor of *The Blue Banner* the next year. The newspaper's basement office at Midtown Plaza was the headquarters. He opened the office every day at 8:00 a.m., returning between classes, and closing at 5:30 or 6:00 p.m. "The office became a hangout not only for my staff, but for their friends. People were coming and going all the time."

Because the paper published twice monthly, the staff met once or twice a week to talk about the next issue. Mr. Tripoli remembered *The Blue Banner* staff as engaged in serious investigative reporting: The student paper initiated the story questioning the OCC Bookstore operation that was eventually picked up by the *Syracuse Herald-Journal* and resulted in indictments and a court case (see Moving To A Permanent Campus).

Other stories included Eugene McCarthy's presidential campaign ("We had a couple of students who were involved in going to New Hampshire to walk the streets for him, so we did a story on his campaign"); local politics ("We met with John Mulroy one time about the future of the school and the budget"); and Vietnam ("We did an article, several articles actually, on students who were veterans who had been to Vietnam, and they brought us photographs. They gave us information about what they did and what it was like"). "The paper was informative. It really gave the students something to think about."

Mr. Tripoli also remembered the fun times at Midtown Plaza: winter weekends, spring weekends, bands brought in from outside, keg parties (the drinking age was 18) and soapsuds in the fountain. "The Club 800— Frank Malfitano [See "Jazz Fest," Chapter 5] used to hang out there. Excellent bar. We would go there for lunch. It was just down the street. They made great sandwiches. Frank would go, not only for lunch, but he would go back at night to listen to the music. Frank would help us plan for the bands; he would bring in people from Top 40 radio."

During those early years, student government was very active. "Elections were big; there were two parties, blue party and white party. Everything had to be run through the Student Government. If you wanted to put up posters, we had to approve them first. We weren't going to let you take shots at the other party. You could say what you stood for, what your platform was. The turnout for elections was amazing. There would be people in line going into the room, and the line would be down the hall."

"Some people came [to OCC] because they wanted to avoid the draft, but then after they came, they got interested in something that took them in a new direction. We had a campus radio station that only broadcast inside the building, a little studio. We would go down there and read the day's weather forecast out of the local paper. We would do the sports section. We had no idea that that was something we might be interested in. [OCC] has just been great for so many people all over the area. It's a great school."

(Interview with Louis Tripoli, A.A. degree from OCC 1968; bachelor's degree from University of Miami; MBA and JD from Syracuse University; currently an attorney with Maguire Cardona Law Firm of Syracuse.)

Louis Tripoli

ADDITIONAL STUDENT ACTIVITIES

Faculty members continued efforts to expand classroom boundaries. Ethnic dish-to-pass meals helped to acquaint students with the cultures of foreign countries being studied, even though it meant considerable extra effort for the faculty. The 1970 *Winter Weekend* dance at Drumlins was an attempt to continue established College traditions. Students also held a formal dinner dance at Le Moyne Manor, a concert at the War Memorial and a snow party at Ironwood Ridge ski slope near Delphi Falls in rural southeastern Onondaga County.

Drama productions were held at the Everson Museum; music concerts were held at the War Memorial. The first *Festival of the Arts* was launched from Midtown Plaza in May 1971 with choir, jazz, percussion, sinfonia and music faculty concerts and a drama, *Whether Pigs Have Wings*. The Festival continued as a cultural highlight of these years. Speakers, art shows and jazz were included in the programs. Rod Serling, who gained fame as an Emmy-winning dramatic writer and *Twilight Zone* producer, visited the campus for the third time in September 1971.

From 1971 to 1976, The *Campus Clipboard* was printed weekly by the Student Activities Office to provide a list of events and announcements for the campus community. One student sought to make the 1971 holiday time brighter for servicemen. The *Home for the Hoildays* drive coordinated by Nancy Singer (General Studies, 1972) raised $22,000 to fly 40 servicemen home from Vietnam to Syracuse for holidays with their families.

In spring 1973, the Onondaga Community College Choir embarked on a European tour that included competing in an International Choir Festival in Holland with 50 other choirs. The OCC choir earned third place in their division. Their participation was the first for any two-year college in the United States. The high quality of the choir led Director Don Miller (Prof. of Music) to enter them in the Festival. After they were selected as competitors, several local clubs helped to finance the trip for the nearly 50 choir members, who also gave local concerts as fundraisers. While they were in Europe, in addition to the competition, the choir performed in Brussels, Belgium; Cologne and Hindleberg, Germany; Luxembourg; and Epinal, France.

In recollection, some faculty members felt their work with the students was the "glue that held OCC together" in the days of controversy among the various College factions, as well as during the anti-war and Civil Rights turmoil that gripped the nation. The physical closeness of the Midtown years provided invaluable experience in learning to get along with others and generated an atmosphere of community despite the ever-present tensions.

> "OCC gave me that chance—I grasped it and ran. I'll always be indebted to OCC for giving me the opportunity to prove myself as a success."
>
> – *Martin G. Preston (COL,USA, Ret.)*
> *(Music, 1968)*

Student announcement at Midtown Plaza posted over a doorway detailing the smoking policy.

View from Midtown Plaza of Downtown Syracuse showing I-81 and Almond Street.

Alumni Snapshot

Karin Franklin-King, '69

- A.A.S., Drama
- B.A., Theater – SUNY Oswego
- M.F.A – Cornell University
- Local TV/Radio Personality, WSYR and WCNY
- Former OCC Foundation Director

Karin Franklin-King came to Central New York more than 40 years ago with nothing but a bus ticket, a couple of bags and big dreams.

"My father told me to get there a month before classes started because I needed to figure out things—like how to use Syracuse's subway system," she says. "So a Greyhound Bus dropped me off along Erie Boulevard, where I walked because there weren't any cabs waiting on the side of the road. And there wasn't a subway system. It was a rude awakening."

She quickly learned that OCC students walked everywhere, no matter what the weather. To get to classes, she walked six blocks from her room at the Mizpah Hotel, across the street from the courthouse, to Midtown Plaza. As a Drama student, she walked to the Syracuse Museum of Fine Arts at James and State Streets, where there was a stage. For other productions, she walked four blocks east to the Regent Theater on Genesee Street, near Irving Avenue, which has evolved into Syracuse Stage. She and her friends walked all over downtown Syracuse. Lunch-counter meals at Grant's and Woolworth's on Salina Street were 50 cents each, and the city's five first-run movie theaters were in full operation nearby. "Friends I met at OCC took me home for weekends and have remained friends for life."

Each young woman at the Mizpah had a bed and shared a kitchen, where all made their own meals. "But you had to be careful to protect your own food supply," she remembered. There was a sign-in, sign-out system, and OCC hired a housemother. All in all, it duplicated the situation at the four-year colleges and universities of the day.

Aspiring to become an actress, Franklin-King left Brooklyn right out of high school for Syracuse and Onondaga Community College. Though she wanted to attend acting school, her mother urged her to put aside that preference and explore the possibility of going to college. Given that Onondaga was one of the only two-year colleges in the state to offer a drama program, it was a perfect fit. "The program was intense. It was personal," she says. "It was exactly what I wanted and needed."

Franklin-King says she became a novelty on campus—as one of the few black women and as somebody who wasn't shy, who got involved and who always had fun. She describes the drama program as "a family," crediting it with transforming her as a person and laying a foundation for the rest of her career.

"At Onondaga, I was given the opportunity to do things in my first year that you can't do at a university until your third or fourth year," she explains. "It helped when I went into broadcasting; I knew what everybody else was responsible for and what they needed to do. And it prepared me for thinking on my feet during live television."

To those searching for a path and looking for opportunity, she has one message: explore Onondaga Community College.

"An immediate 'no' is not no forever," she says. "If you're pursuing something, OCC is a welcoming place. No matter what your situation, there's something there for you, and there's always somebody willing to listen."

ONONDAGA HILL

The first inhabitants of Onondaga Hill were the people of the Ononda'ge'gah Nation *(The People of the Hills)*, who are the Keepers of the Central Fire of the Haudenosaunee—the original Five Nations of the Iroquois Confederacy *(The People of the Longhouse)*. Archaeological evidence of 13th Century villages was unearthed in 1965-1966 through an archaeological dig at the Furnace Brook Site, led by then-SU doctoral student Jim Tuck. Robert Ricklis, a 17-year-old student who was working the dig, discovered buried remains of the longest longhouse (335 feet) uncovered to that point. The sites involved are now the Westbrook Hills Apartments and the Manor Hill housing development.

The American Revolutionary War General John A. Ellis (1763-1820) began the settlement of Onondaga Hill in 1794. He also encouraged other veterans to follow him. Their large distinguished houses on Route 173 and Route 175 are evidence of the settlement's prominence that faded when the Erie Canal made swampy Syracuse the County's commercial and governmental center. On the Route 173 approach uphill from Onondaga Valley are the graves of two soldiers of the War of 1812 who fell ill and died here, one on his way to fight on the Niagara frontier and the other on his way home from fighting. The graves once overlooked the steep-sided and wooded Hopper's Glen, a favorite with artists and picnickers, which was massively changed by road construction in 1969 to give better access to the new College and nearby hospitals.

The County's first jail, courthouse and clerk's office had been established at Onondaga Hill, the seat of County government from 1803 to 1830. West Seneca Turnpike, originally an unpaved trail, was the primary east-west route for settlers heading into western New York State and traversed the center of the town.

By 1962, when County officials offered what was known as the County Farm as the permanent site for Onondaga Community College, Onondaga Hill was a crossroads ham-

Located near Route 173, Hopper's Glen was a popular hiking and picnic area, circa 1890. (Courtesy of Town of Onondaga Historical Society)

This gravesite on the eastern approach to Onondaga Hill (Hopper's Glen) on Route 173 records the death and burial of two soldiers in the War of 1812 who died while camped nearby. (Courtesy Town of Onondaga Historical Society)

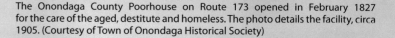

The Onondaga County Poorhouse on Route 173 opened in February 1827 for the care of the aged, destitute and homeless. The photo details the facility, circa 1905. (Courtesy of Town of Onondaga Historical Society)

let, a small community with the traditional array of churches, two grocery stores, a school and post office. The County Farm was attached to the Onondaga County Poorhouse (later known as the Van Duyn Home and Hospital) for aged and incapacitated County citizens. The limestone Poorhouse (1854) and newer brick buildings were a landmark on Route 173, also known as Onondaga Road.

Designation of the County Farm as the College site fulfilled a long tradition of locating colleges and universities on hilltops, with the added advantage of access from two state highways, Route 173 and Route 175, whose intersection marks the approximate geographic center of the County.

Onondaga County had acquired this land (135 acres) in 1909 to expand the farm for its nearby Poorhouse, where residents once worked to help supply their own food. A dairy herd, chickens and at times goats and geese were the mainstays of the Farm, which used the hilly fields for pasturing and crops. The operation had ended with all the equipment and livestock auctioned off in 1965, so the land was fallow when first viewed as a potential campus.

On the site was an earth-covered 500,000-gallon water reservoir built in the 1930s that was 150 feet in diameter and 15 feet deep. It provided the pressure needed by local water systems and replaced a 17-acre open reservoir, about 25 feet deep, that supplied Syracuse with water from 1863 until 1894 when Skaneateles Lake was tapped for the city's public system.

The reservoir, reduced to about 14 acres by 1969, became known over the years as Pogey Pond. It was fondly remembered by nearby farm families for swimming in summer and ice harvesting in winter. For boys living in the Skunk City section of Syracuse along Grand Avenue and Geddes Street, going with older boys up Velasko Road to swim at Pogey was a rite of passage. When dedicated October 29, 1970, the official OCC entrance sign on Route 173 was surrounded by roughly dressed limestone, which was originally part of the 1860s reservoir.

The home of General John A. Ellis, formerly on Route 173. The Ellis family burial ground is located just east of the driveway to the College's storage barn. (Courtesy of Town of Onondaga Historical Society)

Ice cutting on Pogey Pond on February 6, 1924. (Courtesy of Town of Onondaga Historical Society)

Onondaga Hill

COMMUNITY COLLEGE
FUTURE HOME OF
ONONDAGA
COMMUNITY COLLE
CHAIRMAN-
NTY EXECUTIVE
JOHN H

Moving To A Permanent Campus
1968-1973

Since their first meeting in September 1961, trustees had discussed some aspect of a permanent campus at every session. They did not consider privately owned property. Instead, they set their priorities for property owned by Onondaga County, the City of Syracuse, the state or the federal government—in that order. Even before the first academic year ended (1962-1963), trustees hired the local architectural firm of Clark, Clark, Millis, & Gilson to analyze potential permanent College sites. The task of recommending a permanent location was charged to a Site Selection Committee, chaired by Trustee Albert J. Gordon. On August 2, 1963, the Trustees unanimously asked Onondaga County to make available the Onondaga Hill property known as the County Farm, adjacent to the Van Duyn Home and Hospital. But efforts to bolster a faltering downtown and the need to satisfy officials in other towns dragged out the process for two more years. Syracuse Mayor William Walsh and the Metropolitan Development Association made repeated efforts to keep OCC downtown, while suburban town officials demanded studies of their favorite sites. Five locations in Pompey and another in Salina were examined to satisfy members of the Board of Supervisors. Steady pressure from the newspapers and store owners to keep the College downtown led to a cost analysis of five city sites proposed by the mayor.

The newspapers and County officials pressed the trustees to examine all aspects of the College's operation before choosing a permanent site. As a result, the Middle States Commission on Higher Education, a national accreditation organization, was commissioned to conduct a two-year study of college governance, finances, personnel, curricula and students.

In May 1965, the Middle States Commission on Higher Education released its report, which highlighted the poor relations between the faculty and administration as the "Number One problem" at OCC. In addition, the report emphasized that trustees, administration, County officials and faculty each needed to more clearly understand their duties and responsibilities. The report stated that these "stresses are normal in a growing organization where large numbers of students, inexperienced faculty and unclear or not understood goals and purposes exist." Strong action by the College's chief administrator was needed to guide the faculty, the Board of Trustees and the County, the report said. The report suggested better coordination between the County and trustees, who needed to understand more clearly the relationship of the College to the community, and the need for improvements in promoting College programs and services to the community.

UPON THIS HILL

Alluding to the lingering undercurrent of dissatisfaction by some with the Onondaga Hill location, President Marvin Rapp proclaimed the "air is chilly but our hearts are warm" as the permanent campus was dedicated by County and College officials on November 15, 1966, five months after Dr. Rapp arrived on campus. Rapp also wrote a 33-line poem entitled *Lines on the Dedication of Land for Onondaga Community College* that ended, "May the fruit of learning here give strength to body, soul and mind to all who choose to join with us to grow upon this Hill." The ceremony included the site presentation by the County Executive, Mr. John Mulroy, and a dedication by Trustee Rev. Dr. Alexander Carmichel, along with the singing of the Alma Mater written by Prof. Phil Klein (Music).

ARCHITECTS' PLAN

When looked at as a potential location for the College, the County Farm site presented some difficult physical realities. The steep hillsides divided by narrow gorges with exposed shale or bedrock limestone are still visible today, as they were to planners 50 years ago. There was a 130-foot difference in elevation between the highest part of the property and the lowest. The hillside grades ranged from eight percent to more than 15 percent. For comparison, today's steepest road grades are usually only seven percent. Today the winding access road from Route 173 shows how the grade was accommodated. The design of buildings with two or three ground-level entries was another way to deal with the site.

On the positive side, the location received full sun and the view, or "viewshed" as the architects phrased it, was exceptionally wide. However, they noted that buildings should be positioned to reduce walking because of the weather (mainly the snow) and wind on the exposed northerly slope, the main usable part of the property.

Planners found two relatively level positions for buildings on opposite sides of a gorge and outlined a perimeter road and parking areas. The *Master Development Plan* (1967), developed by architect Robert T. Clark of Clark, Clark, Millis, & Gilson, supplied the formal documentation to be examined by College and County officials detail by detail.

The original County allocation to OCC was for 60 acres with the promise of 121 more when the need arose. Architects proposed utilizing the Furnace Brook Gorge to separate the academic buildings—classrooms and the library—from the activity centers, such as physical education and the student center. Square footage for classrooms and offices was determined via a formula, factoring in the anticipated number of students, faculty and staff. Detail by detail, the plans were argued over, refined and eventually approved. All the contracts were awarded to low bidders, following the standard County government procedure.

In order to connect the east and west sections of the campus, the Furnace Brook Gorge had to be traversed. The landscape architects originally called for three bridges: two for the loop road (one at the north end of the gorge and one at the south end) and one for the pedestrian traffic in the center of campus. The costs associated with constructing the bridges were deemed prohibitive. The shortest span (at the north end of the gorge) would have cost $300,000. Instead, County highway workers built a causeway for $170,000. The only bridge that was constructed was the central pedestrian bridge, which was actually presented to the County Legislature as a "utility structure" to carry utilities from one side of campus to the other.

U.S. Department of Agriculture aerial photograph from June 22, 1966, showing the future campus site (then the County Farm), with the old Van Duyn Home and Hospital building (1827-1962) in the upper-right corner. (Courtesy of Institute for Resource Information Sciences, Cornell University)

FIRST CLASSES ON ONONDAGA HILL

A groundbreaking ceremony was held on October 25, 1968, for the first of four buildings proposed in Phase One of the OCC Master Plan. Completion of this structure, eventually to be used for Service and Maintenance, was marked by Opening Day festivities on February 2, 1970, with tours, coffee in the lunchroom and continuous showing of two films President Rapp produced: *Upon This Hill* and *Join With Us.*

That date also marked the first classes on the Onondaga Hill campus. Two hundred Music and Business students began classes in the new Service and Maintenance Building. The low brick structure, originally designed for carpentry shops, other repair facilities and garages, was reconfigured into a large rehearsal room, 15 practice rooms, seven rooms for Music studios and offices, four Business classrooms, a lunchroom and a lounge. The access road was muddy with snow banks on each side, but the new water and sewer lines were working. In a few months, the Drama classes moved in, pushed out of the Midtown Plaza basement by other tenants who complained about the boisterous and noisy behavior of students.

Nearby, rooms at the County's Van Duyn Home and Hospital on the north side of Route 173 were used for classes and offices. For more than 18 months, registration and evening staff offices were on the third floor of Van Duyn. Classes in Human Services, Graphic Arts and Nursing were taught in rooms at Van Duyn, and students regularly greeted the facility's residents whom they found sitting on the stair steps or in rooms nearby. It was more than two years before permanently designated on-campus classroom space became available in the newly built library.

The new campus was officially dedicated on April 21, 1970, with Governor Nelson Rockefeller as speaker. At the same time, ground was broken for the library building. "OCC is officially on its own hill campus," reported the *Syracuse Herald-Journal.* The program had "17 speakers including two preachers," commented the afternoon newspaper. A coffee hour in the new Service and Maintenance building followed, plus a dedication luncheon at the General Hutchinson House restaurant, the historic stone landmark on Route 175, west of OCC, now known as the Inn of the Seasons.

To generate public interest in the Onondaga Hill location, President Rapp persuaded community groups such as the Boy and Girl Scouts, Rotary International and Lions Club to hold seminars and other events on the new campus on Saturdays, even when only the first building was available. By July of 1971, trustees were considering names for the new buildings.

> "OCC provided a strong educational background and a sense of accomplishment, as well as instilled the confidence necessary to succeed in the academic world."
>
> – *Thomas F. Slater, III*
> *(Humanities & Social Sciences, 1970)*

(from left) Board of Trustees Chair Ransom MacKenzie, County Executive John Mulroy and President Marvin Rapp.

County Executive John H. Mulroy and Board of Trustees Chair Ransom MacKenzie (right) operate a two-man saw to cut down some of the trees in July 1967 to symbolically start work on the new campus, while President Marvin Rapp observes.

CAMPUS IN TRANSITION

Many expressed great anticipation for the new location, but others were less sanguine. The new campus was a destination that required a car, so parking quickly became an issue. The campus offered plenty of space, but the lots were roughly graded and dusty when they were not muddy or frozen into deep ruts. "Filled with rocks" was one recollection; "Gravel was too polite a term" was another.

The words "commuter school" came into use just in time to characterize OCC. Students faced the fragmented class locations in Midtown Plaza, the downtown YMCA for Physical Education classes, Van Duyn Home and Hospital, and the actual campus at Onondaga Hill. For a while a shuttle operated from Midtown to Onondaga Hill for workers without cars at the beginning and end of the regular work day, but students were very much on their own in finding ways to get to class. In those years when many did not have cars, students hitchhiked, arranged rides with classmates, or utilized bus service.

For the office staff, having classes in a variety of locations was a challenge. Figuring out who was where and maintaining communication added hours and days to office life. But the greatest challenge was dealing with the new technology, remembered Shirley Singer, the Registrar (1965-1990). She was in charge of space allocation at Midtown Plaza, Van Duyn and Onondaga Hill. The first generation of computers, and their successors, gave everyone repeated lessons in patience as the office went from steady, heavy typewriters to screens with words that disappeared at crucial moments, some never to return. In addition, she remembered that there was the "constant fight with the County" for financial support, along with the steady stream of directions on how to do it "better" from County officials unfamiliar with academia.

Prof. Bruce Haney also recalled learning how to operate computers and dealing with County officials as the greatest challenges of those days. OCC's first programmable computer had a briefcase-sized processor, keyboard and card reader, he said, and this computer was shared by the faculty and office staff.

Throughout all the difficulties of a campus in transition, OCC continued to serve the students without interruption. Meanwhile, plans to have the College totally moved out of Midtown by 1971 fell further and further behind. To showcase its new location, the 1972 graduation ceremony was held on campus with the Service and Maintenance loading dock providing the platform for dignitaries and speakers, who faced an audience seated on the grass.

In July 1972, President Rapp spoke to trustees about the need to "sensitize the County Legislature" about the $19 million cost of completing site work and construction of Phase One campus buildings (the Service and Maintenance building, the library, the Tech Arts building and the Student Center). The large financial commitment was one of the chief obstacles for both County officials and community leaders who were reading news story after news story about controversies involving OCC faculty, ad-

Onondaga Hill campus construction, circa late 1960s-early 1970s.

Students touring the new campus construction on Onondaga Hill, circa late 1960s.

STUDENT CENTER GROUNDBREAKING

(from left) Vice President Harvey Charles, Dean Mary Savage and Student Senate President Ralph Jones turning first ceremonial shovel of dirt on September 9, 1970, to commence construction of the Gordon Student Center.

New York State Governor Nelson Rockefeller turning first ceremonial shovel of dirt, April 21, 1970, to commence construction of Coulter Library.

ministration and students. Regular editorial critiques were offered by the Syracuse newspapers. Rising to the defense of the College, County Legislature Chair Ephraim E. Shapero stalwartly answered the publisher's editorials, reminding the community of the institution's merits. Publisher Stephen Rogers was consulted about the development of the Onondaga Hill campus, but overall opposition by the newspapers to OCC's relocation out of Downtown did not diminish. In addition, some parts of the campus property had great sentimental value to the public. "Modifying" Pogey Pond to fit it into the campus plan was another touchy issue.

In October 1972, Dr. Rapp moved the President's Office to Onondaga Hill, using spartan space in the Service and Maintenance building to conduct College business.

After much public wrangling, the County Legislature in March 1973 approved construction of the Center for Physical Education and the Academic One building to combine classrooms and administrative offices. In May 1973, the Technology Club of Syracuse (now known as the Technology Alliance of Central New York [TACNY]) agreed to sell 24.72 acres of its land to OCC, land that was crucial to expanding OCC's frontage on Route 175. In return, Technology Club members gained access to College buildings and later (1974) had the Technical Building auditorium named in memory of Simon B. Storer, who had originally willed this property to the club in 1946. The Technology Club, founded in 1903 by local engineers, chemists and industrial plant managers, retained ownership of a seismograph building, located on the parcel, which contained telescopes and seismographic facilities. (Due to increased traffic on Route 175 and the resulting vibrations, TACNY eventually was no longer able to use the seismographic equipment. Therefore, in 2005, the Technology Club and the College agreed to demolish this structure to make way for the construction of Residence Halls.)

Alumni Snapshot

Marcia Rees Conrad, '72
- A.A.S., Architectural Technology
- B.S., Architecture – Ohio State
- Registered Architect, Moody Nolan Inc.

Climbing up seven flights of stairs to the architectural technology wing at the Midtown Plaza, Marcia Rees Conrad was pleased to discover a program that promoted acceptance and encouraged her to explore new possibilities.

"I was always the only woman in architecture classes during high school. It was difficult," she shares. "But when I got to Onondaga, I had a chance to do everything—things everybody else did. There was no special treatment. Everyone was treated equally, and I was able to better challenge myself because of it."

Two years later, Conrad walked across a decorated stage at the Onondaga Hill campus and became the first female in the first class of graduates from the Architectural Technology Program. Making the most of her newfound degree, it didn't take long for Conrad to launch herself into the professional world.

"I was always able to find a job thanks to my training from OCC," she explains. "Whenever I interviewed for a job, employers would tell me I got it because of the portfolio the program helped me build and the credibility of a degree. It really opened up a whole new world for me."

Onondaga allowed Conrad to break down barriers and transform herself into a role model for female architects everywhere. And, as thanks for providing her with a career she's been thriving in for nearly 40 years, she's given back to the College by developing a scholarship in memory of one of her dearest role models, Prof. Bill Oliver.

"Bill Oliver put every student in the Architectural Technology program under his wing. He understood us and made sure we knew everything we needed to know to succeed," she says. "I wanted everyone to know and remember the great things he did for students like me and for this College."

The 1973 yearbook reveals the changing face of OCC. Gone are the formal portraits. Casual pictures of students, all unnamed, show longer hair and beards on males, beehive hairdos and bell bottom slacks on females. While informality blossomed in the general classes, Nursing and Dental Hygiene maintained a more traditional atmosphere. Separate graduation ceremonies for these programs were held at DeWitt Community Church, where OCC Trustee Rev. Dr. Alexander Carmichel was pastor. Many of the nursing students combined classes with their work as practical nurses and cherished the formal graduation tea given by the Community General Hospital Auxiliary, which also gave money for Nursing scholarships and encouraged graduates to maintain a close connection to Community General.

Accreditation from the Middle States Commission on Higher Education was granted to OCC in 1973, a significant academic achievement for the 12-year-old College.

> "OCC was the beginning for me.
> Many thanks!"
>
> – *Daniel A. O'Brien*
> *(Police Science, 1971)*

Alumni Snapshot

Thomas Reitano, '72

- A.A.S., Music
- B.M., Music Education –
  Syracuse University
- M.M, Music Education – Syracuse University
- Retired Music Educator – Jamesville- DeWitt
  and East Syracuse-Minoa Districts

Thomas Reitano would not call himself an "achiever" growing up. He didn't have top grades in school. He didn't behave quite as well as he should have. And he didn't make friends with the best crowd.

But thanks to the opportunities offered at Onondaga Community College, Reitano was able to put all of his previous struggles aside, launch a fresh start and take control of his life.

"OCC showed me that I had a chance in life—that I could achieve something greater," he explains. "And it helped me prove to myself that I could be something."

As a lifelong piano player, Reitano thought it was only fitting to select music as his major. His class was the first to experience life at the Onondaga Hill campus—the Music Department was the first to make the move from Midtown Plaza.

The department sat alone in the Service and Maintenance Building. But out of that isolation emerged a camaraderie—not just one among students and their peers, but also one among students and their professors.

"My entire philosophy on music and life came from the College," he shares. "You don't have to be a prima donna to be a good musician. And to be a good music teacher, you need to have compassion. That compassion taught me to never give up on a student, no matter how much they may be struggling."

It's the same philosophy that allowed Reitano to enjoy a successful teaching career. Upon his retirement, the Syracuse Symphony honored him for his outstanding work as an educator for nearly 35 years. And he attributes much of that success to what he learned at Onondaga.

"To this day, I still tell people that I learned more at OCC in two years than I did anywhere else," he says. "I wasn't just another face in a classroom of a hundred students. I was a name. I was a person."

OCC VACATES MIDTOWN PLAZA

The last units of OCC moved from Midtown Plaza to Onondaga Hill in the fall of 1973. The 5,000 students were at last mainly in one location. Physical Education, required for graduation, continued at the YMCA downtown, so not all the commuting problems had ended. Fond memories grew around the 11 years at Midtown Plaza. Everyone missed the closeness that the single building had given the College in its formative years. Now there were new buildings spread out over the raw hillside.

President Rapp at the College's ten-year anniversary celebration.

President Marvin Rapp traveled throughout Onondaga County promoting OCC and its Onondaga Hill campus. He was frequently in touch with County officials and urged trustees to be likewise connected. During Rapp's presidency, faculty and staff initiated several programs, including general interest mini-courses, offerings at the County's Jamesville Penitentiary and Hancock Air Force Base, an evening program for Liverpool School District teacher aides, a guaranteed admissions program for students of the Syracuse City School District and certification programs in technical fields.

In addition, OCC collaborated with the state Department of Motor Vehicles and the local Automobile Club to offer one of the earliest programs for convicted DWI drivers. The Performing Arts faculty presented OCC in Concert, in addition to the arts and jazz programs already underway. And a *Perspective* lecture series was presented by local business, cultural and political leaders.

CAMPUS CONTROVERSIES

For trustees, the new campus represented years of planning, as well as the resolution of multiple controversies and the expenditure of large amounts of money. OCC continued to be a prominent topic in local newspaper headlines. Throughout the early 1970s, the faculty Union was outspoken in making sure their issues were known to the general public. Faculty members attended County Legislature committee meetings, as well as full meetings of the Legislature. Controversies continued between the faculty and administration who still had to have approval from the County in order to grant all salaries, promotions and curriculum changes. Certain provisions of the labor contract, such as teaching load, sabbaticals and the academic year, were not part of the working experience of many trustees who relied on the administration to mediate between the faculty, themselves and the County. Issue after issue went beyond negotiation and into the full range of conflict resolution procedures outlined by state labor law.

Reporters searched for new angles and sought fresh quotes to make news.

The headlines of 1973 included tenure and contract details for faculty, pay for administrators and escalating costs of the new buildings. Board agendas bounced between matters ranging from approving petty cash disbursements of $190.90 to authorizing a $19 million campus construction plan.

In February 1973, the faculty and newspapers demanded the resignations of all trustees. Under duress, trustees reluctantly held a press conference and issued statements to respond to what they characterized as an "emotion-laden controversy" about faculty tenure and overall management of the College. Trustees were clearly stinging as they informed the community that "some of the faculty have chosen to take their grievances directly to the County Legislature and the news media." Trustees also pointed out that OCC was operating in three locations, and the current consolidation at Onondaga Hill was being carried out with little increase in the administrative staff. "The problems now before the College must be resolved by the

The first Commencement Ceremony on the Onondaga Hill campus took place at the Service and Maintenance Building on May 21, 1972.

Graduation procession from the Library to the Service and Maintenance Building.

Library dedication June 24, 1973. (from left) Trustee Don Mawhinney, Trustee Ransom MacKenzie, President Marvin Rapp, Mrs. Sidney B. Coulter, Chair of Legislature Ephraim Shapero, Librarian Mrs. Carolyn Stover and Architect Robert Clark.

Furnace Brook Gorge bridge and Student Center under construction, circa 1971-1972.

Library under construction, early 1970s.

Trustees Albert Gordon, Arthur Hyatt and Ransom MacKenzie review campus design plans with Town of Onondaga Supervisor Clarence Higgins.

Board, Administration, Faculty and Students together" was the conclusion they made.

The decision not to renew the contracts of President Rapp and Vice President Charles came from the trustees as the public, faculty and County officials all focused their ire on the two men at the top of the administration. The constant increases in construction costs, the documented financial losses in the bookstore, uncollectible fees from the evening division and student government overspending (plus the opposition to his administration led by the faculty) agitated trustees and County officials alike, and diminished Dr. Rapp's effectiveness. The State Department of Audit and Control, the County District Attorney and County Comptroller all had investigations underway, with the resulting headlines. Eventually, both sides of the political aisle in the County Legislature called for Rapp's resignation, and he eventually lost the support of the trustees. In March 1973, trustees notified Dr. Rapp and Dr. Charles, the Vice President who had come with him to the College from Long Island, that their contracts would not be renewed in August.

Aroused by the steady faculty protests, students also began to pay attention to how decisions were being made, and they wanted to have a say. In October 1973, the trustees responded by inviting a student representative to attend Board meetings, two years before state law allowed students as full Board members.

THE BOOKSTORE CONTROVERSY

What came to be known as "the bookstore controversy" was headline news. The difficulty went back to 1970 when the bookstore was operated by the Faculty-Student Association. Every full-time student paid $20 a semester into the Student Activity account, also managed by the Faculty-Student Association.

The bookstore manager, first hired in July 1971, had a contract that allowed him to hire workers, order books and merchandise and handle any other details of the store operation with "total responsibility and discretion," according to OCC officials looking back on that year. The part-time bookstore bookkeeper also had charge of the accounts and records of the federally funded student loan programs and issued the checks from this account

Construction on the Technology/Science/Paramedical Building (later named Nicholas Ferrante Hall), circa 1971.

Original entrance sign, dedicated October 29, 1970. The facing limestone bricks were taken from an archway leading into Pogey Pond that had been constructed in the 1850s.

to authorized students. When the management contract was renewed in December 1972, it was learned that the operation had a $79,000 deficit for the previous year. Questions were raised in the local newspapers, based on student and faculty complaints relating to bookstore operations.

Investigations by the Onondaga County Comptroller, the District Attorney and eventually the state's Department of Audit and Control decided that there was $90,000 of missing inventory. Blank checks from the bookstore account had disappeared, and there were numerous questionable business practices. Who had control of the money? Where did it go? Why was it missing? Those were front-burner items for County and College officials who took the heat from the newspapers and the public. A Grand Jury investigation resulted in indictments being issued in 1973. The trial in 1974 and an appeals decision in 1975 resulted in a sentence of probation for the bookkeeper and restitution being paid, with Grand Jury records sealed in December 1975.

In the interim, the County Comptroller took over the bookstore, and trustees searched for a new method of handling the operation. In the County Legislature, the investigations of OCC's bookstore and the student fee led the agenda.

INTERIM PRESIDENT APPOINTED

For Interim President, trustees chose Dr. Roy A. Price, retired head of Social Science doctoral programs at Syracuse University. Francis Wingate, with 13 years experience as SU's Treasurer and Vice President, took those same titles at OCC. The fallout from the dismissal of Dr. Rapp and Dr. Charles continued for several months.

Throughout the controversies and turmoil, County Executive John Mulroy remained firm in his support of OCC and its goal to supply affordable higher education to Onondaga County residents. Although sometimes exasperated during the frequent crises, he reminded the public in 1973 that OCC students have gone on to assume "leadership roles in our community and the College has been instrumental in raising the educational and social level in Onondaga County."

Alumni Snapshot

Jo Anne Bakeman, '73

- A.A.S., Nursing
- B.A., History and Government – Rosary Hill (Daemon) College
- M.S.T., Health Education – SUNY Cortland
- Adjunct Instructor at Onondaga Community College – Health and Humanities; Credentialed Alcoholism/Substance Abuse Counselor

When Jo Anne Bakeman was presented the opportunity to work at Onondaga Community College, she felt her life coming full circle.

"I always had a dream of teaching health at OCC. I always held it in my heart," she says. "So when I was given the opportunity to do so, it was unbelievable."

The dream stems from a special connection Bakeman has with the College—one tracing back to her childhood. Her grandparents' farm was located right down the road from today's Onondaga Hill campus, and she often swam in the former Pogey Pond during hot summer days.

Additionally, her mother worked at the Smith Corona factory in Midtown Plaza that would become the site of Onondaga's first campus. And after the College's campus moved to Onondaga Hill, she started her own business and held an office in Midtown Plaza. But as a student at the College, Bakeman experienced the best of both worlds. She was among the group of students that moved with the College from Midtown Plaza to Onondaga Hill in the early '70s. It's a move she describes as "beautiful," bringing her to a land and an area she held dear.

"I was just blown away by the new campus," she says. "I kept thinking to myself, 'I'm really going to school up here.' To be in this setting, to be down the road from the family farm and near so many memories—it was amazing."

It's a move that will remain with her for the rest of her life.

"I've been connected to Onondaga Community College and Onondaga Hill almost every day for the past 65 years," Bakeman says. "I love coming up to this campus. It's truly a gem in the landscape of Central New York, filled with forward-thinking people with the sense of always making things better and greater. I consider myself very blessed to be a part of it."

INTERCOLLEGIATE ATHLETICS

From the very beginning, Onondaga Community College offered its students the opportunity to participate in intercollegiate athletics. In 1962, both a men's basketball team and a cheerleading squad debuted. Located at Midtown Plaza, the College had no athletic facilities of its own, so games were played at the Jefferson Street Armory. The following year, tennis, cross-country, golf and wrestling were added.

Over the years, the College offered a number of different sports for its students. Sometimes teams were incorporated as official intercollegiate teams; other times students played semi-organized sports under the guise of student clubs. Depending upon funding and student interest, different sports came and went, and some offerings alternated season to season between team and club status. Additional sports included baseball (M), basketball (W), bowling (M), ice hockey (M), lacrosse (M), soccer (M/W), softball (W) and volleyball (W).

The victorious OCC men's lacrosse team in the NJCAA National Championship game against Nassau Community College (May 2009).

In keeping with the strategic enrollment plan and in an effort to offer students the "full college experience," in 2001 President Sydow commenced a build-out of intercollegiate athletics offerings. That year, men's lacrosse was formally reintroduced as a permanent intercollegiate athletic team. Women's lacrosse debuted in 2009. That same year, men's and women's soccer returned. And in 2010, golf and cross-country also returned to the campus, with both men's and women's teams.

By 2011, Onondaga offered students the opportunity to participate in 15 intercollegiate sports: baseball (M), basketball (M/W), cross-country (M/W), golf (M/W), lacrosse (M/W), soccer (M/W), softball (W), tennis (M/W) and volleyball (W).

THE EMERGENCE OF ATHLETIC PROMINENCE

OCC intercollegiate athletic teams compete at the conference (Mid-State Athletic Conference), regional (Region III) and national (NJCAA) levels. In addition to many conference championships, several teams have won championships at the regional and national levels:

• Men's Baseball - Region III: 1984-1987, 1990-1992, 1994
• Men's Basketball - Region III: 1993, *NJCAA: 1993*
• Women's Basketball - Region III: 2009, 2010
• Men's Bowling - Region III: 1980
• Men's Lacrosse - Region III: 2005-2010, *NJCAA: 2006, 2007, 2009, 2010, 2011*
• Women's Lacrosse - Region III: 2010, *NJCAA: 2009*
• Women's Softball - Region III: 1985, 1986, 1990-1992
• Men's Tennis - Region III: 2004, 2008, 2009-*NJCAA: 2008*
• Women's Tennis - Region III: 1992
• Women's Volleyball - Region III: 1985, 1987-1990, 1992-1994, 2000

OCC women's volleyball team plays a match against Monroe Community College in October 2009.

OCC men's baseball team in April 2010 playing Finger Lakes Community College.

OCC's women's soccer team plays Genesee Community College in September 2009.

Basketball game at the New York State Armory during the1968-69 season.

Cross country team 1964-65 (kneeling from left) Jim Molivas, Than Palermo, Ken Landers. (standing from left) Coach Wayne Mousaw, Walter Schlechki, Al Goodin, Phares Noyes, Sam Mahshi.

Student athletes have also achieved notable individual success. Sixteen former baseball players have gone on to sign professional contracts, including former Major League players Archi Cianfrocco and Todd Williams. OCC's men's basketball team moved 38 players onto Division I, II or III programs in the past decade, including Tyrone Albright (Class of 2002), who was a member of Syracuse University's 2003 National Championship team. Thirty-five players from the men's lacrosse team have been named as All-Americans. And 14 women's volleyball athletes also achieved All-American distinction.

In January 2004, the Athletics Department established an Athletics Hall of Fame. An induction ceremony is held each year.

SRC ARENA AND ATHLETIC COMPLEX

When the College moved to its Onondaga Hill campus beginning in the early 1970s, it had the capability to have its own athletic facilities for the first time. The Health and Physical Education Center offered a gymnasium, weight room, training facilities, swimming pool and outdoor tennis courts.

However, as the Athletics program grew, it became apparent that the existing athletic facilities of the College were inadequate. Lacrosse practiced on campus in an open field and played at a variety of off-campus locations, including Liverpool High School, Cicero-North Syracuse High School, the former Griffin Field in Liverpool and Corcoran High School. Baseball and softball also played at the former Griffin Field, and presently play at Hopkins Road Park in Liverpool. Depending on availability, baseball occasionally played home games at Alliance Bank Stadium.

To support the growing Athletics program, in 2008 the College constructed a new $2.9 million facility featuring a state-of-the-art turf field for lacrosse, soccer and other field sports, seating for 2,000 fans, a press box, stadium lighting and a sound system. At the time of this writing, the field hosted games and practices nearly every night of the week as the College's own teams take the field or as other college and scholastic teams in the community utilize the facilities. In 2009, the field was dedicated as the David W. Murphy Field, named in honor of the then-Chair of the OCC Board of Trustees (Member, 1998-2010; Chair, 2004-2010).

Having worked arduously to secure state and local capital funding, OCC broke ground in May 2010 on the 60,000-square foot SRC Arena. In 2007 and 2009, SRC (formerly, Syracuse Research Corporation), an independent, not-for-profit research and development organization and its subsidiary, SRCTec, pledged two gifts totaling $1.525 million to Onondaga Community College's Reach Beyond campaign. In recognition of this substantial support, SRC received naming rights for the arena for 10 years. With flexible seating for audiences ranging from 1,000 to 6,500, the complex features a six-lane regulation track, changeable tennis and basketball courts, a multi-purpose field, concession areas and a press box. This new physical space offers all students the full spectrum of fitness, wellness and intramural sports activities. In addition, the new complex hosts area high school athletic events, intercollegiate tournaments, concerts and a wide range of other events.

In December 2009, the College announced that it would close the 35-year-old campus swimming pool. Despite concerns expressed by some members of the public and the campus community, the College implemented the planned closing in May 2010, citing the rising costs of maintenance and operation in the face of declining public funding. Also in May 2010, OCC and the Greater Syracuse YMCA announced a partnership to build a YMCA on the College's campus as part of the Athletics Complex (the SRC Arena, Murphy Field, and the Health and Physical Education Center, renamed Allyn Hall in December 2011).

Intercollegiate Athletics

The Onondaga Hill Campus
1973-1984

Bringing most of Onondaga Community College to the Hill campus in the fall of 1973 represented vast opportunities: new buildings, more students and a broader selection of courses in a monumental hilltop setting—far different from the industrial Midtown Plaza location. Once the new campus opened, enrollment increased rapidly. In fall 1973, approximately 5,000 students were enrolled. By fall 1977, more than 6,000 students were enrolled. Campus life blossomed with the growing student population.

THE NEW CAMPUS

Characteristic of the College's beginnings, settling in on the Onondaga Hill campus was rocky. Although OCC had left the stark, industrial-style Midtown Plaza behind, the Hill campus was far from being completed.

Classes began in the Service and Maintenance Building in February 1970. The Library was first occupied in January 1972; the Gordon Student Center was partially occupied in 1973. Some indication of the stress shows clearly in the October 1975 trustee minutes, when the architect, Robert T. Clark, assured trustees that "all parts of Academic One will be available January 14, 1976, without fail." The new Health and Physical Education building was delayed by strikes of the building trades and was not occupied until the spring of 1977. That was only part of the work still needed. By 1976, six years after the first building opened, the campus switchboard was overloaded and needed at least $52,000 in improvements. The Library needed new doors, and the main desk with its extensive electrical equipment needed relocation to improve traffic flow.

The bridge spanning the gorge with Gordon Student Center in the distance.

Aerial view of Phase One of campus construction, circa early 1970s. Ferrante Hall and Storer Auditorium are partially built.

Trustees agonized over spending more money to fix roofs, stairs, floors and other parts of "new" buildings. The alterations cost more than two million dollars in the first ten years of the Phase One buildings and made trustees and County officials wary of committing to any more construction.

Faculty offices had not been in the architect's original building plans for Coulter Library, but offices for English, Social Sciences and Modern Languages faculty were jammed into the large open space on the library's second floor overlooking the main floor. Temporary five-foot high partitions without doors were installed. Human Services was shoehorned into the book stack room. One Philosophy professor took a philosophical attitude and hung a string at the top of his opening with a hand-lettered sign: "This is a door." Academic One (renamed Mawhinney Hall June 2006) was authorized in 1973. When the building opened in 1976, faculty office doors were missing. Prof. David Feldman (English) recalled that when his door was finally installed, he posted a *Memorial Notice* on it, mourning the "loss of open space that had existed on this spot for five years."

Winter weather on the wind-swept campus brought its own challenges. Decisions about whether to hold classes in those early days at Onondaga Hill fell to Francis Wingate, Treasurer and Vice President. Without the Internet, the Weather Channel or cell phones, he consulted the sheriff's office about road conditions, evaluated the chances of getting campus roads and parking lots plowed by class time and dealt with the deadlines of the various radio and TV stations. His main decision had to be made by 5:30 a.m. with the knowledge that closing for a day would cost OCC $9,000, he told trustees. If day classes were held, decisions about evening classes could be postponed until 3 p.m. He knew that any decision—whether to close or stay open—would surely draw complaints.

"OCC is dear to my heart, as an alumna, an employee, and a parent. My three children went to OCC and from there went on to other colleges. One son is now a mechanical engineer, another is a registered architect, and my daughter is in business. They all got a good start at OCC."

– *N. Jean Garofano*
(Business Administration, 1978, OCC retiree)

COLLEGE PRESIDENTS

For two years, OCC operated with Dr. Roy A. Price as Interim President while the trustees, County officials and faculty battled over the selection of a new President. Eventually, the disagreements were resolved, and in August 1975, the campus welcomed Dr. Roger J. Manges, of Purdue University in Indiana, as the College's third President. President Manges began by trimming the administrative staff and increasing the faculty support staff, which won approval from trustees.

Students brave the winter weather while crossing the gorge bridge, circa early 1980s.

Gorge spillway into Pogey Pond is visible in lower left corner. Campus loop road dead-ends in upper right corner before the gorge.

Dr. Manges began meeting weekly with the Chair of the Board of Trustees and becoming better acquainted with Onondaga County politics and personalities. He lunched with high school guidance counselors, tried to bring OCC's administration into the computer age, and familiarized himself with the ongoing controversies. His plea, "I ask that the 'ghosts' of the past no longer be invoked," did not, however, receive much consideration. In 1976, President Manges moved the President's Office from the Gordon Student Center into Academic One. (President Rapp moved the office from Midtown to the Service and Maintenance Building on the Onondaga Hill campus in 1972 and then from the Service and Maintenance building to the Gordon Student Center in 1973.) In July 1976, Dr. John Blasi, a long-time Le Moyne College administrator, became OCC's Vice President for Academic Affairs. Throughout the two Manges years at OCC, there were continuous controversies. Manges resigned in May 1977 to return to the Midwest, to Ball State University in Muncie, Indiana.

Dr. Albert T. Skinner, retired President of Cayuga Community College, was appointed as Interim President in July 1977. In only a few months (November 1977), the campus welcomed a new president, Dr. Andreas A. Paloumpis, from Illinois Central College. His academic background was in Aquatic Biology.

OCC's fourth President started another round of reorganization and appointments, along with providing for the expanding services needed to match the increased student enrollment. Dr. Gary Livent was named Vice President for College Services in 1978 (when he retired in 1998, he had become Vice President of Development and Community Relations; and that same year, he was appointed to the Board of Trustees). Dr. Paloumpis brought a direct, decisive management style to the President's Office. He was usually in his office well before 6 a.m. to deal with paperwork so that his days would be free to talk to students, faculty and staff. He is also remembered for his habit of walking the halls, catching up on OCC news as he greeted students and employees.

President Paloumpis quickly fulfilled the expectations of County officials and trustees through careful attention to OCC's financial situation. He not only balanced the budget, but he also ended his first full year with a $300,000 surplus despite having to deal with the failing national economy, inflation, escalating utility costs and the need for more classroom equipment. Dr. Paloumpis also set up the President's Advisory Council of local community and business representatives.

When renewing his contract in 1981, trustees noted that he had brought "stability," improved the community image of OCC and recruited "excellent faculty and administration." The College had developed a viable long-range plan and made substantial progress in reorganizing business procedures.

One of the most controversial decisions came in 1982 when the daily newspapers revealed OCC's plans to discontinue the Drama Department. Faculty members turned out in force to attend the meeting of the trustees to demonstrate Faculty opposition to the action which President Paloumpis claimed would save $200,000. That figure was disputed by the Faculty who maintained that the Drama Department was "income producing" and pleaded to give Drama "a second chance." At the following Board meeting, the Faculty charged that the decision had been made "in great secrecy" with no input from the Drama faculty. Drama students started a court action, pointing out that they had enrolled expecting a two-year degree in Drama. In addition, the faculty union, the OCCFT, filed a grievance that went to arbitration. Both cases ended when OCC agreed to offer courses to permit all eligible second-year students to complete their degree in Drama in 1983 and agreed to a settlement with the affected faculty members.

In October 1983, Dr. Paloumpis announced that he was resigning to become President of Hillsborough Community College in Tampa, Florida. That same month, Dr. Thomas Sheldon, who had served five years as President of Utica College, then a division of Syracuse University, and as state Deputy Commissioner of Elementary, Secondary and Continuing Education, was hired as the Interim President.

Students protesting the discontinuance of the Drama program in 1982.

"OCC was a great foundation for my career in education. A more dedicated staff can be found nowhere else. I am so proud to be an alum and so impressed with the help and support I received at OCC."

– *Margaret "Peggie" Galvagno Pendergast (Humanities & Social Sciences, 1978)*

EPHRAIM E. SHAPERO

Ephraim E. Shapero, a lawyer for more than 70 years, was a member of the Onondaga County Board of Supervisors (later, the County Legislature) from 1958 to 1975, and he served as Chair of both bodies from 1961 to 1975. His 17 years of service in County government spanned the formative time of Onondaga Community College. He was a member of the Board of Supervisors' committee that studied the community college options in 1960. Then as Chair of the Board of Supervisors/County Legislature, Mr. Shapero was responsible for "making it all happen" with the County's elected officials.

Looking back, Mr. Shapero recalled that "money was always tight." His skills as a negotiator and persuader helped OCC overcome some of the opposition that arose as the College's expanding staff and campus required more money. Many times his desire to move OCC forward had to surrender to other County needs, such as new roads or a better trash disposal system.

A graduate of Syracuse University and its College of Law, Mr. Shapero was known for his sharp wit and command of the facts on any issue. He was a tough negotiator and, as leader of the County Legislature, he was able to influence the decisions that resulted in OCC's growth. He was also able to withstand the steady and often vitriolic criticism about OCC that came from the local daily newspapers for many years.

After he died on June 6, 2008, his family asked that donations in his memory be made to the Onondaga Community College Foundation.

STUDENT SUPPORT SERVICES

Requirements for admission to the College were changing. When OCC admitted its first class in 1962, a high school diploma was accepted as the entrance requirement. But in 1973, following new SUNY guidelines, OCC instituted greater flexibility in its admission criteria for students who had not completed a high school diploma. Prof. John MacDonald, former headmaster at The Manlius School, a college preparatory boarding school, is credited with reorganizing the General Studies A.A. program for those students who were academically under-prepared or who had unclear career goals. He came to OCC in 1962 as Director of Admissions and in 1964 became a professor in General Studies.

Support systems for students were part of the pioneering contributions developed by faculty and staff. With the move to Onondaga Hill and the increase in enrollment, these support systems became more formalized. During this time, the English Department organized reading and writing centers, inaugurated English 100 as a course to help students prepare for freshman composition, and continued its English as a Second Language classes. The Assistance in Development (AID) program, later known as Assistance in Matriculation (AIM), helped students to improve their academic averages by enrolling them in a block of basic courses, with an emphasis on the areas of decision-making and communication.

Other support services included Math Labs, the Collegiate Science and Technology Entry Program (C-STEP) and the Educational Opportunity Program (EOP). In addition, a peer tutoring program led by Prof. Norma Foody (Reading) and later, Prof. Baron Duncan (Counseling) matched students with tutors for personalized assistance. Summer-long advisory services were instituted. In the summer of 1974, 49 students held Urban Corps job assignments in 24 departments of Syracuse and Onondaga County government.

Alumni Snapshot

Steven R. Schill, '78

- A.A.S., Electrical Engineering Technology
- B.S., Marketing Management – Syracuse University
- Executive MBA, Business Administration – Syracuse University
- Thin Film Business Line Manager – Inficon, Inc.

Steven R. Schill invested much more than two years into Onondaga Community College. His wife, daughter, brother, mother and mother-in-law all experienced the College and earned their education through it.

"We all went at different times. There have been significant changes in terms of technology and the organization of the College, but we all received the extraordinary experience a two-year community college has to offer," Schill says.

It's an example of one of Onondaga's greatest accomplishments—hosting generations of learning. And though Schill and his family studied at the same institution, the College meant something different to each one.

To Schill, his brother and his daughter, attending Onondaga was the first step in learning a career. To his mother and his mother-in-law, it was an opportunity to advance their careers through higher education. And to his wife, the Nursing program at the College was a second chance—an opportunity to return to school after years in the workforce and switch career paths.

Why did they all choose Onondaga Community College? Schill says that it was simply common sense.

"Students at Onondaga have the ability to be local, to pay a low price and to enroll in modern curricula that allow credits to transfer," he explains. "I don't know why anyone would not go to Onondaga."

Coulter Library and Quad in the throes of a Central New York winter, circa late 1970s.

From the Quad, looking at construction of Academic One (Mawhinney Hall), circa 1973-1975.

An annual holiday Madrigal Dinner was inaugurated during the President Paloumpis years. The Boar's Head procession includes Prof. Don Miller (Music) as a monk (left). Prof. Catherine Hawkins (Radio/Television) addresses the cast of the production (right).

Workers in local industries, such as Allied Chemical, Crouse-Hinds and Carrier, could enhance their job opportunities at OCC. Federal grants helped to launch classes for local Emergency Medical Technicians and surveyors. Federal money also provided library books, energy conservation measures for OCC buildings and services for veterans.

FACULTY COLLOQUIUMS

Starting in 1977, Faculty Colloquiums on a broad range of topics were held for more than six years. Some of the topics were groundbreaking studies at the time: *Profiles of Women Making Non-Traditional Career Choices* in 1979; *Microprocessors: The Second Industrial Revolution* in 1980; *International Terrorism* in 1982; *Mediaspeak: How Television Makes Up Your Mind* in 1983. Others related to topics of personal interest; for example, President Paloumpis spoke on *The Role of Ichthyology in Archaeological Study*. Prof. Frank Doble (Library) presented *The Myth and Magic of a Solar Eclipse*. Prof. Wayne Archer (English) delivered his *Poems To Pop Corn By*, and Prof. Bruce Hutchinson (Business Administration) spoke about *Life on a Coral Reef*.

Professors Lois Easterday (Sociology) and Jim Schofield (Philosophy) present as members of a Faculty Colloquium panel in 1979.

In 1977, the College received a grant under the Comprehensive Employment and Training Act (CETA) and hired Gary Falco as the first Coordinator of the Office of Handicapped Students. Previously, Prof. John Wagner coordinated services out of the Counseling Department. In 1979, the name of the office changed to the Office of Services for Students with Special Needs. Patrick Francher became the Coordinator.

Then in 1980, OCC began to modify the campus to be "barrier-free." Among the projects Mr. Francher initiated were a reader service for visually-impaired students; a student handbook showing the most-accessible campus routes; a tactile campus map (inside and outside of buildings) for visually-impaired students; an audio version of the College Catalog; a dedicated computer terminal for the disabled in the Registrar's Office; a wheelchair pusher system to assist non-ambulatory students in the snow; and an emergency evacuation procedure for the disabled.

"Thank you, OCC, for giving me the tools needed for a fun and rewarding life."

– *Gary D. Kaschak*
(Radio/Television, 1975)

CREATIVE FERVOR

"Creative fervor" was the way Prof. Barbara Davis, Modern Languages and 1978-1980 Faculty Chair, described the state of the faculty in 1980. Their work was recognized nationally with grants from the National Science Foundation, National Education Agency, National Institute of Mental Health, National Endowment for the Humanities, SUNY Research Foundation and others. Prof. Davis created exhibits to commemorate Black History Month for the first time at OCC; she also obtained a federal grant and wrote a book on Syracuse's 15th ward. The Women's Studies program received recognition for its pioneering work. Prof. Jane Donegan (History) researched and wrote about midwifery; English Department faculty member Prof. Donna Cross made the late night TV show circuit with her book *Word Abuse,* appearing five times in one year on the popular *Tonight Show* with Johnny Carson. Prof. Jerry Berrigan taught English Literature courses for residents of the Loretto Home.

In 1978, Prof. David Feldman of the English Department and also advisor to *The Overview,* the student newspaper, developed a Journalism Concentration. The flexibility of the Concentration, a first for OCC, was such a success that many other academic areas followed that path. Concentrations (renamed "minors" in 2009) constitute 12 or more credit hours in a specialized field of study. By 2010, the College offered 18 such minors.

STUDENT ACTIVITIES

A wide variety of clubs and other extracurricular activities developed at the Onondaga Hill campus, in addition to the Festival of Arts initiated at Midtown Plaza in 1971. Clubs formally authorized by OCC received funds from the Student Government. However, many clubs had difficulty in maintaining the paperwork required by the system and frequently sought Phil D'Arms, Director of Student Activities (1977-1993), to help them remain eligible for funding. Students fondly remembered Mr. D'Arms as a man who would "try to make life easier for any student."

A week-long multimedia Arts and Crafts Display and Sale drew entries and viewers from all over New York State in 1974. Later, a Very Special Arts Festival was started, with more than 1,000 students from Central New York usually participating. Jazz concerts were annual events with recurring performances by jazz greats, including Chick Corea and Return to Forever playing in the cafeteria in November 1975. The Roscian Players continued OCC's very active drama tradition, still buying costumes and props at thrift stores and holding yard sales to support the stage shows. Chess and film enthusiasts held meetings and film festivals, such as one featuring classic Charlie Chaplin movies. Participation in all campus activities was enhanced by the inauguration of a College Hour in 1977, which allocated the 11 a.m. to 12:30 p.m. time slot on Monday, Wednesday and Friday for College events. In 1978, women from OCC, with their *I love NY* buttons, joined the national push for an Equal Rights Amendment, marching amidst 100,000 other people in Washington, D.C.

The International Students Association brought together foreign students and local students. In the 1970s, OCC enrolled students from as many as 20 foreign countries, and each year's International Students Welcome, featuring international foods, drew several hundred people. One three-day festival featured the Consul General of Israel as a speaker and concluded with an evening of Middle Eastern dining and dancing.

JAMAA, a service club aimed at bringing racial harmony and cultural awareness to campus, sponsored Black Awareness Weekend for about five years in the 1970s. The three-day 1974 event featured Julian Bond, then President of the Southern Poverty Law Center, as keynote speaker. A panel discussion on *The Role of the Black Student at OCC,* followed by a session with students from Syracuse University, Le Moyne College, SUNY Cortland and SUNY Oswego, was held on Saturday. Sunday featured a church service, a gospel hour and a talk by social activist Dr. Charles Willie, then an SU professor. Dances on Friday and Sunday with a concert on Saturday completed the festivities.

Nationally known speakers appeared at OCC, including Bernie Sanders (then the Socialist Mayor of Burlington, Vermont, and now an Independent U.S. Senator from Vermont); Mitch Miller (recording industry producer and artist, and star of the 1960s television show *Sing Along with Mitch*); Midge Mackenzie (film-maker who chronicled and championed feminism); Senator James L. Buckley (Republican U.S. Senator from New York); Dick Gregory (comedian and social activist); and the Rev. Betty Bone Schiess (one of the first eleven women ordained into the priesthood of the Episcopal Church).

Alumni Snapshot

Kathy Lagrow, '79

- A.S., Human Services
- Bachelor's Degree – SUNY Network
- Graduate coursework – Syracuse University
- Owner, Learn As You Grow Childcare

Kathy Lagrow gained knowledge, experiences and friendships at Onondaga Community College that will last her a lifetime. She remembers the joy of walking onto scenic Onondaga Hill on a cool autumn day. She remembers courses pushing her to explore and think outside of the box.

But nothing tops the memories she holds of her professors. To them, Lagrow wasn't another number. She wasn't another face. She was a person. A human being. An individual.

"They were truly the greatest professors in the world," she says. "You couldn't ask for a nicer group. I worked all throughout college, and the understanding and emotional support they gave me was amazing. It shows that OCC is able to look at the individual, not just the group."

Among the many lessons Lagrow learned at Onondaga, she credits the College with teaching her in particular what it means to serve and give back to the community. As the owner of Central New York's five Learn as You Grow Childcare centers, Lagrow has been involved in projects with the Rescue Mission, the Golisano Children's Hospital and organizations sending Christmas gifts to soldiers.

"I want others to have the opportunities to experience what I did," she says. "OCC taught me the value of hands-on care and assistance, and it introduced me to the experience of giving back."

And for all of her service to the community, Lagrow is pleased at all the College has done to continue its own contributions to society while always focusing on its core mission: the students.

"We're lucky to have OCC in our community. It's maintained and met the needs of the community through its recent expansions—like the dorms and the new arena," she says. "And in spite of all its expansions, it's never lost sight of meeting the needs of the individuals it serves."

Through three successive grants awarded to Professors Ned Hayes and Hugh Bellen (Counseling), the Counseling Department provided career development for students. Pictured above, spring 1976, in the Library (from left) are a student, Prof. Ned Hayes, Prof. John Byrne (Student Personnel Services), Krisanne Sweeney (Technical Specialist in Student Personnel Services) and Prof. Hugh Bellen.

OCC students, circa late 1970s, socializing on the quad.

Alumni Snapshot

Paul Holzwarth, '81 & '83
• A.S., Recreation Leadership
• A.S., Business Administration
• Coordinator, Office of Veterans Affairs at Onondaga Community College

Paul Holzwarth returned from military service in the 1970s only to find himself confused and uneasy with college life.

"I didn't step foot anywhere on campus except for the classroom. I ate lunch in my car for the first month," he says. "I had been disciplined and trained in the military. I was older, and I didn't relate well to other students who were younger."

Like a number of veterans from the Vietnam Era, Holzwarth came to Onondaga Community College in hopes of putting his G.I. Bill benefits to use. Thanks to the Office of Veterans Affairs at the College, he was able to navigate through a maze of numbers, names and paperwork.

But he also found more.

"There wasn't a place where I felt like I belonged until coming to the Vets' Office," he shares. "There's this camaraderie, this sense of closeness. There were activities—chicken barbeques, softball teams, bowling—that gave us a sense of community."

Holzwarth took it upon himself to make sure future student-vets received that same guidance and companionship. Shortly after discovering the College's Vets' Office, Holzwarth accepted a position as one of its work-study students. Today, he continues to serve more than 400 student-vets a year as Coordinator of the office.

"The veteran student deserves as I did—somewhere to go to find the right information, someone to help take off the stress," he says. "You go back to college and already feel like you're behind. But here, there are people to depend on."

The Onondaga Vets' Office remains one of the longest-standing institutions of its kind in the area. And Holzwarth gives the College credit for keeping it that way.

"After the Vietnam grants from the government disappeared, colleges across the nation began to shut down their Vets' Offices," he explains. "But the College stepped up and said 'We'll fund this.' So when more vets returned from Iraq and Afghanistan, we were prepared to help them."

OCC Veterans raising the campus flag in 1975.

Prof. Barbara Davis (Mod. Lang.) took an Honors class to Spain in summer 1980.

Prof. John Merrill (Computer Science) and students at the College computer.

Military veterans continued to be a strong group on campus. They held fundraisers and promoted the veterans' viewpoint in campus affairs. The Ski Club organized lessons and also trips to the Adirondack slopes. The Riding Club staged horse shows in Baldwinsville. The Outing Club took weekend trips to Saranac Lake and Vermont. The Society for Science Fiction and Fantasy met on Saturdays in the Student Lounge. Some clubs related directly to class interests: The Math Club, the Student Nurse Society, the Music Educators Student Chapter, the Dental Hygienists Club and the Women in Technologies, Speech and Broadcasting Club. The Geology Club took spring break trips to the Outer Banks of North Carolina, and the Ecology Club focused on environmental issues.

Maintaining community contacts, students and faculty regularly arranged dinners at the College for residents of the County's Van Duyn Nursing Home. Many Roman Catholic students were members of the Newman Club, and several groups of its more than 200 members offered symposiums and worked in Syracuse's inner city neighborhood centers.

A smaller and less organized group were the two unclothed male streakers who dashed across the bridge over the gorge early one March morning in 1974 and then disappeared into the sunrise in a Volkswagen, making sure OCC was not left out of the college fad of the time.

There were also downsides to Student Activities. Violence at a student clambake at Hinerwadel's in May 1973 drew 13 police cars; on the other hand, in 1979, the clambake "with good security" was attended by 1,200 people. In November 1974, locks on catering cabinets, along with windows, were broken during a campus party. A 1975 controversy centered on the trustees' allocation of a multipurpose room for use by student organizations. Onondaga County officials, as well as OCC trustees, often weighed in as students tested the limits of authority. Defending their public reputation, trustees passed a resolution in 1976 stating that they did not support nor condone the showing of X-rated films on campus.

Despite dramatic highs and lows through the years, the staff of the student newspaper, *The Overview*, tried to keep the commuter campus informed. However, once in a while, their editorializing put *The Overview* dramatically at odds with its constituents. Several staffers recalled the time when an editor barricaded himself in the newspaper office for hours to escape irate readers.

The Student Government Association itself was not immune to difficulties. At that time, the formal organizational structure

FIRST STUDENT TRUSTEE

Since 1973, the OCC Board of Trustees had included a student representative at their meetings. On October 29, 1975, in response to New York state legislation and SUNY Board of Trustees' policy, OCC students held an election for their first official student trustee. Tony Malavenda responded to the opportunity. In an interview, he remembered sitting in the Student Center all day and stopping all other students who passed by to ask for their votes. Among the candidates, he won the election and attended his first meeting as a trustee on November 11, 1975.

Mr. Malavenda recalled the meetings as being held at night in the Student Center. Discussions often focused on finances and personnel issues. The presence of a student trustee was new for the other trustees; some wanted Mr. Malavenda to leave for certain business, especially during discussions of personnel. However, the Chair reminded them that, as a trustee, Mr. Malavenda was entitled to remain. For his part, Mr. Malavenda had no model to follow in his role as student trustee. Generally, his instincts said to focus on listening.

Mr. Malavenda remembered his years at OCC as good preparation for his transfer to Georgetown University and credited his student trusteeship as enhancing his transfer application.

Interview with Anthony Malavenda, student at OCC, 1974-1976; bachelor's degree from Georgetown University; graduate work London School of Economics; Partner, Duke's Root Control, Inc.; current Chair, Hiscock Legal Aid Society Board and Redhouse Art Center Board.

Anthony Malavenda

had little appeal to students. Elections went without candidates, paperwork went undone, and finally in 1976, OCC's Student Government Association, which had served as a liaison between the administration and the corporate Onondaga Student Services Association (OSSA), was dissolved by its own vote in an emergency meeting. By SGA's own observation, since OSSA handled the money passed on by the administration from the mandatory student fees, there was no reason to continue SGA.

FULFILLING EXPECTATIONS
Despite the occasional dispute, OCC amply fulfilled the expectations of the College's founders 20 years earlier. In 1978, 93 percent of OCC students in the Business Department's Insurance Program passed the state's insurance licensing exam, while the state-wide passing average was only 71 percent. That same year, Nursing graduates, with a 95 percent pass rate, scored higher on state exams than students at any other two-

COLLECTIVE BARGAINING

Time and time again (mid 1970s-1980s), the full range of the state's Public Employment Relations Board (PERB) procedures—impasse and arbitration—were invoked on a variety of issues. Contract settlements often took months (the 1977-1980 contract over a year). During prolonged negotiations, there was picketing and mass Union attendance at trustees' meetings, as well as at County Legislature committee meetings and full legislative sessions.

The Union campaigned for more control over working conditions: teaching loads, wages, appointments and tenure. These issues were persistent as the faculty, administration and trustees moved from contract to contract, with the County's attorneys and Personnel Commissioner representing OCC trustees. Contracts were eventually signed retroactively amid charges from both sides of "stonewalling" and "obstructionist behavior." And the faculty repeatedly reminded the public of OCC's ongoing censure by the American Association of University Professors regarding dismissal procedures (see Midtown Plaza Years).

Members of the OCCFT picket during contract negotiations. Professors Edith Schmitz (Modern Languages), Phil Klein (Music), Maxine Stryker (Library); (right from left) Dave Bundy (Biology), Nancy McCarty (History and Political Science) and Jim Doherty (English), Union President.

Picketing on the campus and signs in office windows were visual reminders of the lack of a settlement. When Union pickets appeared at the home of President Paloumpis on a raw, snowy November 25 evening in 1980, he came out in good humor and served them coffee. Some picketers remember they refused as a "matter of principle." Some recall a "silver coffee service," although the newspaper reported he handed out coffee in paper cups.

The dispute over the "OCC 7" is firmly in OCC's collective memory. It occupied the newspaper headlines for weeks. In January 1974, the trustees denied tenure to six faculty members and postponed a decision on a seventh, but the Union slogan demanded a favorable decision on the "OCC 7." The issue of the six denials went through the complete grievance procedure and then on to County court. A settlement came just before the court trial was to begin. Under the settlement, the College agreed to grant tenure to six and promotions to 11 other faculty members not directly cited in the court action. Tenure had already been granted to the seventh faculty member.

MID-LEVEL ADMINISTRATORS UNIONIZE

Prompted by a personnel action against a mid-level administrator in the early 1970s, an administrators' union was organized in March 1974 with 16 members and became the OCC bargaining unit known as the Association of College Administrators (ACA). The first ACA officers included Phil D'Arms, Director of Student Affairs; Margaret (Peg) Hannon, Director of Public Affairs; Bob House, Associate Registrar; Shirley Singer, Registrar; and Al Whitaker, Director of EOP.

The Association of College Administrators union became NYSUT-AFT Local 4596 after affiliation with the New York State United Teachers in 1986. Members were the mid-level professional administrators working in the areas of student services, enrollment services, continued and extended learning, academic services, financial and management services, campus facilities, institutional technology, and institutional research and planning. In October 2004, the respective memberships of the ACA and the OCCFT voted to merge. Effective March 1, 2005, the unions officially became the Onondaga Community College Federation of Teachers and Administrators (OCCFTA).

year school. And for the third year in a row, all Respiratory Therapy graduates moved directly into jobs. A survey of the class of 1983 found that 80 percent of the graduates had remained in Onondaga County, with 90.9 percent either continuing their studies or working in the Central New York community.

In 1982, eight faculty members were recognized for their 20 years at OCC: Professors Jane Donegan (History), Norbert Faltyn (Geology), Janet Harris (Dental Hygiene), Dorothy Harth (Modern Languages), Dorothy Kelly (Human Services), Robert Malek (Biology), Nancy McCarty (History and Political Science) and Carl Oney (Biology). A year later, OCC celebrated its 20 years of service to the community with more than 30 events, including a nuclear arms debate; movies such as *Raiders of the Lost Ark* and *Animal House*; band, choir and jazz concerts; and dancing.

By the close of its second decade, the College boasted an enrollment of over 7,500 students, and the main campus physical plant was well-established with seven buildings in operation: Service and Maintenance, Sidney B. Coulter Library, Albert J. Gordon Student Center, Nicholas Ferrante Hall, Simon B. Storer Auditorium, Academic One and the Health & Physical Education Center.

Students of All Ages Learn at OCC

Rehearsal of the Jazz Lab in 1973, under the direction of Prof. Bill Harris (Music).

OCC FOUNDATION

Founded in 1980, the OCC Foundation, a New York State 501(c)(3) Corporation, serves as the primary fund-raising arm of the College with its mission "To raise, administer and invest funds for the benefit of OCC and its students." During the late 1970s, community college leaders across New York State recognized that initial county and state support of community colleges would likely wane over time and the resulting funding shifts could be catastrophic. One clear solution was through attracting philanthropic support as was already being accomplished by some early community college foundations in Florida, Arizona and North Carolina.

Donald M. Mawhinney, Jr., David R. Robinson and Ralph R. Whitney, Jr. had long recognized the need for generating private support and had also noted the importance of creating a legal entity to protect, invest and shelter any charitable gifts that might flow to the College. As a result, they served as the initial incorporating directors of the new Foundation, Inc. in 1980. In addition, it was felt that protecting such funds within an institutionally related foundation would allow the donor's intent to always be carefully followed and also prevent such funds from ever being used to reduce county and state operating budget allocations to the College.

The College employed Richard J.P. Hanlon, Esq. as its first Director of Development in 1984, and in that position Mr. Hanlon was also Executive Director of the relatively new OCC Foundation. He served in that capacity until 1996 and was familiar with the College and its early days due to his service as Deputy County Executive under Onondaga County's first County Executive and College founder John Mulroy. With Mr. Hanlon's departure, Sharon M. Akkoul succeeded him in the role of Executive Director until 1998, at which time Gene Sirni became Director of Development and OCC Foundation Executive Director.

Dr. Debbie L. Sydow, OCC's seventh president, brought a heightened interest in development and institutional advancement, demonstrating her own philanthropic support by signing

on as an inaugural member of the Legacy Society through the establishment of a leadership planned gift to benefit the College at the time of her passing. In 2001, Sydow hired Thomas A. Burton to serve as the College's Chief Advancement Officer and Executive Director of the Foundation. He had previously served in a similar role at Syracuse-based public broadcaster WCNY.

The 1990 OCC Foundation Tribute Dinner honored Ralph R. Whitney, Jr (left). He received his award from OCC Foundation Director Rev. Dr. Alexander C. Carmichel, III.

Alumni Faces is a display located in the hallway of the Gordon Student Center. Unveiled in 2006, the display features etchings of alumni and brief biographies highlighting their professional as well as service achievements. New recipients are added at an annual College celebration in the Great Room of the Gordon Student Center.

Financial statements dated December 31, 1985, indicate an OCC Foundation, Inc. with total assets of $16,191 with $15,935 of that total made up of restricted gifts. Five years later, the Foundation had grown to hold assets of $243,256 with $241,895 of that sum received as restricted gifts and including a fledgling endowment of $27,500. In 2010 with over $11 million in assets, the Foundation is operated by a 35-member volunteer Board of Directors comprised of business, cultural and community leaders from throughout Central New York.

The Foundation Scholarship Program has assisted thousands of OCC students in achieving their goals through higher education. At the time of the College's 50th Anniversary, scholarship grants exceed $1.2 million with the Foundation administering over 115 different scholarships. The Foundation's overall support of the College and its students, including capital, program and special project support, is well in excess of $4 million. Donor-funded projects range from student-based photo expeditions to Namibia and study of the Aztecs and Mayans in Guatemala and Honduras, to scholarships that open the door to education, to major bricks-and-mortar expansion of College facilities. Through these initiatives, the Foundation plays an ever-increasing role in advancing the College's mission.

In 2006, the Foundation began the "quiet phase" of the Reach Beyond campaign, led by honorary Chair William F. Allyn (who was also instrumental in the success of the previous Today's Choice for Tomorrow's World campaign) and Co-Chairs Allen J. Naples, Region President for M&T Bank, and Robert U. Roberts, CEO of SRC, Inc.

From its quiet start in 1980 to the first ever capital campaign of 1994, to the almost completed $7.5 million Reach Beyond campaign, the largest single fund-raising initiative in College history, the Foundation has grown to become an important contributor to educational dreams in Central New York and is currently engaged in a strategic planning process to double the size and impact of the Foundation.

ONONDAGA COMMUNITY COLLEGE ALUMNI ASSOCIATION

In 1964, members of OCC's first graduating class organized the College's Alumni Association with David Bench as President (Mechanical Technology, 1964). In 2008, with the leadership of then Alumni Association President Miles M. Bottrill (Business Administration, 1982), the Association was dissolved and incorporated into the OCC Foundation as the new Alumni Council, a standing committee of the Foundation. With this shift, the Association became a key element of Foundation operations. Mr. Bottrill served as the first Alumni Council Chair.

In the period leading up to the dissolution of the Alumni Association, a key focus of the Foundation and the College's Institutional Advancement Division was rebuilding the electronic file of alumni dating back to 1964, communicating with almost 40,000 OCC graduates, in some cases for the first time in decades.

Increasing numbers of alumni are now connected to Onondaga, enriching the educational experience for students in myriad ways. From committee and board service to mentoring opportunities, guest lecturing and networking opportunities to fund-raising and planning, alumni are more connected to their alma mater than at any other point in the College's history. In fact, seven alumni now serve on the Foundation Board of Directors. Additionally, the increased outreach to alumni and reconnection with this impressive body of individuals resulted in two alumni appointments to the College Board of Trustees by 2010, Steve Aiello and Dr. Donna DeSiato.

Most recently, the College and the Foundation have embarked on an effort to begin outreach to the tens of thousands of alumni who completed at least 18 credit hours but did not complete a degree. It is hoped that like the previous initiative, identifying and communicating with these students from the past will further enrich the institution's future.

One of the fundraisers conducted by the (former) Alumni Association was the OCC Scholarship Classic, started in 1992. The proceeds from this tournament benefited the Foundation's scholarship fund for OCC students. An extremely popular event, the Classic was hosted at several area golf courses, including Skaneateles Country Club, the Links at Erie Village and the LaFayette Hills Golf & Country Club. The fundraiser hit a high point in 2006 when the tournament raised about $40,000 toward scholarships for students. After a 17-year run, the tournament ended following the 2008 event, due to the financial austerity that hit the nation. Pictured above (from left) are the Skaneateles County Club, Stefan L. Kowalski (student), Prof. Joe Agonito (History), Kenny Roberts (Maintenance Department; Business, 1978) and John "Andy" Breuer (Hueber-Breuer Construction Co, Inc.).

The C&S Companies are proud of the amazing educational resource that Onondaga Community College represents in our community. Many of our employees are graduates of the college, and we are strong supporters of the campus's mission to educate the future leaders of Onondaga County, New York, and the country. Fifty years after its founding, OCC has evolved into a comprehensive community college of more than 12,000 students, distinguishing itself academically as the best community college in the SUNY system.

C&S has been serving the needs of the built environment in Central New York since our founding in Syracuse in 1968. With more than 350 local engineers, architects, planners, environmental scientists, construction professionals and other experts, we are focused on advancing quality of life in our local communities. In 2011, C&S was ranked as the top large company to work for in the fourth annual Best Companies to Work For in New York State awards program. This annual statewide survey and awards program identifies, recognizes and honors New York's best places of employment. "C&S is extremely proud to be named the best company to work for in New York," says company president Ron Peckham. "We have always striven to be the place where the best people choose to work, and the fact that 75 percent of the scoring for this award is based on employee surveys really emphasizes the value our staff places on working in a positive and supportive environment. At C&S, we know that the most important asset we bring to our clients is our outstanding people. Being the best place to work is important to us because it represents our commitment to our employees and the important work they do for our community."

"We are excited about the continued development of OCC and are proud of the many opportunities we have had to partner with OCC to design, build and maintain the campus" says Orrin B "Mac" MacMurray, chairman of the C&S Companies and member of the OCC Foundation Board. The largest catalyst for this significant recent growth on campus has been OCC's current president, Dr. Debbie Sydow. Since her arrival in 2000, Dr. Sydow has focused on a strategic direction, goals and objectives for the college. The college's curricula have expanded to 47 programs, awarding nearly 1,500 degrees annually. OCC recently set new enrollment records, surpassing 10,000 students for the first time. This was the highest rate of growth among all 30 community colleges in the SUNY system. Today, enrollment is over 12,000. With this significant growth in student population, the campus has had to evolve to accommodate the need for more academic, administrative and recreational space.

C&S has been privileged to partner with Dr. Sydow and her team to execute OCC's vision, which has resulted in more than $100 million in capital investment, serving as the catalyst for the strong momentum today. One of the most visible changes to the campus has been the construction of three student housing units, with nearly 500

C&S served as construction manager for the SRC Arena and Events Center and provided mechanical, electrical, plumbing, life safety, security, communications and site civil engineering services.

H1 Hall, formerly a home for the poor and ill in Onondaga Country, contains classrooms, offices, conference and group meeting rooms.

beds near the Route 175 entrance to the campus. These attractive buildings have changed the character of the campus and marked a significant turning point in the history of the college. C&S provided the site/civil engineering services for the development of these dormitories, which are currently fully occupied.

In just the past five years, C&S has played a key role in many of the other major facilities projects at the college. The most significant of these has been the renovation of Storer Auditorium, a campus-wide signage project, the expansion and renovation of Gordon Student Center to create a one-stop student services center (Student Central), the renovation of several science laboratories, the ongoing renovation of Mawhinney Hall and expansion of the parking lots adjacent to Mawhinney Hall.

C&S is just wrapping up the completion of significant renovations to H1 Hall, a historic 45,000 square-foot, four-story building. The innovative project gave the college a "historically modern" building with 16 smart classrooms, 47 offices, three conference rooms and three group meeting rooms. The building, which was originally constructed in 1928 with an addition in 1969, had served as a home for the poor and ill in Onondaga County but had been closed down after new, modern facilities were built. The building stood unused for more than 10 years and needed major renovations. In addition to reconfiguring interior partitions, many elements needed to be replaced, including the roof, exterior doors and windows, all interior finishes and the complete plumbing, mechanical, electrical and security systems. A new elevator shaft was also installed. One of OCC's

primary goals for the project was to reduce the impact on the environment. Reusing the existing building allowed the college to honor a historic property and reduce the environmental impact from new construction.

The college is also opening a new sports complex, the SRC Arena. Onondaga's men's and women's lacrosse teams have already won national championships, as has its men's tennis team. This spring saw the opening of a new turf field, the first piece of the multi-million dollar athletic complex to come that will also include a 10,000-seat-capacity arena and a six-lane track. C&S is the construction manager for this project and provides mechanical, electrical, plumbing, life safety, security, AV/communications and site civil services. The project was designed to achieve a LEED Silver certification from the U.S. Green Building Council.

OCC recently broke ground on a 50,000-square-foot addition to its music department to accommodate the growth. This addition that will ultimately span a 200-plus feet gorge when completed will include classroom, office and music laboratory space, as well as a 150-seat recital hall to complement the school's 350-seat auditorium. C&S is the construction manager on this project. A completion goal of 2013 has been set for this project.

OCC's expansion and contribution to the community has paralleled C&S's growth and commitment to the Central New York area. We congratulate OCC on its 50 years of stellar service and look forward to the next 50 years of academic excellence.

The Syracuse legacy of Lockheed Martin can be traced back to 1942 when the first General Electric (GE) plant opened in Syracuse in a converted streetcar repair shop. Here, 900 SCR-584 radars, an anti-aircraft gun laying system, were built during World War II to help defeat the German Luftwaffe and begin a long heritage of technological innovation in Central New York that continues today.

During the war, GE built another facility in Syracuse to manufacture propulsion turbine generators for U.S. Navy destroyers, as well as radio equipment. That early investment helped GE recognize this region's diverse workforce and close proximity to suppliers, as well as the access to Syracuse University for research. This understanding led to the construction of GE's Electronics Park complex in Liverpool.

The necessity for the facility grew out of the expansion of electronics production as a result of the war. Divisions of the Electronics Department were scattered all over the eastern half of the country. A site was needed to serve as headquarters and an engineering center for the Electronics Department and have a large enough manufacturing plant to take care of practically all business in a normal year. The 150-acre Electronics Park campus became that central location.

In April 1947, the GE Transmitter Building was completed and all of the other buildings, built in the same unique architectural style, finished the following year. The vision of GE Vice President and General Manager W.R.G. Baker resulted in the first facility of its kind, combining research, engineering and production into one site.

The radio transmitters GE's Electronics operation produced when it opened its doors morphed quickly into television receivers and picture tubes by 1948. The public was easily drawn to this exciting new medium and Electronics Park became known as the "Television Capital of the World" as its Central New York workforce pumped out set after set.

While successfully producing televisions, radios and other small appliances for consumer use – much of it an outgrowth of its military work – GE continued to develop radar technology for government and civil use. The AN/FPS-6 radar was introduced into service in the late 1950s and served as the principal height-finder radar for the U.S. for several decades thereafter. Between 1953 and 1960, 450 units of this system were produced. Another early radar was the AN/FPS-8, a medium-range search radar used by the U.S. Air Force Air Defense Command at commercial airports and military bases both in the U.S. and overseas.

With its radar surveillance work on the ground well established, Syracuse researchers turned their attention to the sea and had equal success in developing acoustic technology. Beginning in 1955, engineers demonstrated their know-how with the development of the first variable depth sonar, the first hull-mounted active and passive tactical towed array sonar, and the U.S. Navy's first surface ship anti-submarine warfare system.

While a large and experienced workforce toiled away producing high-profile consumer products and defense systems, a smaller but equally brilliant unit of engineers were hard at work looking to create the next big innovation. In the Syracuse Electronics Laboratory, or E-Lab as it was popularly known, scientists and engineers contributed to many other military, commercial, computer and medical products for more than 50 years.

Key firsts that came out of the E-Lab included the transistor radio, the implantable pacemaker, the CAT scan, high-power video projection systems, Apollo space program simulators, early light emitting diodes (LEDs), digital and analog integrated

The EQ-36 countertarget acquisition radar today helps protect U.S troops from enemy rockets and mortars.

circuits, electronic solid state technology, intercontinental ballistic missile (ICBM) guidance systems and several radar developments. In all, more than 600 patents were awarded for these and other innovations.

In 1992, General Electric Aerospace merged with Martin Marietta Corporation. Just a short time later, in 1995, Martin Marietta merged with Lockheed Corporation to form Lockheed Martin. All combined, Lockheed Martin and its legacy companies has been a major radar innovator across multiple product generations for more than 65 years.

Today, Syracuse is the Radar Center of Excellence for Lockheed Martin and can trace its roots to many firsts in radar technology development. This includes producing the world's first solid-state long range radar, the first simultaneous 3-D radar, the first over-the-horizon radar and the development of the first airborne early warning radar. The airborne early warning surveillance radar program is one of the most successful military programs ever, with four generations of radars on board more than 100 aircraft around the world, including those of the U.S. Navy. That program began in Utica in the 1950s, but moved to Syracuse in 1996.

The diverse portfolio of radar systems spans the frequency spectrum, operating in the air, on the ground and at sea. All produced systems are designed and manufactured to meet customers' exacting mission requirements with built-in scalability to continue performing at a high level for decades. Of the more than 170 long-range radars operating around the world built in Syracuse, none have ever been taken out of service.

The Syracuse site performs work for all four branches of the U.S. armed services and has more international customers than any other Lockheed Martin company. It partners with more than 30 countries around the world to help protect their borders, coastlines and airspace.

Investment and development of new technologies continue in the areas of missile defense, air surveillance, force protection, maritime domain awareness and space situational awareness. Within these large mission classifications, Lockheed Martin has invested heavily in technology and facilities to remain a significant, competitive player both domestically and internationally, and to help keep U.S. armed forces and its allies safe and out of harm's way.

Lockheed Martin is proud to be a vital part of the CNY defense electronics industry base providing surface, air and undersea applications, including radar and surveillance systems, undersea combat systems, and surface combat systems and sensors.

The innovation heritage started decades ago continues on that same Electronics Park footprint today.

The FPS-8 radar was developed in Syracuse in the 1950s.

In 1968, architects Steve Schleicher and Paul Soper set out to open an architectural design firm, Schleicher-Soper Architects, founded on the tenets of culture and community. A few years after its founding, in the early 1970s, the firm, now Architecteam, landed the opportunity to design an office for Syracuse University Chancellor Melvin A. Eggers. The project became a springboard for decades of service to the university and the firm's success in the field of higher education. Since then, Architecteam has completed design projects for Cornell University, Paul Smith's College, Upstate Medical University and numerous public campuses through the State University Construction Fund.

Propelled by word-of-mouth referrals from satisfied customers, Architecteam's proven ability to lead a team of professionals toward innovative solutions to meet clients' design challenges has led to its reputation for design excellence. While the "team" in Architecteam is indicative of the way they do business, the "team" is also currently comprised of seven employees: three licensed architects, two CAD drafters, an intern and a clerical employee. To promote collaboration and teamwork, the firm works in a studio environment. "In an open plan environment, everybody is involved with all aspects of a project," says Brian Hanson, partner at Architecteam. "This creates more well-informed, knowledgeable employees.

Hanson, a 1981 graduate of Onondaga Community College's Architectural Technology Program, has worked at Architecteam for 26 years and has been a partner for 11. He credits his success, in part, to the education he received at OCC. "OCC is a place where opportunity begins," says Hanson. "One can develop his or her skills and enjoy the emergence of their potential at OCC. It was certainly a stepping stone for me."

Like Onondaga Community College, Architecteam is committed to constantly improving the Central New York community. "We are all dependent upon each other in some way," says Hanson. "The stronger we make our community, the lighter the burden. Being community-oriented is about sharing our difficulties and our joys by going the extra mile for a friend or a stranger. That is the essence of a strong community."

Part of Architecteam's commitment to a strong community is reflected in its sustainable design practices. Hanson is an accredited professional in the USGBC's Leadership in Energy and Environmental Design (LEED) initiative. "We have learned to respond to environmental concerns and create designs that are environmentally responsible," Hanson says. Architecteam's sustainability initiatives are helping to provide a safer and more manageable environment for future generations.

As Onondaga Community College celebrates its golden anniversary, the college continues to grow and evolve. "There has been quite an effort to expand and develop the OCC campus, and it has been great to see," says Hanson. Architecteam congratulates OCC on its anniversary and wishes the college continued success in living out its mission of "making high quality educational programs and services accessible to our diverse citizenry, empowering individuals to explore and discover their inherent potential and to transform themselves to live, work and thrive in our global community."

Winnick Hillel Center at Syracuse University

Haylor, Freyer & Coon has a long-standing commitment to supporting education.

I n the 1920s, Barney Haylor was just getting started in Syracuse as an aspiring insurance salesman. Sadly, his father, a district chief with the Syracuse Fire Department at the time, died of smoke inhalation. After his father's death, Haylor set out to serve and insure local firefighters and quickly found his niche. In 1928, the firm that would eventually become Haylor, Freyer & Coon officially opened its doors in downtown Syracuse.

Since 1928, HF&C has grown from a four-person firm into the international insurance brokerage that it is today, expanding its niche well beyond insuring firefighters to offer all types of insurance, from group health to personal and commercial property casualty. All along, HF&C has remained true to its local roots. Headquartered in Syracuse, the firm now employs 150 people in Syracuse and a total of 210 employees throughout Central New York.

The firm's impact on the community goes well beyond its physical presence. HF&C Chairman Vic DiSerio explains, "Part of our corporate vision is a commitment to support the community by working with non-profits and charitable organizations." True to its word, the firm supports a wide array of organizations, including Peace Incorporated, United Way, YMCA and Upstate Medical University Foundation. Haylor's employees also lend their time as directors and volunteers for several non-profit groups, including the Onondaga Community College Foundation, the Kidney Foundation, Samaritan Center, Paige's Butterfly Run and the Syracuse Corporate Challenge.

HF&C has a long-standing commitment to supporting education. The firm insures several educational institutions, and its collegiate department focuses on providing insurance for college students. The company provides an annual scholarship at Cazenovia College, as well as the HF&C scholarship offered to the child of any Haylor employee attending college. DiSerio stresses that by supporting OCC, Haylor is supporting the community as a whole. "Onondaga Community College plays an important part in the future of the community and the future of education in the community," he says. "With the cost of education being what it is, OCC offers many students an opportunity

Haylor, Freyer & Coon Chairman Vic DiSerio

they might otherwise not have to obtain a college education, both because of the cost and the fact that it's local."

Whether in the community or in business, HF&C brings the same passion for people. "There are many competitors selling insurance," says DiSerio. "We distinguish ourselves by providing exceptional service." Because of its status as an independent agency, Haylor, Freyer & Coon is not tied to any one insurance company. "We represent the client, not the insurance company. That means we can utilize the insurance marketplace to develop programs that are best suited to our clients."

This attitude and commitment to the community has earned Haylor, Freyer & Coon the 81st spot in *Business Insurance*'s Top 100 Brokers in 2011. "We're proud to compete on a regional and national level from right here in Syracuse," says DiSerio. Even as the agency continues to grow, HF&C has never lost touch with what matters—the community. "This is where we started," says DiSerio. "This is our home."

"Several partners of Hiscock & Barclay are proud to call themselves OCC graduates."

I n 2012, Hiscock & Barclay, LLP celebrates 157 years of continuous service to clients in the U.S., Canada and beyond. From its roots as a small rural firm established by L. Harris and Frank Hiscock in 1855 to its expansion across New York State and the Northeast with 200 attorneys practicing in 30 areas of law, the Firm is deeply connected to Central New York. It continually attracts superior talent and strives to be a workplace of choice, operating on principles of diversity and a commitment to professional excellence.

The Firm's proud history includes important philanthropic and civic contributions that continue to improve the quality of life in Central New York and throughout each of the eight communities in which offices are located. From its earliest roots, the Firm and its partners have been instrumental in helping to establish important charitable organizations such as the Central New York Community Foundation, the Rosamond Gifford Charitable Corporation and Hiscock Legal Aid Society. It continues to be actively engaged in a wide range of charitable organizations, educational institutions, health care facilities and countless other organizations committed to improving the communities in which we live. The Firm supports its attorneys' involvement in terms of both a significant investment of dollars and thousands of hours of *pro bono* time as well.

Hiscock & Barclay played an integral role in the formation of Onondaga Community College in 1959-1960 through the work of its partner, Donald M. Mawhinney, Jr., who was a member of the Onondaga County Board of Supervisors, charged with researching the establishment of a community college in Onondaga County. In 1961, the Board of Supervisors approved the establishment of OCC, with Hiscock & Barclay supporting the growth and transformation of the College throughout its 50-year history. Mawhinney has served as a founding member of the Board of Trustees since 1961 and is the longest serving community college trustee in the United States. He continues to be an OCC trustee today, having served as Chairman of the Board, Chairman of the Campus Building Committee and numerous other leadership positions. In June 2006, the Board of Trustees rededicated the Academic One building in his honor as the Donald M. Mawhinney, Jr. Hall.

Donald M. Mawhinney, Jr. has served as a member of the OCC Board of Trustees since 1961.

The Firm continues to assist OCC, including the OCC Foundation, in meeting its mission. With the guidance of Firm partner John Sindoni, who served as a Director of the Foundation, Hiscock & Barclay provided assistance related to the largest gift of real estate made to the OCC Foundation, provided support with a major gift to the *Reach Beyond Campaign* and continues to work with the College on other matters. Several notable partners of Hiscock & Barclay are proud to call themselves OCC graduates, including Syracuse Managing Director Gerald Stack and partner Richard Capozza.

Hiscock & Barclay is honored to have been associated with Onondaga Community College for these past 50 years and looks forward to contributing to OCC's success in the years ahead. Hiscock & Barclay salutes and congratulates OCC on its 50th Anniversary!

Colleges and universities play a pivotal role in a region's economic, social and cultural success. This is especially true in Central New York, where Onondaga Community College and Le Moyne College share a commitment to providing an education that benefits not just the individual learner, but also the community as a whole. Le Moyne is proud to collaborate with OCC in this mission.

We salute and congratulate OCC's faculty, staff and alumni as they celebrate 50 years of success. Le Moyne draws more transfer students from OCC than from any other institution. We understand that education, at its core, is a source of unparalleled opportunity, and are proud of our shared commitment to first-generation college students. Both schools provide the region with a talented and diverse workforce. Upon graduation, 60 percent of Le Moyne alumni and over 80 percent of OCC alumni establish careers and raise families in Central New York.

Together, Le Moyne and OCC are significant drivers of the regional economy. According to the Commission on Independent Colleges and Universities, in 2009 Le Moyne had $160 million of local economic impact on the region, both direct and spillover. A 2010 article written by OCC President Debbie Sydow, Ph.D., that was published by the New York State Association of Counties, indicates that OCC generates "approximately $52 million in regional income each year due to its operations and capital spending and (contributes) to an economy that is nearly $900 million stronger due to the College's operations." These efforts encourage new businesses to establish roots in Central New York, assist existing companies and promote long-term economic stability and growth.

Beyond a commitment to undergraduate students, both institutions provide opportunities for professionals to enhance their current skills through customized training programs. As it shares in the celebration of OCC's golden anniversary, the Le Moyne community gratefully acknowledges the visionary leadership of President Sydow. During her tenure, the College has invested heavily in new and existing campus facilities, leading to record enrollment and the development of various programs that have expanded community access to higher education. Her efforts have facilitated this growth and ultimately made a positive impact on our community.

"On behalf of Le Moyne College, I would like to congratulate the OCC community for its tremendous success over the past 50 years," says Dr. Fred Pestello, president of Le Moyne. "Onondaga Community College plays a critical and unique role in the region's vitality and growth. We are honored to share OCC's commitment to serving a diverse population, to excellence in higher education and to this beautiful and historically significant region in the heart of New York State."

Le Moyne College salutes OCC's many impressive achievements over the past five decades, while looking forward to a future of limitless possibilities.

The first structure built on the Heights, Grewen Hall remains the landmark, and most recognized, building on the Le Moyne College campus.

M&T Bank has built a track record as one of the nation's most successful regional banks. M&T was one of the only banks to remain profitable throughout the U.S. financial crisis, posted the lowest loan losses among peer regional banks and did not cut its shareholder dividend.

M&T has a deep history serving Upstate New York, where it has been headquartered for more than 155 years. The bank employs more than 520 people in the Central New York Region, which is managed from its regional headquarters on South Salina Street in downtown Syracuse.

The regional bank's team is one of the leading commercial and industrial lenders in Central New York, maintaining relationships with a large percentage of the Syracuse area's top businesses. Through its strong government lending division, M&T also provides financial services to Onondaga County, Onondaga Community College and a host of local governments and school districts.

Known for its conservative financial culture and consistent returns for shareholders, M&T has also built a strong reputation for community involvement. M&T leads by example. Bank employees serve on the boards of dozens of local arts, cultural and civic organizations.

M&T Bank Regional President Allen Naples sits on the Onondaga Community College Board of Trustees. He chaired the OCC Foundation board for six years and led a highly successful capital campaign to raise millions of dollars for the continued growth and development of the campus.

The bank understands the important role strong community colleges play in economic development. As the U.S. transforms to a service- and knowledge-based economy, with job growth coming in information technology, environmental sciences, health care and other fields, community colleges help produce and train new workers needed to grow those industries.

Additionally, M&T has become known as the dominant small business bank across Upstate New York and has led the Syracuse area in loans made through the U.S. Small Business Administration for years. The bank understands the role small business plays in creating most new jobs in Central New York and across the United States, and it serves as a primary ally to local small business, providing both financial support and management expertise to clients.

The bank's local leaders have expanded on their position in small business lending by serving as one of the founding members of the New York's Creative Core Emerging Business Competition. The annual competition gives entrepreneurs and small businesses a chance to showcase their business plans and technologies to venture capitalists.

Through the leadership of M&T Bank, the New York Business Development Corporation and Center State CEO, the grand prize for the annual contest has grown to $250,000, making it one of the largest privately funded business contests of its kind in the nation. The final presentations made by competing businesses are hosted each spring in OCC's Storer Auditorium.

OCC President Dr. Debbie L. Sydow and OCC Foundation Executive Director Thomas A. Burton congratulate Allen J. Naples, CNY Regional President of M&T Bank, and Robert U. Roberts, CEO of SRC., Inc., co-chairs of OCC's Reach Beyond Capital Campaign.

MVP Health Care is a regionally based and nationally recognized health insurance provider offering health plans to members in Central New York, as well as Eastern and Western New York, New Hampshire and Vermont. MVP consistently rates among the nation's top health insurance companies and continues to raise the bar for quality, innovation and wellness, all while seeking new ways to improve health care processes and practices. Our regional approach gives us closer relationships with hospitals and provides us with richer knowledge about regional health care systems.

At MVP Health Care, being a non-profit company allows us to take a longer view of our business without having expectations for the next quarter's results. We don't have to make short-term decisions and can think of our members' interests in the long run.

Our regional approach enables us to work closely with hospitals and providers in Central New York to design innovative products offering competitive pricing and substantial benefits. Perhaps most important, our local relationships and innovativeness have created better partnerships with doctors and hospitals, making the health care experience work better for our members and their providers.

At MVP, we see wellness at the center of efforts to improve quality and improve the long-term health of our members. Our approach empowers members to reach their personal health goals. Going far beyond typical medical coverage, MVP enables employers to offer greater everyday value in their health insurance benefits.

Technology makes it easier for customers to work with MVP. We partner and collaborate both nationally and regionally to develop the systems we use for managed care e-commerce and plan administration. This approach dramatically improves the way employers select, purchase and administer health plans; enhances members' access to personal plan details; and streamlines numerous internal processes. We use technology to empower people with the tools and information they need to make the health care choices that are right for them.

MVP Central New York develops innovations for a strong health care experience.

Active in Our Communities

Beyond the innovative benefits of our health plans, MVP is advancing wellness through a broad range of community events and activities.

Our GenerationGo program is dedicated to stemming the tide of childhood obesity and related conditions by positively instilling healthy habits in the children of our region. Through a combination of live events and online resources, GenerationGo provides information and inspiration to kids, parents and youth team coaches across MVP's service area.

GenerationGo emphasizes positive role models — leveraging the personality and popularity of elite athletes, including United States Women's National Soccer Team player Abby Wambach and legendary lacrosse star (now Syracuse University coach) Gary Gait. These athletes bring the message of healthy lifestyle choices directly to hundreds of kids each year.

The Right Plan for You

MVP Health Care offers a wide variety of health plans for people and businesses throughout Central New York. MVP brings a healthy approach to health care.

Congratulations to OCC on celebrating 50 years! Morrisville State College is changing the face of the four-year-degree institution with unprecedented advances in higher education. An action-oriented, interactive learning lab, Morrisville is a national leader in technology, integrating it into all aspects of campus life. From being the first to implement a completely wireless campus to the newest transformation of a historic barn into a 25,000 sq. ft. architecture design center, Morrisville State College is moving toward providing a better future for its students.

See applied learning at its finest. The campus allows students and faculty to engage in ways that go beyond the traditional classroom environment with a 19 to 1 student to professor ratio. Hands-on learning is not only one of Morrisville's best-kept secrets; it's also a major key to student success after graduation.

Athletics are also an integral part of the educational and personal development of all students. Boasting 15 intercollegiate athletic teams and dozens of intramural athletics, Morrisville provides students with a balanced, total college experience, not to mention a new million dollar stadium which also doubles as a working lab for students in hospitality-related majors.

With more than 80 bachelor and associate degrees and literally hundreds of student-run campus activities a year, it's hard not to find something that interests students as well as faculty.

The Sheila Johnson Design Center, originally a barn, was turned into state-of-the-art learning space.

Sysco began in 1936 in New York State as a single company, Albany Frosted Foods. Founder Herbert K. Liebich started the company by selling frozen vegetables, packed by Birds Eye, to restaurants, hotels, hospitals and institutions. Liebich was later joined in business by his brother, Werner, and former Birds Eye salesman, Paul Dickinson. Albany Frosted Foods became incorporated in 1937. As Albany Frosted Foods expanded, a retail distribution business was added (Syracuse branch), supplying frozen foods to markets and independent grocers. Today, only the foodservice companies remain. But the original operation, now known as Sysco Albany, is the oldest continuously operated frozen food distribution company in the United States.

In 1947, Albany Frosted Foods purchased a Syracuse branch, Veteran Foods of Syracuse, and later, branches in Rochester (1948) and Elmira (1960). In 1964, Werner Liebich and Paul Dickinson retired, making Herbert Liebich sole owner of Albany Frosted Foods.

John Baugh founded Sysco in 1969 when his company, Zero Foods, and eight other companies joined together to form the SYstems and Services COmpany. The original Board of Directors included Herbert Liebich, making Syracuse one of the founding operating companies of Sysco Corporation. Liebich's four branches would later become known as Sysco Frosted Foods.

Sysco Frosted Foods in Syracuse continued to expand and absorbed the Rochester branch. In 1984, Sysco moved to its present location on Warners Road and in 1985 separated from the retail distribution (River Valley Foods) and concentrated its efforts in wholesale distribution.

A $2 million expansion in 1990 increased the Warners Road location to 148,000 square feet. In 1991, Sysco acquired the foodservice portion of the S.M. Flickinger Company. With this acquisition, the Sysco Syracuse operation would be known as Sysco Food Services of Syracuse, and a new fold-out operation began in Jamestown. Sysco Jamestown would distribute to and service the Erie, Pennsylvania, Jamestown and Buffalo markets.

Two more expansions occurred at Sysco Syracuse; one in 1996 and another in 2011 bringing the Warners Road facility to its current size of over 443,000 square feet on 31 acres.

At the present time, Sysco Syracuse has over 500 employees, with diverse and dedicated expertise in sales, merchandising, marketing, transportation, warehousing and customer service. In addition to the operation on Warners Road, Sysco Syracuse has sales offices in Buffalo, Rochester, Utica and Elmira. The Sysco Syracuse distribution range is north to the Canadian border, west to Niagara Falls, south into the northern areas of Pennsylvania, and east into the Adirondack Park.

Today, Sysco Corporation is the global leader in selling, marketing and distributing food products to restaurants, healthcare and educational facilities, lodging establishments and other customers who prepare meals away from home. Its family of products also includes equipment and supplies for the food service and hospitality industries.

Sysco is the oldest continuously operated frozen food distribution company in the United States.

American Food & Vending Corporation is proud to be founded here in Central New York. We are the leading provider of vending, on-site foodservice, catering and refreshment services in our area, and have rapidly grown to serve over 35 cities across the United States in 15 states, as well as 16 foreign countries. As a family-owned business headquartered in Syracuse, we are now one of the largest independent foodservice providers in the United States.

From Columbus to Kansas City, Montana to Montego Bay and, most importantly, our home in Central New York, we have earned a reputation for outstanding customer service and culinary innovation. Our chefs have won many awards, and our unique management style and customer focus have been the subject of industry textbooks and publications. We are most proud of our many talented and dedicated employees, and the fact that American Food & Vending is an example of locally based companies that have grown and brought many families to our wonderful region.

From its headquarters in Liverpool, New York, American Food & Vending Corp. serves customers in 17 countries.

Thompson & Johnson Equipment Company and Bobcat of Central New York are committed to the Central New York area and support OCC as a very important resource for our area. Serving the material handling and compact construction industries with industry leading brands, including Bobcat, Crown, Toyota and Clark, T&J provides solutions to customer problems with a well-trained sales representative and inside staff, supported by 60 mechanics, over 300 short-term rental units and a $1.5 million parts inventory.

T&J and Bobcat of CNY's core values of honesty, work ethic and loyalty are reflected in our workforce, which boasts a 13-year average tenure. This translates into more creative ideas for solving our customers' problems.

As a family-owned and operated business, we appreciate the benefit of a well-trained workforce and congratulate OCC for educating the local population for 50 years.

Based in East Syracuse, New York, Thompson & Johnson Equipment Company and Bobcat of Central New York serve the material handling and compact construction industries.

CH INSURANCE FORMS COMMUNITY PARTNERSHIPS

CH Insurance is a locally owned independent property/casualty and benefits insurance agency based in Syracuse, New York. Started in 1999 by Joe Convertino Sr., CH Insurance's mission is to develop long-term relationships with clients in the Central New York region. "Our customers are our most important asset," says Convertino, President.

As a local business, CH is dedicated to making the local community the best it can be. A member of the Manufacturers Association of CNY, Convertino also works with CenterState CEO on a committee to help local colleges develop insurance and risk management studies. Executive Vice President Joe Convertino Jr. is a past president and current board member of the Independent Agents and Brokers Association of Central New York.

CH Insurance provides Worker's Compensation, claims management and loss control services for OCC. CH's Paul Evans works with the college and is committed to making recommendations and assisting the college.

As OCC celebrates its 50th anniversary, it is building for the future. "The expansion of OCC's campus and the quality of its educational offerings are a major plus for the community, and it's happening right in our back yard," says Joe Jr.

Joe Convertino Sr. and Joe Convertino Jr.

CITIZENS BANK IS ALL ABOUT COMMUNITY

Citizens Bank believes that good banking is good citizenship. Every day we focus on serving our customers well, delivering the best possible banking capabilities and giving back to the communities we serve.

We are honored to be included in this publication. For Citizens Bank, community is central to how we do business. We believe that when a community prospers, we all prosper. Through the Citizens Bank Foundation, we provide support to nonprofits throughout the Central New York region to help build and improve the communities in which we live and work. Through our banking relationships in the area, we are helping to foster a vibrant business environment.

We are proud of our affiliation with Onondaga Community College. In 2005, Citizens Bank provided financing to OCC's Housing Development Corporation for the college's first student housing. We have continued to be a banking partner to the college as it has grown into a powerful regional economic engine.

We congratulate Onondaga Community College on its 50th anniversary and salute the work that the college does to provide an educated, skilled workforce in the region. We celebrate the college's rich history, and we look forward to the college's promising future.

Jim Gaspo, President of Citizens Bank in New York

COMMUNITY BANK PRESIDENT AND ALUMNUS SALUTES OCC

As a proud graduate of Onondaga Community College, I am gratified to see the continued effectiveness and engagement of the College in preparing our community's students for success in advanced education and in the work force. The quality, accessibility and affordability of an education at OCC are powerful opportunities for the future of our community. An exceptional faculty focused on education, combined with a broad offering of degree and certificate curricula, makes OCC one of the most vitally important institutions in our community. As a banker, I well understand the concept of return on investment. There is no better investment one can make than in an education or financial support of Onondaga Community College.

Mark E. Tryniski, President & Chief Executive Officer of Community Bank System, Inc., is also a 1981 graduate of Onondaga Community College.

COYNE TEXTILE SERVICES: SUPPORTING THE COMMUNITY SINCE 1929

Congratulations to Onondaga Community College for achieving 50 years of service to the community and its students. Coyne has long supported the valuable work of the College through partnerships, including the J. Stanley Coyne EXCELL Center.

Coyne began in Syracuse and has grown to become one of the country's leading privately owned industrial laundry firms. From its first day of operation, the company built its business and reputation on the premise that reusing is better than discarding—long before the EPA and concerns about the environment.

Today, Coyne cleans and returns to its customers millions of reusable cotton wiping towels to replace pollution-laden paper products destined for landfills; professionally cleans tens of thousands of industrial uniforms and work garments each day; and provides other safety and environmentally friendly products, including floor mats. Through Coyne's state-of-the-art cleaning process and wastewater treatment systems, the company has successfully recovered over 12 million gallons of hazardous residuals from these items that might otherwise end up in the environment. Now Coyne has introduced its own proprietary

line of reusable absorbent products, called Green Bull, to capture oils and liquids used in the manufacturing process.

For more information about Coyne Textile Services, please visit www.CoyneTextileServices.com.

DELTA STRATAGEM HELPS REVITALIZE LOCAL MANUFACTURING

Delta Stratagem specializes in business transformation. "We take companies from a traditional way of operating to a more contemporary, lean operational style that is geared to compete in the 21st century," says founder Tony Mangione. Delta Stratagem goes beyond improving processes to changing the way people think and behave, from company culture to organizational culture and working habits.

Beginning in 2001, the Delta Stratagem team applied this philosophy to help develop the Lean Institute at Onondaga Community College. The certification program aimed to help Central New York manufacturing companies eliminate unnecessary waste from their processes through classroom and on-the-job training. "Companies saw improvements in productivity and competitiveness, and the workforce was re-energized," says Mangione. "Helping to revitalize CNY manufacturing was our most important contribution."

Delta Stratagem helps companies throughout the United States and internationally. Offerings range from speaking engagements, seminars, training and consulting to adjunct management services, hands-on implementation and the outright running of companies.

Where many lean experts focus on engineering alone, Delta Stratagem understands that operational change is not sustainable without first changing minds. "We help companies see that their employees are the true profit and productivity generators. Success begins with educating and energizing the people."

Delta Stratagem Founder Tony Mangione

EXCELLUS BLUECROSS BLUESHIELD MAKING A DIFFERENCE IN THE PLACE WE CALL HOME

Excellus BlueCross BlueShield congratulates Onondaga Community College on 50 years of serving the educational and economic development needs of Central New York.

Employing some 1,000 people, Excellus BlueCross BlueShield celebrated an anniversary of its own in 2011 — its 75th year of providing health insurance needs for local residents.

Over the years, Excellus BlueCross BlueShield has grown to be part of a $5 billion family of companies that finances and delivers vital health care services to nearly 1.8 million people across upstate New York.

As New York's largest nonprofit health plan, Excellus BlueCross BlueShield is committed to assuring that as many people as possible have affordable, dignified access to needed, effective health care services. The company has a product at every price point, giving employers options to keep coverage affordable. We continue to help reduce the number of uninsured in our community by supporting government safety-net programs.

Excellus BlueCross BlueShield employees work and live where their members, providers and employers do. The company supports programs and services that enhance quality of life in Central New York.

Excellus BlueCross Blueshield is proud to recognize OCC on its anniversary and celebrate its commitment to offering high-quality educational programs and services.

Excellus BlueCross BlueShield in Syracuse, New York

ounded in 1880 and currently managed by the fifth and sixth generations, Hueber-Breuer Construction Co., Inc. is the largest continuously operating, family-owned construction management and general construction company in Central New York. Since 1880, we have built some of the most notable landmarks in the region.

Our portfolio of successfully completed educational facilities is second to none, and we are proud of our ties with Onondaga Community College. We hav helped shape the growth of the college with two of the most notable expansions to the campus. Both the Whitney Applied Technology Center and the 600-bed residence halls are facilities we developed and constructed. This trusting working relationship continues today day with the new Academic II Building scheduled for completion in 2012.

Like Onondaga Community College, Hueber-Breuer understands what it means to be dedicated to our local community. With OCC celebrating 50 years of guilding and educating our students, we salute the effort and hard work invested into developing a premier center of higher education. We are pleased to be part of this commemorative book, and we pledge our continued support and partnership in the future as Onondaga Community College looks to the next 50 years. Congratulations!

Onondaga Community College residence halls were constructed by Hueber-Breuer.

KEUKA COLLEGE **PARTNERS WITH OCC**

n the past decade, Keuka College's Accelerated Studies for Adults Program (ASAP) has forged partnerships with colleges throughout New York State to bring educational opportunities to place-bound students.

Meeting the needs of adult learners at more than 20 locations, Keuka College's adult student enrollment has grown to more than 900 with nearly 1,600 ASAP graduates.

Keuka's longest standing adult education partner is Onondaga Community College. Since the partnership began in the early 2000s, over 300 students have earned Keuka College degrees at OCC.

When the partnership was finalized with a single bachelor's degree offering, OCC President Dr. Debbie L. Sydow said that she expected the program to expand. She was prophetic. Keuka now offers seven programs at OCC:

- Bachelor's degrees in criminal justice systems, nursing for RNs, organizational management and social work

- Master's degrees in criminal justice administration, management and nursing.

Each degree program is designed to meet the needs of busy, active adults. Classes are held one night each week, one course at a time. Students attend class at a location close to home with the same group of people.

ASAP programs begin three times a year—in fall, spring and summer—and applications are accepted year-round.

Keuka College meets the needs of adult learners at more than 20 locations.

MACNY CONNECTS AND COLLABORATES

On behalf of MACNY, The Manufacturers Association, and its collective membership, congratulations to Onondaga Community College on its milestone of 50 years in providing our region with quality education and training opportunities for thousands of students!

MACNY and OCC share a rich history in working together, and a collective goal in offering top notch education, training and programs that enable students and certified workers to succeed in acquiring the skills, degrees and credentials needed for high-wage, high-skill employment right here in our region. For 50 years, OCC has been working with local organizations such as MACNY to ensure programs and offerings are connected, collaborative and beneficial in creating a skilled workforce.

On behalf of the MACNY membership who have benefited from the 50 years of service and education to our region, we congratulate OCC and wish you many more years of success!

Manufacturing Careers Day, sponsored by Partners for Education & Business/MACNY, recently hosted OCC students from the Mechanical/Electronic Technology Programs for a tour of Lockheed Martin's manufacturing operations.

MVCC PUTS "UNITY" IN COMMUNITY COLLEGE

Established in 1946, Mohawk Valley Community College was New York State's first community college. Throughout its history, MVCC has responded to the changing needs of the community to create a transformative learning environment. As Matthew Snyder, MVCC director of marketing and communications, explains, innovation is often best achieved through partnership.

As sister community colleges in the SUNY system, MVCC and Onondaga Community College collaborate in pooling knowledge and sharing best practices. MVCC's relationship with OCC is a productive two-way street for both faculty and administrators. As testament to this bond, MVCC recently studied OCC's approach to the One-Stop Student Service Center while developing a similar program within its own institution. "Our colleagues from OCC really welcomed us with open arms, sharing their ideas and what they've learned in a true spirit of collaboration," says Snyder.

Increasingly, students, families and local businesses are calling on community colleges like OCC and MVCC as their colleges of choice. "All of us here at MVCC commend and appreciate what our colleagues at OCC have done for the community over the past 50 years," says Snyder. "We are excited to collaborate with OCC moving forward. Together we can create a rising tide of awareness that lifts all ships."

Mohawk Valley Community College Student Service Center

MORSE MANUFACTURING: A SYNERGISTIC PARTNERSHIP

A few years ago, Morse Manufacturing Co. sent ten employees to the Lean Manufacturing Institute at Onondaga Community College. Nate Andrews, Morse Vice President, says, "A partnership with OCC provided our employees with the knowledge required to implement lean practices within our company." Those lean business practices learned at OCC continue to support the family-owned company's ability to continually grow, regardless of the economic conditions that can plague its competitors.

Established in 1923, the manufacturer of drum handling equipment relies on a locally trained workforce that routinely outperforms its global competitors.

Bob Andrews, president of the company says, "The liaison between the manufacturing community and the school has helped to create a real-world education, coupled with classroom learning that is priceless." As a board member of the statewide Small Business Development Center, Andrews believes that the training offered at OCC provides local businesses with an educated workforce that is in the best interests of the local business community. He adds, "Our partnership with the College allows us to continually upgrade our employees' skills in order to maintain our international leadership position, measured by the number of products we manufacture, the support we provide our customers and the dollars we generate."

Morse Manufacturing Co. does business across the globe from its headquarters in East Syracuse, New York.

NATIONAL GRID: SAFETY, COMMUNITY, PRESERVATION

National Grid strives to build strong, local ties to the communities we serve. Over the years, National Grid has enjoyed a close working relationship with Onondaga Community College. Members of our Central New York leadership team are also active members of the OCC Board of Trustees, and National Grid employees support the college in a variety of ways.

National Grid is taking action to address the challenges of workforce development with its "Engineering Our Future" initiative. To date, the company has invested more than $3 million in the program to encourage students of all ages and backgrounds to study science, technology, engineering and math, collectively known as "STEM."

Beginning in 2007, National Grid partnered with Onondaga Community College to implement its new utility worker training program. The one-year certification, approved by the NYS Department of Education in 2010, encompasses traditional training and sets math and science standards for those entering the field. The curriculum also encourages students to achieve higher levels of education following their certification.

National Grid is pleased to honor Onondaga Community College on its 50th Anniversary. We look forward to collaborating with the college for many years to come.

Since 2007, National Grid has partnered with OCC for its new utility worker training and certification program.

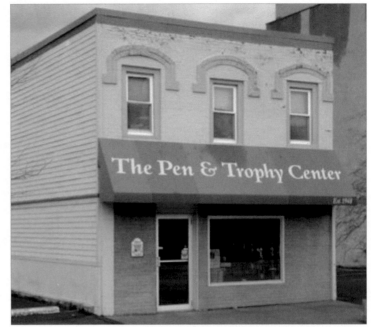

When it's time to acknowledge the accomplishments of others, The Pen and Trophy Center is front and center. In the hands and on the shelves of high-achieving Central New Yorkers, The Pen and Trophy Center has played a part in marking significant honors and milestones since 1948.

A fixture in Syracuse for 63 years, The Pen and Trophy Center salutes Onondaga Community College as it marks its 50th anniversary of providing service and education. Like OCC, The Pen and Trophy Center is known and recognized for quality, achievement and success. High quality craftsmanship combined with the latest engraving technologies and years of experience in the art of engraving and award production techniques are used to create trophies, plaques, awards, promotional items and more.

The Pen and Trophy Center is proud of its long tradition in Central New York, and celebrates this milestone with Onondaga Community College.

The Pen and Trophy Center has been a fixture in Syracuse for 63 years.

PIONEER COMPANIES HELP BUILD THE FUTURE

The Pioneer Companies, a division of CP Realty, LLC, is proud to honor and recognize Onondaga Community College on its 50th Anniversary.

Like OCC, Pioneer has strong roots in our community and is committed to remaining an important contributor to the growth and success of Central New York. Pioneer has partnered with the college on several important projects, including the sale to the college of what is now the J. Stanley Coyne Hall and oversight of the construction of the residence halls.

CP Realty is a national, privately held real estate owner, operator, property manager and developer with headquarter offices in Syracuse, New York, and Denver, Colorado. Over its 50-year history, the company has established itself as a full-service, vertically integrated company with acquisition, leasing, development, construction management, property management, brokerage, asset management, receivership, legal, accounting and finance functions. CP Realty is a consortium of related entities, each with an established track record in its given market. Entities within CP Realty include the Pioneer Companies based in Syracuse, New York; Continuum Partners based in Denver, Colorado; and affiliate partners in Arizona, Florida and South Carolina.

Washington Station, a 126,000-square-foot Class A, LEED-certified office building located in Syracuse's Armory Square district houses the corporate offices of the Pioneer Companies.

$3,569,391
Raised through tonight

$6,000,000
Goal

PRO-TEL PEOPLE CREATES OPPORTUNITIES

Students and recent graduates at Onondaga Community College are discovering that there is more to staffing agencies than meets the eye, thanks to PRO-TEL People. According to Pro-Tel Staffing Operations Manager Lindsay Drake, using an employment agency is a powerful way to network and open doors.

With partnerships in place at local schools, PRO-TEL People is in tune with students' needs. Along with permanent placement and paid internships, the agency helps job candidates with career counseling, résumé services and mock interviews.

By sitting down one-on-one with job seekers, PRO-TEL can offer objectives to help candidates succeed. "During an interview, it's more than just work history," says Drake. "Employers want to know what skills candidates have to offer and if they are knowledgeable about what's going on in the world."

Where PRO-TEL People separates itself from other staffing agencies is in its emphasis on the employee; yet the agency offers no shortage of services for employers. Along with staffing solutions, PRO-TEL People provides HR, payroll, IT and engineering services.

For PRO-TEL, helping employees is helping the community. "PRO-TEL and OCC help mold people in the beginning of their careers," says Drake. "These are the future leaders of our community."

PRO-TEL People's Staffing Operations Manager Lindsay Drake assists new hire Tami Clark-Linger (seated) update her résumé for her future employer.

RICCELLI ENTERPRISES: IN IT FOR THE LONG HAUL

You see them on the highways every day. Wherever you travel throughout the Northeast and beyond, the 400 owned and operated trucks of Riccelli Enterprises are there hauling crushed stone, wood chips and other bulk commodities, transporting scrap metal and construction debris, delivering steel beams and taking away recyclables. Whatever needs to be moved from Point A to Point B, Riccelli Enterprises gets the job done.

Getting the job done is what Riccelli Enterprises does best and, to that end, has been a strong presence on the OCC campus as the College renovates and builds-out new projects. Riccelli Enterprises is dedicated to the CNY community and the continued success of OCC and its long-term commitment to improving the region. President and COO Richard J. Riccelli Sr. explains. "An educated and informed population makes for better law, better regulations and great employees." In fact, Riccelli Enterprises' Senior Vice President of Administration and Finance, Mike Relf, is an OCC alumnus.

As OCC builds its future on a strong foundation, Riccelli Enterprises is proud to be part of that growth and to reap the benefits of an educated and skilled workforce.

Joe Riccelli (right) borrowed $600 from his father to start Riccelli Enterprises in 1971. Now headed by Joe's son, Richard, the company is the largest trucking company of its kind in Central New York.

SECNY Federal Credit Union is 100 percent local, owned by its members and overseen by volunteer Board of Directors and committee members. With nearly 15,000 members and a 40-year history of outstanding financial service, SECNY takes great pride in its partnership with Onondaga Community College. The credit union's primary mission is to "provide financial responsibility through education," a seemingly perfect match with not only the college's visions and goals, but also for neighboring residents and school districts.

SECNY membership is free and is open to everyone living, working, worshipping, attending school, as well as businesses and legal entities in the Central New York area, which consists of Onondaga, Cayuga, Madison and Oswego counties.

With five Central New York branches (three of which have opened within the last three years), SECNY has experienced positive growth in the communities it serves. Each branch houses technology to provide all the conveniences of everyday banking with a friendly face who knows you and your family.

These ideas, combined with the understanding that nothing is as personal as one's financial well-being, have deep roots on Onondaga Hill, and are spread throughout Central New York.

SECNY Federal Credit Union's Onondaga Hill Office

SENECA IN THE COMMUNITY

For more than 30 years, Seneca has maintained a longstanding tradition of giving back to the communities in which we do business. For Seneca, helping those around us is a natural part of doing business. Whenever possible, we encourage our partners and customers to join us in this commitment. Visit any Seneca facility in Syracuse, Liverpool or Alpharetta, Georgia, and you'll see a community of employees known for their dedication, positive work ethic and commitment to superior manufacturing services.

At Seneca, we recognize that we are only as good as our employees. That's why we are committed to giving every Seneca professional an opportunity to grow and advance in their roles and responsibilities. Onondaga Community College's Lean Manufacturing Institute was instrumental in helping our employees gain the knowledge to be more competitive at a pivotal moment in our history and helping Seneca meet the challenges of a changing marketplace.

By first empowering and then listening to our employees, each is given an opportunity to contribute to Seneca's corporate improvement and evolution. Insights from throughout the organization enable us to better adapt to and meet the changing needs of our customers and the marketplace.

OCC's Lean Manufacturing Institute helped Seneca employees gain the required know-ledge to meet the challenges of a changing marketplace.

OCC Welcome LEADERS of TOMORROW

SUNY CORTLAND, THE NEXT BIG STEP

S UNY Cortland is an institution of opportunity. More than 40 percent of our students transfer here from schools like Onondaga Community College. Why? SUNY Cortland is a student-oriented college that offers a unique educational experience focused on academic excellence, individual and community wellness and opportunities to apply classroom lessons to the real world. We have the largest accredited teacher education program in New York State. Our students are engaged in international study in more than 30 countries, and our student athletes compete successfully at the highest level of NCAA Division III sports. Academic programs are available in a wide variety of fields, providing the strong theoretical, cultural, personal and practical foundation needed for lifelong success.

SUNY Cortland is a place where students build momentum toward their future; a campus alive with the energy of an active student body involved in research projects, clubs, community service and many other activities. Our dedicated and distinguished faculty love to teach,

and educating students is their top priority. The campus culture inspires students to be a champion in every aspect of life. It's part of what contributes to our success in the classroom, on the athletic field and in the competitive world beyond college.

SUNY Cortland inspires students to be champions in every aspect of life.

UPSTATE AND OCC: A HEALTHY PARTNERSHIP FOR CENTRAL NEW YORK

O nondaga Community College and Upstate Medical University share a unique partnership that has produced hundreds of exceptional health professionals to serve the region.

Every degree program at Upstate is aimed at improving health. It solely offers junior and senior years of college and graduate programs, so students come from OCC to pursue bachelor's and master's degrees for a range of health careers. Onondaga and Upstate are just five miles apart, so students who transfer to Upstate can maintain continuity in their jobs and personal lives.

Over the years, the OCC/Upstate partnership has resulted in alumni who succeed in careers as therapists, scientists, doctors, advanced practice nurses, professors and more. Our graduates have led clinics, cured patients, taught students and performed research—and the majority stayed to contribute their talents to Central New York.

Both institutions also share common values. As part of the State University of New York, Onondaga and Upstate are committed to the role of public education as one that opens doors to every member of our society and contributes to the common good. Upstate congratulates Onondaga on five decades of service and is committed to keeping their connection equally healthy in the years ahead.

Upstate Medical University's partnership with OCC results in successful alumni who share their medical skills with the local region.

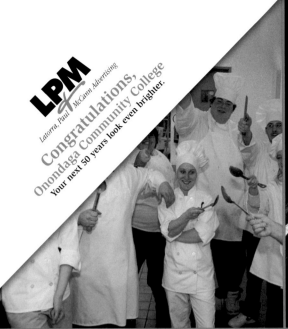

SYRACUSE UNIVERSITY AND OCC: PARTNERS IN ACCESS AND OPPORTUNITY

As neighboring institutions of higher education serving Central New York and beyond, Syracuse University and Onondaga Community College have forged a deeply collaborative relationship centered on our shared commitment to access and opportunity and vision of education as a public good.

For 50 years, OCC has been a vital pipeline for students seeking to continue studies at SU, and today it is the single largest source of SU transfers. Recently, we took this relationship to a whole new level, launching a precedent-setting 2+2 admission agreement for students seeking to continue at SU after completing their coursework at OCC. The agreement assures qualifying students with guaranteed transfer into an array of SU programs and predictive financial aid packages. Together, we're reducing students' financial burden while assuring them of a world-class education.

As increasing numbers of students launch their higher education careers at top-quality community colleges, SU is a proud partner with OCC in pre-paring the diverse next generation for leadership in the workplace and in the world. Congratulations to President Debbie Sydow and all who have played a role in making OCC the vital community asset and success story it is today.

A variety of transfer support services eases students' transition into Syracuse University.

UTICA COLLEGE: LEARNING THAT MAKES YOU STRONGER

Utica College (UC) is a private, independent college founded in 1946. Our 20,000 alumni have founded enterprises, built communities and distinguished themselves in health care, government, education and many other fields all over the world. Wherever their dreams may lead them, UC graduates make remarkable contributions using the tools they develop at Utica; tools that include essential knowledge about the world and how it works, as well as the confidence to lead.

From the moment students arrive on campus, they join a vibrant community of scholars that includes our remarkably accomplished faculty and an engaging and diverse student body. They soon discover strengths they never knew they possessed, building self-confidence through continual intellectual challenge and enriching extracurricular opportunities.

With 37 bachelor's degree programs, UC's undergraduate curriculum combines advanced learning in liberal arts with innovative practical study in a number of professional disciplines. UC also offers master's degree programs in a variety of fields, as well as doctoral programs in physical therapy.

Our campus features cutting-edge facilities and technologies that support programs in the health professions, economic crime and justice studies, public relations/journalism, life sciences and other fields.

Utica College offers a unique blend of liberal and professional studies.

The College Matures
1984-2000

I ncreased enrollment came with each economic downturn. Allied Chemical in Solvay, once the County's largest employer and tax-payer, ended production at its 104-year-old plant in 1985. General Motors closed its local plant in 1993. Unemployment rose as major industries, such as Carrier and General Electric, continued to cut jobs. Trustees and employees alike had to wrestle with the fact that when the opportunities that the College offered were most needed, its resources were most strained. Originally designed for 5,000 students, OCC enrolled approximately 7,100 students in 1985 and approximately 8,100 students in 1993. From the promise in 1961 of funding one-third of the annual operating costs, the County's share of the College operating budget had decreased to 18.9 percent by 1999-2000.

On a more positive note, during the 1980s and 1990s, local newspaper reporters became less interested in breaking-news controversies at OCC and more aware of the College's value to the community.

NEW PRESIDENT: BRUCE LESLIE

Dr. Bruce H. Leslie, selected as the fifth President in 1984, came to Onondaga with a résumé featuring administrative experience in urban colleges. "We've got to get this place back on the right focus—educational excellence," was his initial statement.

Controversy surrounded his appointment when supporters of Dr. John Blasi, Vice President for Academic Affairs, maintained that he had not received fair treatment in the search process. Faculty members protested both the choice of Dr. Leslie and their stalled contract negotiations. The controversy surrounding Dr. Leslie's selection continued for months, and Dr. Blasi began legal proceedings. After dropping his legal challenges and saying that he would stay at OCC, Dr. Blasi resigned in 1985. A *Post-Standard* editorial said he was an excellent administrator who had been "constantly in contention with the new president and the board." Dr. Blasi said his resignation was "in the best interests of the college."

Given the economic situation, one of Dr. Leslie's goals was to train workers for the new jobs appearing both in the service sector and in old-line industry. Providing this training meant developing direct links to local firms such as Crouse-Hinds, Backus Ford, Lakeside Printing, New Process Gear (New Venture Gear, 2002; Magna International, 2004), Carrier, Niagara-Mohawk (National Grid, 2002), Welch-Allyn and Anaren, as well as to hotels, convenience stores and drugstore chains. To enhance student success in the job market, faculty began to design classes around industry requests and employment opportunities. Thus in 1985, when Allied Chemical closed its Solvay Process plant, OCC offered intensive six-month retraining courses focused on employment at jobs that were immediately available.

Dr. Leslie's plans to offer classes for County employees close to their worksites helped improve OCC's status with the County. Classes in American Sign Language, Business, English, Communication and Spanish were among those offered at the Civic Center. He also started using the local public television station, WCNY, to air classes for those at home, thereby launching distance learning.

President Bruce Leslie (center) played his bagpipes regularly with local pipe bands and marched in the St. Patrick's Day parades in Syracuse. At the 1995 Commencement Ceremony, he played as part of the processional with the Oran Mor Pipe Band.

Dr. Gary Livent, Vice President for Development & Community Relations, presents Assemblywoman Joan Christensen with a piece of student artwork in recognition of her support.

In 1991, at Dr. Leslie's request, a Faculty committee was formed to work with him to resolve a 19-year dispute with the American Association of University Professors (AAUP). Members of the committee were Professors Joe Agonito (History), Jim Doherty (Union President and English) and George Matthews (Mathematics). The efforts of Dr. Leslie and the Faculty committee ended the 1972 censure OCC received for the firing of Prof. George J. Dmohowski (Mathematics), one of the original faculty members. Trustees had given him a one-year notice that he would not be rehired. The ensuing protests by faculty led to the AAUP censure (see Midtown Plaza Years).

Public opinion about the College was changing after years of steady criticism. In 1992, the afternoon daily newspaper, the *Syracuse Herald-Journal*, editorialized that OCC had a "crucial presence in the community" and suffers from "an undeserved identity problem." With the variety of programs offered to business and industry trainees, as well as the 40 degree programs offered, OCC was "an unrecognized gem—a smart school" fitting into the technological future. That same year, trustees authorized design and engineering work for an Applied Technology

During President Leslie's tenure, the College memorialized retirees and the deceased members of the campus community by an annual tree-planting ceremony in October.

Center. As enrollment increased year after year, the limitations of a campus built for an estimated 5,000 students had become evident. The Center would be the first new OCC building in 16 years, and the College launched its first private fundraising campaign. An up-to-date facility to train the next technological generation was in sight.

Dr. Leslie also brought a fresh perspective to labor disputes. In the past, new contracts were usually signed well after the expiration date of the previous contract. Dr. Leslie proposed Mutual Gains Bargaining, which centers on reaching a new contract in a timely fashion by resolving issues together rather than by each side coming into negotiations with predetermined positions. In fall 1985 before beginning negotiations for the upcoming contract, representatives of the OCCFT, the ACA and the College participated in Mutual Gains training led by members of Cornell University's School of Industrial and Labor Relations. Representatives from PERB (Public Employment Relations Board) also attended. Through Mutual Gains Bargaining, negotiators arrived at an agreement on a four-year contract (1996-2000) only 18 days after the expiration of the previous contract. Union President Jim Doherty (and Prof. of English) noted that this agreement was the quickest resolution in two decades. However, as the OCCFT and the College approached negotiations for the next contract (January 2000), the College would not agree to Mutual Gains Bargaining.

In 1996, just as plans for the Applied Technology Center were moving forward, President Leslie announced his resignation. Trustees accepted his departure "with reluctance and great pride" in his appointment to Chancellor of the Community-Technical Colleges of Connecticut. In his farewell, Dr. Leslie asked Onondaga County residents and their County legislative representatives to "give OCC the respect it deserves." To serve as Interim President, trustees turned to one of their own, Barrett Jones, a trustee for 10 years and a retired bank CEO.

"I am very happy that my career started at OCC. The training I received came from the phenomenal staff in the Architecture Department. I have always loved architecture and construction, and I am proud to list OCC on my résumé."

– Thomas Cullen (Architectural Technology, 1986)

KEEPING STUDENTS FIRST

"Dealing with the real world," was the way Dr. Les Crowell, Dean of Student Services (1976-1994), summed up OCC. Based on his two decades at the College, he pointed out that many students held jobs, and all were going home each night to their families and community responsibilities, which could stretch out the years needed to earn a degree. Part-time students outnumbered full-timers in 11 of 16 years, 1984 to 2000.

In the 1980s and 1990s, the College expanded earlier Student Support Programs and developed new ones. After-Semester Workshops, organized by Nancy (Berring) Hazzard (Director of the Learning Support Center) and Professor Sharon Testone (Mathematics), helped faltering math students to prepare for the next semester. Math Diagnostics, a competency-based, independent study program, also assisted students. An earlier peer tutoring program became the Content Tutoring Center in 1994 through the efforts of Deborah Knight (Coordinator of the Learning Disabilities Assistance Program), Nancy (Berring) Hazzard, and Prof. Gloria Battaglia (Counseling). In the Center, successful students were enlisted as tutors in their subject area. The Supplemental Instruction/SI Plus Program was developed through the leadership of Prof. Barbara Risser (Reading; later Vice President of Student and Academic Services before becoming President of Finger Lakes Community College). Through SI Plus, student-led study groups were attached to high-risk courses such as Chemistry, Economics and Accounting. During these years, Prof. Jim Martin (Counseling) also led a Multicultural Math/Science Tutorial Program that provided peer and professional mentoring.

Through the Office of Services for Students with Special Needs, the College continued to pioneer in adapting the campus for physically disabled students. By 1986, all offices and classrooms were accessible to wheelchairs. Of the state's 64 SUNY campuses, OCC ranked fourth highest in its population of disabled students.

New academic programs reflected rapidly changing fields: Automotive Technology (1990), Computer Information Systems (1994), Emergency Management (1999) and Environmental Technology (2000). New courses in photo film processing matched the beginning of in-store developing technology. OCC's photo lab courses led to jobs at NASA's Johnson Space Center in 1997 when James Suits and Todd Munson, fresh from their OCC classes, joined Steven Clere, who had been at OCC 10 years earlier, to process the photos from the space shuttle. In a January 1993 meeting of the Trustees, Dr. Gary Livent noted that graduates from OCC's Radio/Television Program were members of crews sent by all three local television stations to Somalia to cover Central New Yorkers involved in the military's *Operation Restore Hope*.

In the 1980s and 1990s, voice mail and, later, the Internet transformed campus communication and interaction. When registration by touch-tone phone became available via the STAR (Student Telephone Assisted Registration) system, OCC was the first two-year college in Central New York to implement this innovative technology. Campus computers were just becoming available for student use. In 1999, there were 25 open access computer stations. Other student computers were available in academic departments such as English, Business Administration and Computer Studies. (By 2010, students had wireless access throughout the campus, numerous Internet cafes, and 110 computers in an open lab, in addition to computer labs in academic departments.)

OCC exhibited its philosophy of accommodating those with special circumstances when Maria Regina, a two-year Catholic college for women, closed in 1988. Because some of those students decided to attend OCC, the College added two curricula, Medical Records Technology and Physical Therapy Assistant, so that the students could continue their education.

In 1992, OCC chose its first student commencement speaker. David Borowski of Camillus had returned to the classroom after 10 years of working in County parks. He completed his degree as a physical therapist assistant and, as one of the 1,329 graduates, was eager to share with others what the College had done for him. Most graduations were held in Onondaga County's War Memorial in downtown Syracuse; 1987 at the Landmark Theater; 1993 and 1994 at the Le Moyne College Henninger Athletic Center.

Alumni Snapshot

Deraux Branch, '88
- A.A., Humanities
- B.A. in Sociology – University at Albany
- MBA, Columbia College
- President and CEO, Branch's Driving School

Deraux Branch came to Onondaga Community College at the tender age of 17—young, immature, indecisive, looking for discipline and structure.

"My father told me to pick up the phone and call OCC so I could work, make money while I was going, and get an education," he says. "We didn't have the money to attend a different school."

It's a decision that introduced new experiences, new ideas and new challenges. Branch needed to know if college was the right fit, that he could conquer it and move on to even greater endeavors. And he needed to discover it all at a place that offered direction and guidance.

"The whole college thing was frightening at first—making friendships, building rapport with professors, and learning about relationships," he shares. "But I was learning interpersonal skills. I learned to become a better speaker through classes and events. It was a nurturing environment."

Attending Onondaga allowed Branch to stay local and continue working full time at the family business: Branch's Driving School. It's a business that's remained a staple in the Central New York community for the last 48 years, with Branch now carrying on its mission of service.

Thanks to the help of Onondaga, Branch learned what it means to uphold that mission and become part of something greater.

"The biggest impact it had on me was teaching me to care for and become involved in the community. I'm involved today because of the things my professors said and did," he explains. "You have to give back when you take. Learning to become involved in the community was part of my growing process—OCC was a byproduct of it."

That's not the only thing he took away from the College. Branch recalls the advice a professor gave him from time to time—one that still rings true today.

"A professor told me to aim and shoot for the stars, that you can achieve anything whether people think you can or not," he says. "That advice set me on a different path, not mediocrity."

Graduates often remained in Onondaga County after completing their studies. Of the 542 respondents to the 1985 Graduate Survey, 89.5 percent were working in Onondaga County. Of the 604 respondents to the 1999 Graduate Survey, 85 percent were working in Onondaga County. After 30 years, alumni were becoming the County's business, educational, economic and political leaders. Roy A. Bernardi, a student in 1963-1964, was mayor of Syracuse and later went to Washington as Undersecretary of Housing and Urban Development for President George W. Bush. John Dillon, Class of 1967, and Kevin E. Walsh, Class of 1973, served as Onondaga County Sheriffs. Syracuse Police Chief Thomas Sardino was Class of 1967, and Chief Gary W. Miguel was Class of 1971.

"Thanks for helping me gather the tools I needed to be successful."

– Mary E. Foltz
(Hotel Technology, 1997)

SCHOLARSHIPS

The variety of clubs, organizations, businesses and individuals that offered scholarships for OCC's students was matched only by the wide range of recipients. An Honors Endowment Fund from Trustee Donald M. Mawhinney, Jr. helped students who demonstrated high academic achievement. The Trustee Ralph R. Whitney award went to a faculty member who contributed to "the advancement of the college within the community." The honored faculty member then chose a student to receive the scholarship based on outstanding achievement. In 1997, Dr. Helen Etherington and her husband, John, established a scholarship especially aimed at helping "non-traditional" female students. That was what Dr. Etherington herself had been when she attended OCC in 1962. She went on to receive her doctorate from Syracuse University, joined OCC's faculty in 1970, and later chaired the Business Administration Department. In 1984, she became Vice President of Academic and Student Services, retiring in 1993. In 1985, she received OCC's Distinguished Alumni Award and in 2007 was an Alumni Faces inductee.

A scholarship for those of Irish heritage living in Central New York was established by James T. Walsh, a Syracuse native who represented Onondaga County in the U.S. House of Representatives from 1988 to 2008. State scholarship grants, begun in 1988, helped African-American, Latino and American Indian students and were matched by funds from the Minority Honors Scholarship Breakfast started in 1990. In 1994 while President Bruce Leslie was in Germany on a month-long Fulbright Scholarship, students raffled off his parking space to benefit the College's Minority Scholarship fund.

When he was Syracuse Police Chief in 1988, Leigh Hunt taught a Police Administration class on his lunch hour. He donated his salary for two scholarships awarded to city high school minority students enrolled in the Criminal Justice pro-

Students crossing the bridge in between classes, circa late 1980s.

gram. Recognizing the critical need for volunteer firefighters and emergency service workers, local agents for the State Farm Insurance Company supported scholarships for Fire Protection, Emergency Management and Emergency Medical Technician students who planned to serve in a volunteer department for

ADJUNCTS UNIONIZE

In spring 1985, OCC's adjunct faculty gained the right to union representation under the OCCFT. At that time, the Union represented 215 full-time faculty members, and the College reported an additional 230 adjuncts, who taught approximately 40 percent of the class sections. Adjuncts employed in the same field that they were teaching brought real-life and specialized knowledge into the classroom, plus they provided the flexible workforce needed to accommodate enrollment fluctuations, and to fill in when full-time faculty were on sabbatical or other leave. However, adjuncts were concerned that they did not receive benefits, often were without permanent office space, and had no assurance of rehiring.

The Adjunct Faculty Bargaining Unit Committee included Professors Jim Doherty (Union President and English) and Jim Jones (Biology), adjunct Mary Salibrici (English) and NYSUT Field Representative Jim Mathews. The first negotiations established work assignment procedures, evaluation procedures, limited benefits and a salary schedule. Fall 1987, the OCCFT held elections for the first adjunct officers: Vice President Milton Hicks (Health), Delegates Mazan El Hassan (Economics), Chris Heppeler (English) and Gretchen Roberts (Library).

at least three years after graduation. William H. Meyer, a County Legislator and State Farm agent, organized the scholarship program in 1991. And from 1988 to the time of this publication, Community General Hospital (now Upstate University Hospital at Community General) has awarded five scholarships annually to Nursing students. Another cooperative effort, initiated by the County Legislature's Health Committee, provided up to 40 scholarships of $500 to disadvantaged students to enable them to complete coursework required to enter into one of the College's Health Professions programs, such as Nursing. Additional $500 scholarships to help students complete the training were linked to a requirement to work in Onondaga County after graduation.

DIVERSITY

The diversity of OCC students was both local and global. International receptions and dinners each year brought students together, echoing the work of faculty in the Midtown Plaza years. Starting in 1987, a Multicultural Honors Scholarship dinner recognized achievements of African-American, Latino and Native American students. The traditional American Thanksgiving dinner served for international students was another annual activity, and the International Festival showcased countries and cultures represented by students of the College.

Snapshots through the years show the diversity of international life at OCC. Praise for the welcoming atmosphere for foreign students came from a Le Moyne professor who sent a South African student to OCC to become accustomed to American academic life. A young Kurdish refugee hoped to use his OCC degree as a step on the way to medical school. After a year of English as a Second Language study, he was an "A" student. An introduction to Pakistani cuisine was available each year to students in Biology Professor Mahtab Shaikih's Anatomy and Physiology courses. During his 28 years at the College, he estimated that at least 2,800 students visited his home to eat the Pakistani chicken meal that he prepared.

Studying abroad also became possible for students in 1994 when the Office of Study Abroad opened with Prof. Lucille Pallotta (Modern Languages) as Coordinator. OCC was part of the College Consortium on International Studies (CCIS) and sent students to Canada, China, Costa Rica, Ecuador, England, France, Ghana, Ireland, Italy, Japan and Spain. Most of the students remained abroad for one semester. The program ended in 1997-1998 due to campus budget cuts. In 2002,

Study Abroad and International Education became part of Academic Initiatives, administered by Dianne Fancher, Director. Through the SUNY Consortium, OCC students usually went abroad during the summer, often to Italy through SUNY Oswego. In 2007, the oversight for Study Abroad was moved to Diversity Services.

Women's History Month, Hispanic Heritage Month and others brought special programs to campus, but one of the most enduring ethnic observances was February's Black Awareness Month, which was celebrated in many different ways as the years went on, with national speakers and entertainment emphasizing African-American culture. JAMAA, active since the Midtown Plaza days, continued to take the lead in maintaining awareness. In 1991, minority alumni came back to OCC to help minority students understand how their College studies could help them to attain their goals in the corporate world. "OCC helped me get my academic life in order," said one graduate, a senior employment supervisor at Mutual of New York.

In 1993, students from the Native American Club approached History Professors Joe Agonito, Hiram Smith and Jim Dupree to re-introduce Native American courses (first offered in 1970).

Alumni Snapshot

Kim Colasanti, '93

- A.A., Math and Science
- B.S. in Computer Science – Syracuse University
- M.S. in Computer Science – Syracuse University
- Quality Assurance Manager, Welch Allyn

Kim Colasanti came to Onondaga Community College with a full plate. She worked a full-time job. She was changing careers. And she hadn't stepped foot in a classroom for years.

"When I graduated from high school, I didn't go directly to college," she says. "I always intended to go back to college, but things kept getting in the way."

But all of that didn't stop her from realizing her potential and making the most of her time at Onondaga. Despite working jobs in administration and arbitration, Colasanti's true passion remained in mathematics and computers. PCs were on the rise, and the software niche started to boom in the early '90s.

Colasanti knew she needed to be a part of it.

"I looked at a lot of different options. Seeing as I was in a low-paying job, money was a big factor," she says. "I realized I could get a two-year degree from OCC, transfer all my credits into SU and get a full bachelor's degree with SU's name on it."

Earning a perfect grade point average and joining the Phi Theta Kappa Honor Society are just a handful of Colasanti's accomplishments at Onondaga. But her desire for success went beyond academics. She saw the college experience and earning a degree as an opportunity to make her more independent.

"I wanted to be able to support myself. I couldn't support myself on the money I was making," she says. "My driving force that kept me going was that I did not want to rely on anybody to support me."

Colasanti later transferred to Syracuse University. She earned a master's degree. And she worked her way up to quality assurance manager at Welch Allyn in Skaneateles, New York.

But she'll never forget where it all started.

"Any time someone brings up the College, I will say loudly and clearly, 'I went to OCC. It's a great college. I loved my professors and my teachers.'"

In 1996, students spent three weeks studying ceramics and drawing at a residential art center located in a village just outside Barcelona, Spain. Pictured above are the students, along with Professors Andy (Art) and Engracia (Modern Languages and a Barcelona native) Schuster and their sons, Andrew Jr. and Alex. At the top of the photo is Msgr. Josep Poch, who hosted the Schuster family. (Courtesy of Prof. Engracia Schuster)

In the fall semester, a North American Indian History course was taught. As a follow-up, Bernadette Mendonez-Russell (Dean, Center for Arts, Humanities & Social Sciences) created a Native American Advisory Committee, including members from the local Native American community and from the OCC campus community. In fall 1996, Prof. Hiram Smith, committee Coordinator, presented the Native American Studies Concentration (now Minor). The format was similar to that of the African-American history classes the faculty pioneered in the 1960s with Prof. Dupree as the instructor. Prof. Tara Ross (History), who had created the first African-American Studies course at Radford University in Virginia, came to OCC when Prof. Dupree retired in 1994. She organized a cohesive program of study that resulted in a Concentration (now Minor) in African-American Studies.

Promoting diversity was part of Prof. Ann Felton's life (Human Services) and a key aspect of her contribution to the College. Her life's goal was to assure minorities that there was a way to get an education. In 1989, an Office of Multicultural Resources and Diversity Awareness (now known as Diversity Services) opened with Prof. Felton as Director; advisory committees were

formed to help with diversity training for the staff and faculty. Through the Diversity Awareness Program, Prof. Felton had a direct impact throughout the institution; she also shared her vision on a national level. Her unexpected death in 1992, after an illness, draped the campus in sadness. At the time, President

CENTER FOR TEACHING EXCELLENCE

OCC's Center for Teaching Excellence resulted from a spring 1991 Teaching and Learning project organized around the examination of program, staff and institutional effectiveness. President Bruce Leslie noted in his remarks to the Faculty at the start of the 1991-1992 academic year that there was "strong interest in developing a means by which the College could ensure that all the challenges of teaching, whether related to curricula development, technologies used in the classroom, student learning styles, or utilizing different teaching techniques could be addressed." Through the leadership of Prof. Ellen Douglas (Human Services), Prof. John Rogers (Business), Prof. Virginia Tilden (Nursing) and Bernadette Mendonez-Russell (Dean of Arts, Humanities & Social Sciences), the Teaching Center was created.

In 1994, Prof. Patricia Waelder (English/Reading) was appointed as the Center's first Coordinator in its location in Coulter Library. She oversaw the development of the mini-grant process to fund faculty travel to conferences, course tuition and classroom projects. The Center also offered on-campus faculty development through workshops. In 1996, Prof. Ellen Douglas took over the Coordinator's position and launched two additional Center initiatives: the newsletter, *It's Academic*, and the Readers' Group, a small-group discussion of professional readings. Prof. Georgia Schneider (Modern Languages) stepped into the role of Coordinator in the fall of 1997 and oversaw the transition of the Center's initial Advisory Board to a Standing Committee of the Faculty, which continues even now as the primary source of faculty input regarding Center programming and direction.

In 2000, President Debbie Sydow launched the President's Incentive Grant program to provide a new opportunity to fund faculty innovation through competitive grants. Prof. Kathy Eisele (English) became Coordinator in fall 2001. She refined the process for managing the incentive grants and oversaw the Center's relocation to Academic One (now Mawhinney Hall). The Teaching Center also began a collaboration with the new Multimedia Instructional Designers (MIDs), Professors Karl Klein and MaryPat Root (Computer Studies), who shared the Teaching Center space for a time. Under Prof. Deb Irwin (Reading), who began her term as Coordinator in 2006, the influence of technology, study abroad, service learning and the partnership with the Diversity Awareness Office became increasingly evident in the programming. In 2010, Prof. Jamie Sindell (English) became Coordinator, followed by Prof. Ednita Wright (Human Services) in 2011.

Still today, the core mission of the Teaching Center remains providing opportunities for faculty development and innovation.

OCC offered students many internship/work opportunities. For government-oriented students, the Minority Leaders Fellowship Program offered summer work in Washington, D.C. In addition, students interned in state offices in Albany. Walt Disney World continues year after year to recruit at OCC through the Disney College Program initiated in the 1980s when Prof. Jim Drake (Business Administration) made the first contact with Disney. Students are placed in entry-level positions throughout the Walt Disney World Parks and Resorts. They earn 12 to 15 hours of College credit while working in the entertainment capital.

ONONDAGA NATION FLAG RAISING

In an interview, Carol Cowles (Assistant to the President 1985-1994; Dean of Students 1994-1998) remembered the close relationship between the College and the Onondaga Nation that developed by working with the Clan Mothers and the OCC students from the Nation. An active Native American student club included members from several tribes (Onondagas, Cayugas, Senecas, Cherokees and Seminoles). She also remembered the Native American social dances (as opposed to dances with religious significance) held on campus when "lots and lots of families from the Onondaga Nation would come," as well as many people from the wider community "for a fun evening."

Ms. Cowles recalled "powerful speakers for some of the Native American celebrations [such as Onondaga Nation Chief] Irving Powless taking a sack out from underneath the podium and bringing out a wampum belt that George Washington had touched" and "[Onondaga Nation Chief and Tadodaho (Firekeeper) of the Six Nations Confederacy] Leon Shenandoah coming and speaking in this very, very quiet voice about things that he had seen in dreams that had come to reality." By 1994, there were 125 Native Americans enrolled. That year, 43 people associated with OCC went to the Red Earth Native American Cultural Festival in Oklahoma. The link between the College and the Nation continued year after year as Onondaga Chiefs and Clan Mothers continued to speak to students.

President Bruce Leslie and Carol Cowles raising the Onondaga Nation Flag on May 5, 1995.

Professor Ann Felton, Director of the Office of Multicultural Resources and Diversity Awareness (1989-1992), confers with student Nashid G. Shakir (Business Technology, 1992).

Bruce Leslie said, "She shared her vision of change," a vision that is still carried on today in OCC's Ann Felton Multicultural Center and Gallery, a venue for local, regional and national art and activities, which opened in Ferrante Hall in 2003.

FACULTY SCHOLARS

While classroom teaching was the hallmark of the College's faculty, they also were earning national and international recognition for a wide range of accomplishments. Prof. Jane Donegan's research resulted in *Hydropathic Highway to Health: Women and Water Cures in Antebellum America*, published in 1986, bringing the History professor national acclaim. *Pope Joan*, a book published in 1996, brought Donna Cross, English professor and Writing Skills Center Coordinator, international recognition. *Publisher's Weekly* congratulated her on the historical romance that grew out of her ten years researching the tale of a Ninth Century woman who, disguised as a man, took over her deceased brother's persona and was eventually crowned Pope. In October 2009, Berlin, Germany, held the world premiere of the movie version, and the Syracuse premiere was held at the Palace Theater in spring 2011.

In July 1989, the Syracuse Symphony Orchestra, under the direction of Neal Gittleman, premiered Music Professor Don Miller's composition the *Finger Lakes Suite* in a Skaneateles, New York, performance. In its three movements, the Suite celebrated the geography and history of the Finger Lakes region: the beauty of the lakes; the yearning for equality (Native Americans, African Americans, women); and the bounty of the countryside. Prof. Miller's later composition *Here Rests in Honored Glory* set music to the inscription on the Tomb of the Unknowns and was designated as the official hymn of mourning by the Veterans of the Vietnam War and the Paralyzed Veterans of America. In November 1991, student choristers from OCC, Le Moyne College, Oneida High School and the University of Maryland sang it during Veterans Day ceremonies at the Tomb in Arlington National Cemetery under the direction of Jeffrey Welcher, Oneida Choral Director. Members from the Oneida High School Brass and Percussion Ensemble joined them. In the fall of 2009, the composition received the George Washington Medal of Honor, given by the Freedoms Foundation at Valley Forge.

International acclaim also came to Prof. James MacKillop, of the English faculty, for his *Anthology of Irish Literature* (1987) and for a 1989 conference held at OCC of the interdisciplinary American Conference for Irish Studies (ACIS). Over 350 people attended from seven countries, including Irish intellectual Conor Cruise O'Brien as the keynote speaker. Subsequently, Prof. MacKillop became President of ACIS. In 1998, the Oxford University Press published his *Dictionary of Celtic Mythology*. Prof. MacKillop also collaborated with Prof. Donna Cross (English) in authoring *Speaking With Words* and contributed theater commentary and reviews to local newspapers. Prof. Doug Brode, who organized the Cinema Studies Concentration (now Minor) in the English Department, was a film critic for Syracuse newspapers, including the *Syracuse New Times*. In addition, he wrote film scripts and published several books about films, including *Films of Steven Spielberg* and *Shakespeare in the Movies*.

Dr. Helen Milewska Etherington, Vice President for Academic and Student Services, was a noted student of Polish literature, culture and economics. She received a full scholarship for the summer session at the Marie Curie-Sklodowska University in Poland in 1998. And that same year, Geology Professor Meg Harris discovered a 245-million year old trilobite at Pratt's Falls in the southeastern Onondaga County Town of Pompey. The new species of insect, which was named *Kennacryphaeus Harrisae* in her honor, earned her a listing in geology manuals and museums throughout the world.

Alumni Snapshot

Karen Webster, '95
- A.S., Business Administration
- Onondaga Nation Clan Mother
- Office Manager, Ganigonhi:yoh

To Karen Webster, Onondaga Community College provided more than just an education. She says it blessed her with a second family.

"No matter who you were, what your background was, or who you knew or didn't know, there was always someone there to help," she explains.

And it's a family that's accompanied and guided her for decades. Webster began her degree at Onondaga in 1970—bussing back and forth between Midtown Plaza and the Onondaga Hill campus for classes. She eventually left the College to pursue a career and a family but returned more than 20 years later to complete her education.

"I lost my job in '93. I could get another job or get an education," she says. "So I decided to go back. I received support from my boyfriend—he said that I might need it later in life."

Webster embraced her second opportunity and became actively involved around campus. As a work study, she assumed a role in the Ann Felton Multicultural Center as a counselor for Native American students. She also served as a leader in the College's Native American Club.

"There's so much diversity up there—you can't get that from many local places," Webster says. "And there are so many things going on at campus. I was glad to be a part of all of it."

She also played a key role in raising the Iroquois Confederacy flag on the College's main flagpole. With the help of fellow Native American students, Webster organized an event well attended by local politicians, college officials and Onondaga Nation leaders to commemorate the occasion.

The flag still remains there today—flying high, right next to the New York State and United States emblems, acting as a symbol of unity.

"OCC is a big part of our lives," she shares. "We wanted to share with everyone how lucky we are to have the school here—right in our backyard. I would never trade it for anything."

Performance of *Here Rests in Honored Glory* at Arlington National Cemetery, November 11, 1991. (Courtesy of Donald & Mary Miller)

WHITNEY APPLIED TECHNOLOGY CENTER

By 1992, OCC was being hailed as a primary provider of workforce training in Central New York and, thus, an important contributor to economic development. Authorized that year, the new 183,000-square-foot Applied Technology Center (ATC) was designed to carry out that part of the College's mission. A combination of county, state and federal sources funded the $29.5 million project. The firm of Mitchell/Giurgola Architects (New York City) was awarded the contract for building design. The architects won two awards for the design: Recognized Value Award (2001), given by the School Construction News and Design Share Awards, and American Architecture Recognition (2004), sponsored by the Chicago Athenaeum: Museum of Architecture and Design.

Whitney Applied Technology Center in fall 2008, with the Gordon Student Center to the right. The campus buildings on the west side of the Gorge are visible in the background.

Architect's scale model of the proposed Applied Technology Center.

RALPH "ROY" WHITNEY, JR.

Ralph "Roy" Whitney dedicated nearly 40 years of service to Onondaga Community College. He served as a member of the Board of Trustees (1967-1983), including two terms as Chair, and as a member of the OCC Foundation Board of Directors (1980-2005).

Coming from the New York Investment Banking Firm of Hammond, Kennedy & Co., Inc. (now Hammond, Kennedy, & Whitney), Mr. Whitney brought his background in finance to the OCC Board and Foundation. As a trustee, he served on and chaired the Finance Committee. As a founding member of the Foundation, he helped establish fundraising initiatives at the College, including the "Today's Choice for Tomorrow's Future Campaign," the annual giving campaign, and numerous other corporate and individual campaigns to support student scholarships and other College initiatives.

Dedicated in November 1999, the light brick and white steel building featured contrasting angular and curved details. The Center was a striking architectural contrast to the campus' earlier dark brick structures. The ATC was named in honor of Mr. Ralph Whitney and his wife, Dr. Fay Whitney, who contributed a substantial gift to the "Today's Choice for Tomorrow's Future" campaign. Mr. Whitney was a member of the Board of Trustees (1967-1983) and of the Foundation Board of Directors (1980-2005). "We believe education is the key to people's lives," said Dr. Whitney, a college nursing educator, when she explained the couple's philosophy and donation.

The new Ralph and Fay Whitney Applied Technology Center provided a learning environment to meet the demands of rapidly changing technology fields. The programs that relocated benefited from custom-designed space, such as Architectural Technology (spacious studios with an urban view), Automotive Technology (a high-bay area), Photography (a state-of-the-art darkroom), and Electronic Media Communications, formerly Radio-Television (a professional television production facility and radio station). The new radio and television studio also provided the opportunity for a state-of-the-art radio station. Previously, the College's radio station WOCC (Supermix.us, an Internet radio station, in 2010) had been audible only through the public address system in the Gordon Student Center.

Included in the original design for Whitney was a suite of offices to accommodate the president and senior administrative staff, which as a result of a change order issued by President Raisman, continued to work out of retrofitted classrooms in Mawhinney Hall through the 2008-2009 academic year. In summer 2009, ten years after the building opened, the President's Suite relocated to the Whitney ATC from Mawhinney Hall, creating three additional classrooms in the vacated space.

![R.I.T. without D.E.B.T. billboard]

R.I.T. without D.E.B.T.
$26,922 Off
OCC
Where to start!
LAMAR

A North Campus had been perennially discussed ever since OCC left downtown Syracuse in 1973. Finally, in 1999, an agreement was reached on leasing space at Seneca Mall, Route 57 in Liverpool, to accommodate the estimated 1,000 students expected. Enrollment from the area, where 40 percent of the County's population lived, topped all expectations. For the first fiscal year (2000-2001), the North Site enrolled 2,048 students in 101 credit sections and 819 students in 69 non-credit sections (duplicated headcount).

Shortly after he arrived, President Neal Raisman began utilizing billboards in the city of Syracuse as an advertising campaign for OCC, creating an excitement in the Central New York community about the College and its potential.

Employees and students participate in the Syracuse St. Patrick's Day parade in the mid-1980s. Prof. Rob O'Boyle (Library) in the white sweater rides on the float, while College Nurse Betty O'Connor walks alongside it.

NEW PRESIDENT: NEAL RAISMAN

In 1997, Dr. Neal O. Raisman, former President of Rockland Community College (near New York City), was selected to be OCC's sixth President. He arrived in August of that year. Dr. Raisman promised to give OCC a "new look" and immediately started an advertising campaign for the College. His goal was to help the region overcome what he saw as its own sense of self-defeat.

As plans for the upcoming budget (1998-1999) began and a $2 million deficit became apparent, Dr. Raisman proposed a sweeping administrative and academic restructuring. His reorganization plan met opposition from the faculty and other employees. One proposal was to organize academic departments as clusters, thus eliminating long-standing department chairs. "Painful" as the plan was, Dr. Raisman said, "The college has hit a financial wall," with prospects of a larger deficit the following year if immediate action was not taken.

In the end, 18 layoffs in administrative and support staff occurred, including the elimination of four deans: Center for Community Education, Center for Arts and Sciences, Center for Health and Community Professions, and Student Services. Dr. Raisman did insist on maintaining a core of full-time faculty to teach a minimum of 60 percent of courses rather than reducing costs by increasing the number of adjunct faculty, and in the end, no full-time faculty were laid off.

Under President Raisman's tenure, the final planning, construction and preparation for the opening of the Whitney Applied Technology Center occurred. He also initiated the Honors Program, using as a model the program at Rockland Community College.

President Raisman often found himself out of step with County officials. As one observer commented, he "never really got the feel of the community." Dr. Raisman resigned in June 1999. Board Chair Anne Messenger was succinct: "He submitted his resignation and we accepted it." Dr. Raisman said he was "disappointed" about how his 22 months at OCC had ended, "but I guess I knew we were headed in this direction."

Less than a month after Dr. Raisman's departure, Dr. Joseph Bulmer, retired after 17 years as President of Hudson Valley Community College in Troy, was chosen as Interim President, and a Presidential Search Committee was established.

Alumni Snapshot

Jason Dudzinski, '94

- Criminal Justice
- Member of 1992-1993 Championship Men's Basketball Team
- Head Coach of JV Men's Basketball, Henninger High School

Jason Dudzinski came to Onondaga Community College knowing one thing: he wanted to play basketball.

"I'd seen that the team had good success the year before, but I noticed they had no big guys on the team," he says. "I thought it's what they needed. I had it. So I joined."

Dudzinski became one of the tallest players on the team—and he was only a few inches over six feet. And it's that lack of size that made the Lazers underdogs throughout the entire season. They weren't nationally ranked. They didn't post an undefeated record. They didn't garner much attention at all until entering post-season play. Still, it didn't stop them from winning the program's first national championship.

"Every single person on that team loved the game of basketball, all the players and the coaches. They weren't playing just to stay in shape or for something to do," Dudzinski shares. "We were one of the hardest working teams out there. Nobody took a day off."

Thanks to a successful regional bid, the Lazers were dubbed "the giant killers" for beating some of the game's top teams. The discipline, energy and tenacity displayed in the regional tournament earned Onondaga the opportunity to compete for the national championship.

Dudzinski remembers it all—traveling east to Oneonta and stacking up against a powerhouse Minneapolis Community College team in the finals. Only a dozen people showed up to watch, a consequence of the harsh Blizzard of '93 that buried New York state in mounds of snow.

But the Lazers didn't let it faze them. They defeated Minneapolis 84-78 to capture the national title.

"It's hard to explain that feeling—to be number one in the United States at the end of the buzzer," he says. "It doesn't matter at what level the game is played: a national championship is a national championship."

What led an underestimated, underrated Onondaga team to success? Dudzinski credits the maturity of the players and the dedication of the coaching staff.

"The coaches knew what they were doing. If they asked us to run into a wall, we didn't ask why—we just did it," Dudzinski says. "They had all of our respect, even with two-and-a-half and three-hour practices."

But Dudzinski also gives his academic "coaches" credit for helping him through everything—working, going to school, playing basketball and raising a child all at the same time. Without their help, he may have never experienced both the thrill of a national title and the thrill of earning a college degree.

"It was hard. I wanted to quit many times," he admits. "But my professors urged me to keep going. They showed me that I could do it."

In 1988-1989 and 1989-1990, the men's basketball team won the Mid-State Athletic Conference Championship. In 1992-1993, the team (pictured above) defeated Minneapolis Community College (84-78) to capture their first NJCAA Championship. Coach Mike Rizzi is pictured on the right, holding the trophy with County Executive Nick Pirro. The championship game was played at SUNY Oneonta, when a Northeast blizzard made it too dangerous to travel to SUNY Delhi, where the game was originally scheduled. The game, played on March 14, was still delayed a day due to the storm.

COMMUNITY EDUCATION

In 1990, Onondaga Community College signed a lease for the 30,000-square-foot Unity Mutual Insurance Building near the Route 173 entrance. It became the EXCELL Center (now J. Stanley Coyne Hall) when the Center for Community Education relocated there from the Gordon Student Center. When the building was purchased in 1994, it was the first major expansion of the campus beyond the initial core buildings. In 2000, the College connected the EXCELL Center to the rest of campus by constructing a causeway (Collegiate Drive) from the main campus loop road (Ransom G. MacKenzie Drive), bisecting the site of the former Pogey Pond.

The Center for Community Education, led by Dean Patricia Pirro, generated some of the College's nationally recognized and most popular community-oriented programs: the Rural Women's Work Readiness Project, Displaced Homemakers Project, ENCORE-Enrichment Courses for Retirement, and a Child Development Project for P.E.A.C.E. (People's Equal Action and Community Effort, Inc.) were some of the early OCC programs housed in the EXCELL Center. During the 1980s and 1990s, popular non-credit courses were offered: Real Estate Sales, Insurance Agents & Brokers, Aerobics/Step Aerobics, Social Ballroom Dancing and Financial Planning. The Center also developed numerous winter recreation classes for young children and parents, and for several years organized the Daddy/Daughter Valentine Dance for the Ronald MacDonald House. Popular non-credit courses in 2010 included classes in SAT Preparation, Defensive Driving, Basic Motorcycle Rider Safety, Phlebotomy and Notary Public.

SPECIALIZED PROGRAMS

During summers, the campus was filled with elementary through high school age students who participated in a variety of academic and recreational courses. College for Kids, sports camps, driver education and the remedial summer school classes brought a new perspective and introduced local parents to OCC's campus, academic opportunities and facilities.

Entrance to the Home Office of Unity Mutual Life Insurance Company from Onondaga Road (Route 173).

College for Kids program with the Syracuse Police Department.

A Community Education class at a garden in front of Storer Auditorium.

Main entrance to H -1 Hall on the former County Poorhouse property, which was renovated in 2010-2011.

By summer 1999, classes had expanded to offer Pre-College Mathematics, Biology, English and Physics to help recent high school graduates get an advance start on college. A regional summer school was also offered free for several years for students from the city's Southwest Community Center and the Spanish Action League. Children in grades three though eight attended classes in Language Arts, Mathematics, Study Skills, Science and Social Studies.

The Liberty Partnerships Program at OCC began as a high school tutoring program for students who needed assistance graduating. In the first 20 years, the Program served more than 2,300 students and graduated approximately 85 percent of its seniors. Over 75 percent of the LPP students go on to higher education.

In 1994, the College was awarded a School-to-Work grant, one of the first initiatives that developed partnerships with school districts, colleges and the business community to address the needs of all stakeholders. A major focus was the infusion of work-based experiences, such as job shadowing and internships, into curricula at both the high school and college levels. The College administered this grant until 2001 when the funding was eliminated at the federal level. More than 20 school districts participated in the initiative, which had an impact on thousands of students, teachers and College faculty.

In the late 1980s, College for Living began offering classes for students with developmental disabilities. Courses included Money Math, Aerobics and Listening Skills. Since 2001, College for Living has also operated a group day-habilitation program that assists students with independent living and employability skills. Approximately 250 students have enrolled annually (2007-2010) in courses geared to their unique needs.

In 1984, the Small Business Development Center (SBDC) was located at the Sam Williams Business Center in downtown Syracuse and staffed by a director and a part-time advisor. As a start-up incubator for small businesses, the Center was so successful that the actual building was expanded to double its size. However, no classes were offered, only business advice. In the early 1990s, when on-campus space became available, the SBDC moved to the EXCELL Center. With additional staff, the SBDC began offering classes in basic business start-up. At this time, a partnership with the Department of Labor began, and the Self Employment Assistance Program (SEAP) was developed. Eventually, the SBDC moved to the Whitney Building and began offering an expanded array of classes. In 2011, the SBDC moved to the newly restored H-1 Hall on the former Poorhouse property. New programs and services include Operation: Start Up and Grow (a veterans' business conference); a Green Business advisor stationed at the Northside Collaboratory on N. Salina Street; and advisors at North Campus and other locations.

Community Education

Fire and emergency personnel practicing a coordinated emergency response using a model city.

A student participates in a College for Living course.

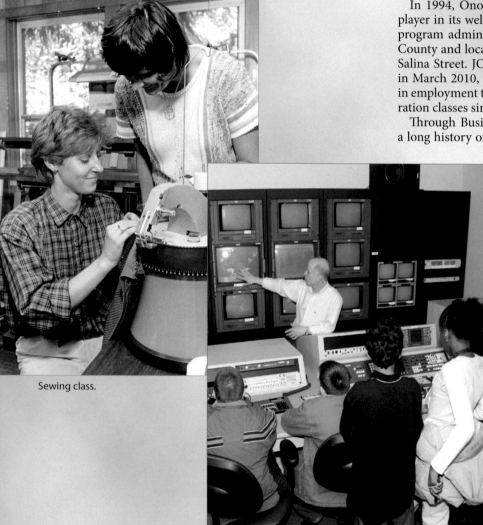

Sewing class.

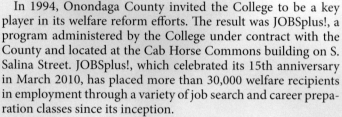

Prof. Anthony Vadala (EMC) provides an overview of video equipment in a studio at OCC to students from Van Duyn Elementary School.

In 1994, Onondaga County invited the College to be a key player in its welfare reform efforts. The result was JOBSplus!, a program administered by the College under contract with the County and located at the Cab Horse Commons building on S. Salina Street. JOBSplus!, which celebrated its 15th anniversary in March 2010, has placed more than 30,000 welfare recipients in employment through a variety of job search and career preparation classes since its inception.

Through Business Workforce Development, the College has a long history of supporting local businesses and employers by providing customized training.

President Sydow secured funding in the early 2000s to embark on a new and innovative initiative to support the local manufacturing base through a Lean Manufacturing Institute and the Industrial Readiness Certificate. Business sectors, such as healthcare, advanced manufacturing, building science and information technology are supported through non-credit programs: Lean Six Sigma (a partnership with Rochester Institute of Technology); Certified Production Technician; Broadband Technology; building performance certification through the Center for Energy Efficiency and Building Science (a partnership with Hudson Valley Community College); and computer programming courses through the Center for Business Information Technology.

The College also forms partnerships directly with businesses and organizations, such as Anheuser-Busch, Excellus, Verizon, Centro and National Grid, to deliver content that is specific and unique to their companies.

The Fire Protection program began in 1970 at the request of Syracuse Fire Chief Thomas F. Hanlon and quickly began to draw students from far beyond Onondaga County. In 1987, the County Fire Chiefs

Police Academy recruits training on the campus perimeter road, with residence halls visible in the background.

Stella Penizotto enjoys a special moment with two children at one of the three Shining Stars Daycare centers, which she founded in the Syracuse area with assistance from the Small Business Development Center at OCC.

Association began providing scholarships for Fire Service training through state grants. This funding led to National Certification (1995) for OCC's Fire Service Certification Program by both national accreditation bodies, a first in New York State.

In 1975, the Police Academy moved from downtown Syracuse to OCC, where it was affiliated with the Criminal Justice Institute under the direction of retired Syracuse Police Captain Larry Lynch but still managed by the Onondaga County Sheriff's Office and the Syracuse Police Department. In the late 1980s, the Academy became part of the College's Community Education programs and eventually moved from the main campus to the EXCELL Center (now Coyne Hall). In 1994, the Syracuse Police Department left the College's Academy to form its own.

Recognized statewide as a leader in public safety training, the PSTC now includes credit courses and programs in Law Enforcement (Police Academy), Fire Protection, Homeland Security and Disaster Preparedness. In addition, the PSTC provides non-credit training for local businesses in disaster management, security personnel and OSHA requirements, and non-credit courses in police training and fire protection.

President Debbie Sydow presents JOBSplus! Director Janice Mayne with a plaque to commemorate the 15th anniversary of the program.

Participants in a community education class.

Community Education

The New Millennium
2000-2011

T ransformation" was the theme of OCC's 40th anniversary celebration, which commenced in September 2001, on the heels of opening the new Whitney Applied Technology Center and welcoming a new president. The College's initial five academic programs had expanded to over 50. Its graduating class had grown from the first one of 177 (1964) to 906 (2001). And by the fall of 2002, enrollment totaled 8,205 students, compared with the first class of 1,294 in fall 1962. There was much to celebrate.

The College kicked off its celebration on September 9 with a barbeque on the campus quad. Students, alumni, faculty and staff joined President Debbie Sydow in commemorating four decades of service to the community. Local political and community leaders were also in attendance, including Congressman Jim Walsh, County Executive Nick Pirro, Senator John DeFrancisco, Mayor Matt Driscoll and County Legislature Chair William Sanford, who in his remarks mused that the College and its president were both "40 years young" and were both "poised to do great things for Central New York."

"Transformation" took on a dramatically different meaning, however, when two days later, on September 11, devastation resulted from terrorist attacks on the World Trade Center and other U.S. targets. It was against this backdrop that Onondaga Community College entered its fortieth decade. There were not many other celebratory events held on campus that year.

FRAMEWORK FOR SUCCESS

When in 1998 Onondaga received its ten-year reaccreditation from the Middle States Commission on Higher Education, the Middle States team advised, "As the Onondaga community changes, the College needs to reinvent itself to the extent necessary to meet the needs of a changed society…[and it] should raise the priority of the activities designed to attract new students and retain them once they choose to attend OCC." The College was at another crossroads. Trustees had concerns about the economy, budget shortfalls and the leadership necessary to navigate forward. Realizing the need to be proactive, trustees came together to work on a strategic plan. Trustee Gary Livent described it as an "intense process, much easier to reach consensus on vision than on the more specific priorities and goals." According to Dr. Livent, "an additional benefit of the strategic plan is that it proved helpful in the presidential search process that began later that year. Trustees were able to agree on the qualities and expertise we sought in the next president and to share our vision for the future with candidates."

Prof. Larry Weiskirch (Biology) in a Biology lab.

Students enjoying a game of Frisbee on an early fall day on the Quad in front of Mawhinney Hall.

A NEW PRESIDENT FOR A NEW MILLENNIUM

On July 1, 2000, Debbie L. Sydow, Ph.D., who had risen through the faculty and administrative ranks of the Virginia Community College system, became OCC's seventh (and first female) president. As the College welcomed its fifth chief administrator in five years, the campus community was seeking stability in its leadership, and the Board of Trustees was looking for someone to help the College realize the goals outlined in its new strategic plan. Both trustees and faculty agreed that Sydow was the top candidate. "I'm glad I was OCC's choice, because OCC was my choice," she said as she conveyed her enthusiasm for her new position. Presidential Search Committee Chair David Murphy predicted that Dr. Sydow would lead "quietly but with conviction." Not even the 191.9 inches of snow that fell during her first Syracuse winter could dim her enthusiasm for OCC and the Central New York community.

A *Post-Standard* editorial declared, "New OCC president faces daunting challenges with energy, enthusiasm," noting that Sydow "comes on board in the wake of the controversial, two-year tenure of her predecessor." With decided optimism, the editorial concluded as follows: "Experienced as an acting president at another community college, [Sydow] has the energy and leadership skills that could serve OCC exceptionally well. We bid her a warm welcome to this special community."

REINVENTING THE COMMUNITY'S COLLEGE

With a clear sense of purpose, President Sydow immediately set to work to translate the Board-approved strategic plan, *A Framework for Success*, into a plan of action with measurable objectives. She solicited input from employees and retirees, alumni and students, business leaders, community members and elected officials. She engaged local civic and social organizations in discussions about their views of the College and appeared in television, newspaper and radio interviews. These conversations with campus and community stakeholders set the course for change. Although it had adapted and changed over the course of 40 years, relatively few community members were aware of all that the College had to offer. Reintroducing the local community to OCC emerged as a top priority, as did the need to re-align internal systems in direct support of student success.

In response to student concerns, a team of professionals from New York and Virginia was formed by President Sydow to recommend improvements to enrollment services. The final report reads, "A consistent theme that emerged in our discussions was the need to transform and improve services in order to provide a more efficient and effective learning-centered operation. These sentiments support a One-Stop Center concept and design. Such a Center would provide integrated service and informa-

The Automotive Technology Vehicle Laboratory is located in the Whitney Applied Technology Center. The Automotive Technology Program was one of the first in the nation to include Emissions Diagnostics (clean air training) and alternative fuel vehicles in its curriculum. In addition, hybrid and plug-in hybrid vehicles were added.

Hospitality Management Prof. James Taylor (black hat) supervises students preparing meals in the kitchen of the student-run restaurant, the Bistro, in the Gordon Student Center. (Courtesy of Stephen Cannerelli, *The Post Standard*)

tion, coupled with convenience." The team went on to say, "We believe such an approach would support the OCC mission as a student-centered institution with a student-learning focus."

Simultaneous to re-thinking enrollment services, President Sydow tapped Prof. Tara Ross (History) to lead a study to review the effectiveness of evening, weekend and off-campus offerings. The report revealed considerable unmet demand. A few selected courses could be completed at off-site locations or at times convenient for working adults. However, it was largely impossible for non-traditional students to complete course requirements for a degree or certificate at times and places convenient for them.

In 2003, President Sydow recommended, and the Board of Trustees approved, a comprehensive realignment of College operations designed to prioritize and improve student recruitment, retention and success. Extensive operational changes were implemented during the 2003-2004 academic year, resulting in centralized, one-stop enrollment services (Student Central) for students, and online access to full degree programs. Programs and services to support a planned residential population were expanded, including athletics. And capital investment necessary to support realignment and the anticipated enrollment growth was secured.

> ## "OCC changed my life."
>
> *— Mary Barber Terry (Accounting, 2003)*

CAPITAL PROJECTS: RENOVATIONS, NEW BUILDINGS AND NEW PROPERTIES

In addition to being faced with contract negotiations, stagnant enrollment and the controversies surrounding her predecessor's departure, upon her arrival, President Sydow was confronted with the realities of a 40-year-old campus with aging buildings

and a history of deferred maintenance. "Solid but aging" was the reported condition of campus facilities. A six-year *Facilities Master Plan* was approved by trustees in 2001 with projects totaling $79 million. Efforts proceeded to secure necessary state and local funding to proceed with extensive capital renovation and construction.

Over the next decade the focus on student recruitment, retention and success guided capital improvements, and the campus was literally transformed. With new capital funding support from the state and the county Coyne Hall, Mawhinney Hall (formerly Academic One), Ferrante Hall, the Gordon Student Center, and the Health and Physical Education Center underwent extensive renovation. There was also new construction: Student Central, residence halls, Murphy Field, SRC Arena and Academic II (a Performing Arts Center) were added, and the Children's Learning Center nearly doubled in size. Property acquisitions included 8 acres adjoining Coyne Hall, 14 acres and 3 buildings adjacent to the College on Route 175, and the 48-acre/two-building former County Poorhouse property across Route 173 from the campus. All except the 14-acre acquisition came about through negotiated donations. In addition, interior signage was upgraded in the interest of improved campus navigation for students and visitors alike, and in 2009, crumbling concrete signs at both entrances were replaced by sturdy granite signs with electronic messaging capability.

A RESIDENTIAL CAMPUS

For the previous 40 years, one feature of the student body had remained the same—everyone commuted to campus. But change became a constant on campus in the first decade of the new millennium. Community interest in a residential option at OCC led to a feasibility study that was completed in 2002. The study documented demand for up to 600 beds. It took four years to implement, but a whole new student experience and new challenges came when OCC introduced a residential option in

Students relaxing and socializing in one of the residence hall suites in 2008.

Students moving into the residence halls on the first move-in day, September 2006.

the 2006 fall semester. For the first time, 500 students were living on campus, many participating in formal learning communities. Two- and three-bedroom suites included a shared living room, eating space and a small kitchen. All buildings were equipped with high-speed Internet access and contemporary laundry facilities. As one student described it, "Living on the OCC campus, close to home but still on my own, has been a dream come true."

Once ground was finally broken for the buildings in June 2005, construction of the three residence halls took just over a year to complete. Starting on that first move-in day (September 2006), volunteers stepped forward to welcome students and to help them move into the residence halls.

Along with enhanced support systems (food, library, security, etc.), the residential option brought new social activities and educational programming. Movie nights, health education and money management programs were scheduled. Buses were scheduled for shopping center trips. Day trips to local attractions, such as the Everson Museum of Art, Corning Museum of Glass, Museum of Science and Technology (The MOST), area sporting events (Syracuse Crunch ice hockey and Syracuse University football), Syracuse Stage, Crouse Hinds Theater and more were arranged. Other programs centered around college life, such as healthy relationships, stress reduction and Midnight Breakfasts before finals.

The success of the residence halls led to subsequent reconfigurations, resulting in accommodations for a total of 585 students by 2007. And by 2008, plans for a second phase of student housing were already underway. "Choosing to live on campus was one of the best decisions I could have made," says Kayla Spivey '09, Nursing, President of the Whole Earth Club.

THE PROMISE OF SELF-DISCOVERY

In its first four decades, Onondaga Community College established a strong presence in the Central New York community. However, by 2000 the community's overall perception of the College was outdated at best, and inaccurate at worst. Research conducted by the College revealed a stark disconnect between prospective students' perspectives of Onondaga prior to enrolling and their educational experience upon arrival. References like "OCC on the Rock" or "Harvard on the Hill" were often used by those unfamiliar with the breadth and quality of academic programs available at Onondaga. And despite the presence of thousands of successful alumni in the local community, few graduates were eager to publicly claim their alma mater.

Students indicated in research that they wanted to feel proud that they chose to attend OCC. In an attempt to address this concern and to align perception with reality, in 2003 the College embarked upon an extensive research project, the *OCC Identity Project*, that led to clarity regarding the core promise of the institution (*Promise of Self-Discovery*) and a new credo: Explore. Discover. *Transform.*

Understanding the Promise and the Credo was only the first step. In the months and years following the *Identity Project*, extensive effort was invested in aligning community perception with the reality of the Onondaga Community College educational experience. More and more individuals came to campus to participate in more and more community events and programs, and more and more students enrolled. Seeing was believing, for visitors were "stunned by the changes on campus," and word of mouth eventually led to a renewed community interest in Onondaga Community College.

The College began to receive national accolades for academic quality, accolades that helped the institution to gain more widespread recognition for excellence, which previously had been relatively unknown outside of the inner circle of students, alumni and faculty and staff. For example, Onondaga's Math Department was selected by the Carnegie Foundation for the Advancement of Teaching in 2010 to participate in the national Quantway Networked Improvement Community program in recognition of its innovative approaches to mathematics education.

The addition of new transfer agreements throughout the decade dramatically strengthened the educational pathways available to students. In 2008, Onondaga Community College and SUNY College of Environmental Science and Forestry signed an innovative articulation agreement to enable Onondaga graduates in specified degree programs to continue their studies at SUNY-ESF through a series of seamless transfer agreements and a level tuition rate consistent with that of Onondaga. In 2010, Onondaga and Syracuse University announced a partnership to provide qualifying students with dual admission and guaranteed transfer into 33 degree programs at Syracuse University. These dual admission agreements with prestigious institutions such as SUNY-ESF and Syracuse University, combined with the addition of three state-of-the-art residence halls in 2006 and a growing number of national championship sports teams, also enhanced appreciation in the community for Onondaga's academic excellence and student life programming.

IMPROVED RELATIONSHIPS: COUNTY GOVERNMENT AND COMMUNITY

In presenting the 2001-2002 budget to the Onondaga County Legislature, President Sydow pledged to continue to improve services and programs for students. Her prediction that "enrollment will follow quality" was fulfilled in the years that followed with enrollment surging by more than 65 percent from 2000 to 2010. In contrast to earlier years, negotiations in advance of the College's budget submission helped the official public hearings run smoothly. Frequently no one appeared at public hearings after 2001. These hearings were sometimes over in less than a minute, unlike the drawn-out battles of the early years.

By 2001, County Executive Nick Pirro declared that "Dr. Sydow is the first president in quite a while who is interested in how we spend our money up there." In his State of the County address that March, County Executive Pirro asked the County Legislature to approve technology upgrades on campus. Up to 2008 and the financial crisis of the time, Pirro and the Legislature would continue to support substantial investments in College operations and the physical plant as steady enrollment gains provided irrefutable evidence of local demand.

The annual report for the 2003-2004 academic year stated that OCC had hosted events bringing 75,000 local residents to the campus, and had saved $1 million through efficiency improvements and technology upgrades. In a statistic that the County Legislature could appreciate, Sydow announced that OCC was named one of the most cost-efficient colleges in the State University of New York, as measured by net cost per full-time equivalent (FTE) student. County legislators were also pleased when a 2004 economic impact study showed that the College and its related activities accounted for $56.1 million annual economic activity in Central New York.

When in 2007 news broke that Sydow was a finalist for the presidency at Broward Community College in Ft. Lauderdale, Florida, the public reaction when she announced that she would be staying to finish key projects on campus was best summed up in an editorial headlined "Staying, and Welcome." "Sydow is a leader whose talents will continue to draw notice. OCC shouldn't expect to keep her forever. For now, however, the college and the community are lucky to have her," the editorial read.

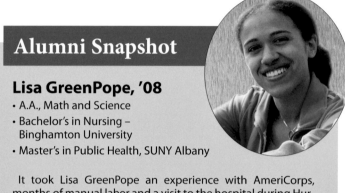

Alumni Snapshot

Lisa GreenPope, '08

- A.A., Math and Science
- Bachelor's in Nursing – Binghamton University
- Master's in Public Health, SUNY Albany

It took Lisa GreenPope an experience with AmeriCorps, months of manual labor and a visit to the hospital during Hurricane Katrina to realize the true value of a higher education.

"We had to go to a department store being used as a hospital during Hurricane Katrina. I was surprised to see that the nurses and doctors were solid despite their lack of materials," she shares. "It made me realize that if I wanted to go into the medical field, I needed to become well-educated and more professional."

That realization was fulfilled at Onondaga Community College. GreenPope needed a place to renew her abilities, build her confidence and develop an impressive résumé. She enrolled with a clear-cut plan: earn her associate's degree and transfer to a four-year institution.

"I knew exactly what I wanted to experience," she says. "I had been to College before but dropped out. I wanted to be more serious and focused this time."

But she discovered more at Onondaga. She became engaged with service projects in the community as Vice President of the College's Phi Theta Kappa chapter. She tutored fellow students in the Collegiate Science and Technology Entry Program and Educational Opportunity Program. And she attended a number of conferences and completed internships thanks to her various roles.

"I wouldn't have been able to have these active opportunities at a bigger or four-year school—these opportunities to organize, coordinate and create," she says. "And I was looked out for here. There are people who care about students and seeing them be successful."

GreenPope carried that success with her, crediting Onondaga's small classes and approachable professors for teaching her relevant, practical skills. And she credits the College for opening up a wealth of scholarship opportunities that benefitted her after she transferred.

"Onondaga taught me to work hard and take advantage of all the opportunities available to me," she says. "I didn't want to attend a huge school and feel average. And thanks to the support I received here, I got it right this time around."

SUSTAINABILITY

Students entering campus during the College's 50th anniversary year in fall 2011 find at OCC a campus dedicated to advancing the principles of sustainability through its academic programs, campus and community service initiatives, and campus operations. Onondaga's strong commitment to sustainability can trace its roots back to 1979 when the College first formed a Recycling Committee. Under the leadership of Charlie White (Director of Campus Facilities, 1982-1997), efforts first centered on the recycling of paper. Two decades later, during the 2003-2004 academic year, the College began installing separated recycling containers in the hallways of all buildings. In addition, electronic and other equipment, scrap metal and even food scraps (composting) were routinely recycled.

In 2000, OCC received a $500,000 Congestion Mitigation Air Quality (CMAQ) award from the Syracuse Metropolitan Transportation Council (SMTC) to train environmental technicians. The resulting Environmental Technology degree was reconfigured in 2009 to add a new option in Biotechnology, emphasizing biofuels, biomaterials and alternative energy technologies.

The College's sustainability initiative gained added momentum in 2007 when President Sydow signed the American College and University Presidents' Climate Commitment. In becoming a signatory, OCC agreed to develop and implement a plan to become carbon neutral by eliminating the College's greenhouse gas emissions. The same year the College received a $700,000 grant from the New York State Foundation for Science, Technology and Innovation (NYSTAR) to develop sustainability-related workforce training and academic programs, including Automotive Technology, Environmental Technology and Architectural Technology programs. A Sustainability Task Force, chaired by David Wall (Director of Corporate and Public Partnerships), developed a *Sustainability Action Plan* in 2008.

OCC made campus operations more sustainable by improving energy efficiency in lighting, heating, cooling and other areas. During a decade marked by extensive capital improvement and expansion, as existing buildings were renovated and new ones were built, sustainable, green and efficient construction techniques were utilized. Among the features of the 2006 renovation of the Gordon Student Center, outside shading louvers were installed to avoid overheating from the midday summer sun. Day-lighting via windows mounted high on walls allowed

As part of the *Sustainable Landscape Master Plan*, sections of the College grounds that were previously mowed now grow wild, creating patches of natural wildflower gardens.

deeper penetration of sunlight. In some locations, sensors were installed to control and dim artificial lighting when sufficient daylight was detected. And the floor of the Great Room was constructed as a concrete slab with radiant warm water tubing embedded throughout to save energy and provide a more uniform, comfortable heat.

During the mid-1990s, Jim Manwaring (Central Stores and Mail Manager, 1984-2009) suggested to then-President Bruce Leslie that the College could stop mowing certain areas of campus and create meadows. The project only lasted a short period

OCC'S THIRD SEAL 2005-PRESENT

On April 4, 2005, the Board of Trustees adopted a new College logo as part of the College's Identity Project. The design was based upon research completed by Jennifer Wolfe Design.

The Crest is made up of five main components: the "O", the Flame, the Quills, the Book and the Wordmark (text). The "O" is made up of two facing letter "C"s, for "community" and "college." The Flame represents both the "dancing" flame of "Self-Discovery," as well as the flame of the Longhouse. Its tip bends toward the horizon symbolizing a pathway toward the future. The Quills represent the great triad of a centered individual: a well-developed mind, body and soul. The Book symbolizes knowledge, its open pages giving way to the burning flame and triad of accomplishment.

of time. Mr. Manwaring brought the same proposal to President Sydow. The *Sustainable Landscape Master Plan*, created in 2009, identified opportunities to reduce lawn mowing and increase planting of native vegetation to decrease fuel use and improve natural habitat. Utilizing the expertise of a local landscape architect, nearly 20 acres of previously mown grass was methodically returned to meadows, beginning that same summer.

Through educational activities associated with Earth Day and Campus Sustainability Day, the College reached out to the campus community. Under the leadership of Prof. Peter Kraai (Biology), a student club, called The Whole Earth Club, was created in 2005-2006. Projects undertaken include advocating for composting of kitchen waste, campaigning to eliminate bottled water and selling refillable water bottles as a fundraiser, presenting displays on Earth Day and handing out seedlings, and screening various films to raise awareness. In 2009, the Architecture and Interior Design Club (in existence since the early 1980s) became one of the first clubs in the nation to join the U.S. Green Building Council Students with the assistance of Prof. Ken Bobis and USGBC New York Upstate Chapter Executive Director Tracie Hall. On campus, the Green Suites Program encouraged office suites to demonstrate their dedication to sustainability by pledging to a list of sustainability-related practices, such as reducing paper use and energy consumption. In 2010, OCC earned first place in New York State in the waste minimization category of the RecyleMania contest, a national recycling competition among colleges and universities. Also in 2010, the College further committed to advancing campus sustainability by hiring Sean Vormwald as its first Director of Sustainability. The College continued incorporating green building design principles into its new construction projects, such as the SRC Arena and Events Center. In 2011, Onondaga installed a 21.16kW solar array on the Whitney Applied Technology Center.

> "I will never forget my experience at your wonderful school and the caring people who helped me along the way. Thank you! A community college is what it implies—a community, and more than ever at OCC."
>
> – *Floyd V. Mills (Criminal Justice, 2007)*

ADVANCES IN TECHNOLOGY AND ONLINE LEARNING

Students who started in 1962 at Midtown Plaza took their class notes on paper notebook pages. In 2011, computers, laptops and tablets provided support for instruction and contact with the entire world. Blogs, chat rooms, social and business networks were available, as well as data management systems. Individual cell phones, smartphones and other types of personal wireless devices allowed instant and constant commu-

Alumni Snapshot

Tom Dannan, '04
- A.A., Humanities and Social Sciences
- B.A. in Public Policy – Syracuse University
- Director of Development, John Dau Foundation

At 26 years of age, Tom Dannan's accomplishments eclipse some individuals' lifetime experiences. He earned a two-year college degree. He earned a four-year college degree. He volunteered with the Peace Corps in Morocco. And he's recently helped with the relief effort in the Southern Sudan. But his journey started right here in Central New York at Onondaga Community College.

"It's something I can always look back on and be happy about," Dannan says. "When I come back here, I always have fond memories of the learning that went on, the experiences I had, and the people that I met."

Dannan arrived at Onondaga after applying to several four-year universities but not receiving suitable amounts of financial aid. He calls his family "working class," sharing that he had to work all throughout high school and college, and that going to an expensive college simply wasn't viable. But that's not to say he coasted through his time at Onondaga Community College.

"I never felt cheated out of the college experience," Dannan shares. "The people I met in the classroom inspired and moved me more maybe than at a more traditional college. I remember sitting in the classroom with people who hadn't been in school for 30 years, people who were single mothers raising three or four kids, people who were war refugees—all in one classroom together. It was a pretty amazing experience. There's nothing like it that could replace it."

Dannan embraced the opportunities given to him—becoming heavily involved in the student newspaper, assuming a position as vice president of the Phi Theta Kappa Honor Society, and thriving in the academic environment. He developed a love for learning, for knowledge and for service to the world around him.

"It's the kind of environment that really spurs learning," he says. "OCC really expanded the world to me. Even though I went to a diverse high school and watched the news, getting here was the first time I really lived it and met people who were coming from all over."

"Living" those experiences encouraged Dannan to go forward in the world and make a positive impact. And though he's more than 5,000 miles away at times, he recalls his Onondaga experiences often—sharing them around the globe and spreading good news about all it has to offer.

"When I put on my résumé that I graduated from OCC, that I was a member of the Honor Society with a 3.8 GPA, I feel good about my time here," he says. "A lot of the classes, even though they were 100- and 200-level classes, really hit on some pretty cool pockets of knowledge and experiences. I'm proud to say I'm an OCC alum."

nication throughout the campus and across the globe. The 1990s brought the convenience of touchtone phone registration and grade reports (via STAR). Thanks to rapid advances in technology, by May 2003 students could use WebAccess to check their grades online. To accommodate the shift of students to online resources, the College stopped mailing grade reports in fall 2007 and permanently ended the STAR program in November 2008. Moving into cyberspace, OCC streamed its commencement live online for the first time in May 2009.

When the Whitney Applied Technology Center opened for classes in fall 1999, OCC unveiled its first four multimedia lecture halls. Three years later, the first sixteen "smart" classrooms, consisting of technology such as an instructor computer, projector, document camera and audio/video equipment, were installed with at least one such classroom in each academic building, including at the North Site. By fall 2011, over 120 of the College's classrooms were equipped with "smart" classroom technology.

In 2001, the College dedicated its Academic Computing Center in Academic One (later Mawhinney Hall). Those 101 computers and two laser printers were only the first step in an extensive plan to invest in long-overdue technology upgrades across a campus that at the time lacked the very infrastructure necessary to support advanced academic and administrative computing. Upgrades and expansion of campus technology in the early 2000s included construction of a robust IT infrastructure, general and program specific computer labs, internet cafes and a wireless network.

In fall semester 2001, the College offered its first set of four online courses through the SUNY Learning Network (SLN). Prof. Nancy Gabriel (Teacher Education), Prof. Patricia Martin (Teacher Education), Prof. Peggy Przybycien (Nursing) and Prof. Sharon Testone (Mathematics) were OCC's pioneers of online learning. A strategic goal of establishing 11 complete online programs by 2011 was achieved early. By fall semester 2010, there were 3,756 students enrolled in 218 online sections of courses (duplicated headcount).

In the first 10 years of offering online courses, Onondaga Community College drew students from all 62 counties in New York, 38 U.S. states, and nine other countries from around the world. Technology also enabled professors to share their expertise with an international audience. In 2002, President Sydow greeted and Prof. Ramesh Gaonkar (Electrical and Computer Engineering Technology) delivered an address to 400 engineering students at India's Pume University, via Web conferencing.

Although technology increased the speed and ease of campus communication, electronic communication mirrored the sentiments that were previously expressed on fliers taped to bulletin boards across campus. No matter what physical form the messages took, or the year in which they were written, they showed the care that characterizes the OCC community. E-mails about helping one of their own "through a tough time" or a health problem were familiar. "Sad News" was the subject line of notices about deaths of staff members, their families and retirees. And from the College's United Way campaign to the annual mitten drive, employees remained actively engaged in support of the local community. Campus communications,

no matter the technology, show a chain of caring that has linked the campus community and woven strong bonds for the OCC family from its Midtown days through its 50th anniversary year.

Alumni Snapshot

Casey Knapp, '10
- A.S., Business Administration
- Studying Animal Science at Cornell University
- Family Owns Cobblestone Valley Farms in Preble, New York

Casey Knapp's passion for green agriculture and an eco-friendly lifestyle was a natural fit for Onondaga's Whole Earth Club—so natural that he became its president and played a key role in many campus sustainability initiatives.

"The College was definitely open to the idea and understood the importance of sustainability," he says. "They took big steps in enhancing the biodiversity of the environment and atmosphere."

Growing up on a farm, Knapp always found himself fascinated with green and sustainability movements. His perspectives on the environment, composting and organics, along with the Whole Earth Club's philosophy of green discovery, naturally complemented Onondaga's Sustainability Master Plan.

"One of the things we specifically did was remove plastic water bottles from campus," he shares. "It's a silly concept—paying a dollar for water that's expensive to manufacture. Eighty percent of the bottles end up in dumpsters. People needed to be educated, and it wasn't hard to open their eyes to it."

Knapp, with the help of the Whole Earth Club, left a lasting legacy on the campus. They held composting workshops. They advocated for gardens. And they praised the College's own sustainability efforts—enacting a sustainable landscape plan, purchasing more electricity from sustainable sources, establishing LEED requirements for new buildings and more.

But Knapp's interest in Onondaga extended beyond sustainability. To him, the College was a catalyst to achieve a larger goal: studying agriculture at the prestigious Cornell University.

"When I talked with someone from Cornell, they were excited and encouraged that I wanted to go there," he says. "Onondaga sends good students to Cornell, and they know that. Studying business couples well with agriculture—running a farm is running a business."

And though it didn't click altogether until later, Knapp now realizes that Onondaga allowed him the opportunity for self-discovery through interactions both in and out of the classroom.

"I didn't notice I was changing while I was there. But when I left, I realized that I had grown intellectually and changed the priorities in my life," he says. "I see clearly now what OCC did, and it's a really great stepping stone."

GORDON STUDENT CENTER & STUDENT CENTRAL

In 2003-2004, President Sydow unveiled a plan to centralize student enrollment services in one location, initially dubbed "The One Stop" and later "Student Central." Establishing the One Stop fell under the purview of the new Vice President for Student and Academic Services, Barbara Risser (2004-2007). When first launched, Student Central temporarily operated in renovated space in the lobby of Academic One (Mawhinney Hall). The re-engineered operation provided students with a one-stop location for all core admissions and enrollment services, which were previously housed in 14 separate offices spread across five different campus buildings. For ideas about providing these centralized services, the College looked to the nation's premier customer-oriented business—Disney—rather than to other academic institutions.

Student Central was part of the first major campus construction project undertaken during Dr. Sydow's tenure—a $9.9 million addition and renovation of the Gordon Student Center, in use since January 1973. The architecture firm of King + King designed the project, and Lil Green, who joined Onondaga as an adjunct professor in Interior Design, served as Senior Interior Designer for King + King on the project team. In addition to the new specialized space, the renovation involved upgrading all the plumbing, electrical, heating and ventilation systems within the Student Center, utilizing green and other specialized construction techniques. According to Prof. Ken Bobis (Architecture & Interior Design), "The design in many ways is 'cutting edge,' and on occasion our students and faculty had access to the construction site and the construction drawings, which proved very valuable to teaching and learning." The end result of the renovations, concluded in spring 2006, was a revitalized, light-infused Gordon Student Center, complete with modern dining facilities, a Great Room (for hosting campus events), the Bistro and a 16,000-square-foot addition to house Student Central.

At Student Central, service is provided to community members and students from the inquiry stage through graduation and beyond. In 2009, Student Central handled nearly 100,000 incoming calls and served nearly 50,000 students at the front desk. Launched in spring 2008, a "SmartCard" provided students with centralized access to services such as buying books and meals, checking out library materials, and entrance to campus labs and residence halls.

With the centralization of the enrollment processes, students and parents praised the courteous and helpful attention students received. Working at enrollment time needs "patience, skill and a good measure of humor," wrote President Sydow when she complimented those working in Student Central in 2009.

A DIVERSE AND ENGAGED FACULTY

The growing student body was well served by OCC's dedicated faculty members who continued to deliver the personalized attention that is the hallmark of the College. In 2003, retirements meant that OCC lost 537 years of classroom expertise. In response, the College launched an expanded orientation and mentoring program to help new faculty become familiar with OCC and its unique mission. An annual Employee Appreciation Event was launched to celebrate individual and team accomplishments, and the Horizon Leadership program sought to grow internal leaders. Even as new faculty joined the ranks, the focus of the College's first 50 years remained the same, a deep and abiding commitment to students and their learning experience. Additionally, the faculty (both new and veteran) continued to gain local, state and national recognition.

Prof. David Abrams (Music) served as a critic and columnist with *The Post-Standard* from 1992 to 2008, earning nine Syracuse Press Club awards. He also established an online critique blog, called CNY Café Momus. His opera reviews as a contributing writer, including those of the Metropolitan Opera simulcast, have been posted at the international website Musical Criticism.com.

Beginning in September 2001, Prof. Kevin Moore (Music) launched a three-year concert program to present all 32 Beethoven piano sonatas. The performances were delivered through Civic Morning Musicals at the Hosmer Auditorium in the Everson Museum of Art.

Beginning in 2002, WCNY public television aired *The Ivory Tower Half Hour*, a weekly round table discussion providing commentary on local, regional and national news events. One of the original panelists, Professor Tara Ross (History) helped to make the show Central New York's highest-rated, locally produced non-news show.

Prof. Barbara Davis (Modern Languages) produced exhibits marking OCC's first commemoration of Black History Month

On the set of WCNY's *The Ivory Tower*. (from left) Bob Greene, Cazenovia College; Tara Ross, Onondaga Community College; Bob Spitzer, SUNY Cortland; David Rubin, Syracuse University.

DONALD M. MAWHINNEY, JR.

In 1961, Donald M. Mawhinney, Jr. was appointed as one of the founding trustees of Onondaga County's new community college by John Mulroy, Chair of the County's Board of Supervisors. Mr. Mawhinney was a logical choice to be part of the new venture. Since 1958, both he and Mr. Mulroy had been members of the County's governing body. Additionally, the two had voted in favor of the legislation, in 1961, which recommended that a community college be formed.

In the years since that initial appointment, Trustee Mawhinney has served in numerous capacities. He was Chair from January 1976 to July 1978 and again from October 1986 to August 1991; Vice Chair for two, two-year terms; Secretary for two, two-year terms; and Chair of the Finance, Building and Grounds and the Public Relations Committees. He also has been the College's state and national legislative liaison for many years. In addition to his work as a trustee, he was a founding member of the OCC Foundation Board of Directors, serving for 22 years.

Recognizing his "unparalleled contributions" to the College, the Board of Trustees rededicated the Academic One building in his honor as Donald M. Mawhinney, Jr. Hall in June 2006. In his remarks, Mr. Mawhinney noted that community colleges were finally receiving well-deserved recognition in the SUNY system. In May 2007, he received the New York State Community College Trustees Founding Trustee Award, recognizing his 46 years of service (at that time) and his tenure as the longest serving trustee in the SUNY system. And for being one of the longest serving trustees in the nation, the Association for Community College Trustees presented him with a Trail Blazers award in 2010.

"We are fortunate that we have such a committed supporter of our community college in Don Mawhinney," said County Executive Joanie Mahoney when she reappointed him as a trustee in 2009. "His guidance and knowledge are of great advantage to the College and community alike, and I am grateful for his continued service to Onondaga County."

Donald M. Mawhinney, Jr.

and contributed the African American photograph collection housed in OCC's library. Her book *Syracuse African Americans* was published in 2005, and her book *Jewish Community of Syracuse* was published in 2011.

In the classroom, History Professor Joe Agonito's students could expect a thorough analysis of events, especially those relating to the United States frontier and the Plains Indians. After ten years of intense research, he and his wife, Rosemary, pieced together fragments of details to bring to life *Buffalo Calf Road Woman: The Story of a Warrior at Little Big Horn*, an award-winning publication that added to his acclaim for earlier articles and documentaries.

OCC faculty provided the backbone of many local community theater groups. Prof. Donna Stuccio (Criminal Justice) used police officers as her protagonists in two plays, *Blue Moon* and *The Job*. The sequel to *Blue Moon*, *elegy in blue*, was produced at Jazz Central in Syracuse in 2010.

For more than 20 years, Prof. David Feldman (English/Journalism) was a playwright and the guiding spirit of local community theater productions, especially as artistic director for the reading of new works by local and national playwrights. Prof. Feldman's own plays were produced in the Boston area, New York City and Los Angeles, as well as in Central New York. An endowed Journalism Scholarship was established in his name upon his retirement in 2002.

In 2007, Prof. Karl Klein (Computer Studies) received OCC's first "e-nitiative" grant from the Kauffman Foundation through a partnership with Syracuse University, which enabled him to expand entrepreneurship opportunities for students by creating an online course focusing on "ecopreneurship."

In April 2007, Prof. Marty Martino (Meteorology) used funding from a President's Incentive grant to install a wireless, solar-powered weather station on the roof of Ferrante Hall. The data, which is used for Meteorology courses, is updated continuously and available on the OCC Weather Website. In its first winter of operation, the station fell victim to a series of ice storms. The wind vane and anemometer (measuring wind speed) froze with a quarter-inch coating of ice. Prof. Martino climbed onto the roof of Ferrante Hall in the dead of winter and melted the ice with his bare hands. Although he was able to get the instruments thawed after the first ice storm, the second one encased the station in a half-inch coating of ice, so it was left to Mother Nature to eventually thaw out the equipment.

In 2007, Prof. Theresa Mohamed (English) published a book entitled *Essays in Response to Bill Cosby's Comments About African American Failure*. Prof. Ednita Wright (Human Services) contributed an essay for the book, "Substance Abuse in African American Communities."

OCC adjunct faculty members were also familiar faces and voices throughout Central New York. Gretchen Kinnell, adjunct in the Human Services and Teacher Education Department and retired from Child Care Solutions, has written *No Biting: Policy and Practice in Toddler Programs* for parents and early childhood educators. Kevin Stack, adjunct professor in the Architecture and Interior Design Department, President of Northeast Natural Homes and nationally recognized leader and expert in green home building, sustainability and Biomimicry, built the first LEED-certified Gold home in New York State on Skaneateles Lake (certified by the USGBC in 2007).

Psychology adjunct Elizabeth Fern has supported the local theater and the performing arts community through work with The Talent Company, Salt City, Opening Night Productions and through performances with the Coachmen Band.

Prof. Paul Bertan (Chemistry) instructing a class in fall 2008.

Prof. Marty Martino (Meteorology) atop Ferrante Hall with the campus weather station in October 2009.

Prof. Donna Stuccio (Criminal Justice) (second from left, back row) with the cast of her most recent play *elegy in blue*, fall 2010. (Courtesy of Prof. Donna Stuccio)

"I met many friends and mentors with whom I still keep contact. It was an amazing two years. OCC has the most wonderful Math Department of all SUNY schools."

– Patricia A. Owens (Adolescence Education, 2007)

DIVERSE AND ENGAGED STUDENTS

OCC welcomed its first international students in its very first year of operation (1962-1963). Since that time, the College has continued to enroll students from around the globe, and the campus on the hill was seen as welcoming by many international students. In the spirit of continuing and expanding the internationalization of the College, in November 2000, President Sydow created an outreach program with the South African nation of Namibia, beginning with her visit to that nation before she came to OCC. She invited a delegation from the University of Namibia (UNAM) to visit Onondaga, and prior to the departure of Vice Chancellor of UNAM Peter Katjavivi, a sister college agreement was established. This agreement led to several exchange visits between OCC and UNAM, including a 2003 trip to Namibia for Prof. Victor Lisnyczy's photography class, which resulted in an extensive photo exhibit.

By 2006, OCC had students on campus from Brazil, Canada, China, England, Germany, Ghana, Israel, Ivory Coast, Japan, Latvia, Mongolia, Nepal, Nigeria, Poland, Senegal, Saudi Arabia, South Korea, Sweden, Tanzania and Thailand. The College also welcomed dozens of students from Sudan, including several "Lost Boys of Sudan" who in 2008 presented President Sydow with a plaque expressing their gratitude to the College that had "made so many opportunities available" to them. Among the various student clubs and organizations, an International Students Club carried on the tradition of the 200-member International Club of the 1970s.

While opportunities for students to study abroad had existed since the 1970s, the 2000s saw a blossoming of opportunities and increased college support for students to engage in learning off-campus and around the world. For example, beginning in 1995, Prof. Meg Harris (Geology) partnered with Dr. James Haynes of SUNY Brockport to offer Geology of the Bahamas, a two-week field course on the island of San Salvador. In 2001, six OCC students in a service-oriented international study course taught by Dr. Emmanuel Awuah built houses in the West African nation of Ghana.

Starting in 2008, students could join Professors Rick McLain and Hiram Smith (History) for a summer study-abroad option in Latin America. The enthusiasm of students led to an expansion of the program. In 2010, Professors McLain and Smith, along with Prof. Arnaud Lambert (Anthropology) and Prof. David VanArsdale (Sociology), presented a study-abroad program to Mexico.

CAMPUS SAFETY AND SECURITY

One of the consequences of opening residence halls was a rethinking of campus safety and security. At that time (September 2006), a contract security guard agency provided those services. However, the 24/7 residential student population required coverage that had not previously existed on campus. One of the first solutions was to hire off-duty Onondaga County Sheriff's Deputies on nights and weekends, but it did not take long to realize that law enforcement and campus security require different skill sets.

Utilizing recently passed New York State legislation, the solution was to hire and train Campus Peace Officers, who would possess most of the rights and responsibilities of a police officer on campus, including carrying firearms. The College hired Frank Lawrence (Director of Campus Safety and Security, 2007-2008; center of photo) to create the Peace Officer training program and the Public Safety force.

To prepare new officers, OCC developed a 13-week, 480-hour professional law enforcement training program at the College's Public Safety Training Center (PSTC) in Coyne Hall. The first class of 16 Campus Peace Officers graduated in August 2007. The 24-hour security offered by the Campus Peace Officers and the Blue Light emergency phone system throughout the grounds also demonstrated the expectations of a post-9/11 world.

Under the leadership of Doug Kinney, Vice President of Campus Safety and Security, Onondaga continued to enhance campus safety, rolling out an innovative Student Patrol Program, instituting new protocols, and implementing a new campus emergency notification system designed by Fred Carpenter, Enterprise Systems Administrator, that saved the College an estimated $200,000 and was recognized by the League for Innovation in the Community College with a 2011 Innovator of the Year Award.

Prof. Meg Harris (yellow shirt) instructs students in her Geology of the Bahamas course in January 2005. (Courtesy of Prof. Meg Harris)

The Lost Boys are among thousands in Sudan who fled their villages due to the violence of a long-standing civil war. After spending years in refugee camps, several Lost Boys were resettled in Syracuse and some became OCC students. In October 2008, three of them presented a plaque of appreciation to President Sydow. Pictured above (from left) are Carl Oropallo from St. Vincent de Paul Church, OCC students Kerubino Kang Guot and Atem Anyang Abik, President Debbie Sydow, Gabriel Bol Deng (Mathematics & Science, 2004), Adjunct Prof. Penny Kim (Counseling) and Eunice D. Williams, OCC Chief Diversity Officer.

In summer 2009, Prof. Christine Kukenberger (Art) offered an art course in Italy. In the month that students lived in the city of Florence, they studied the history of the art and culture of Renaissance Italy and related periods. They visited every major museum of the city, studied the Italian masters and toured dozens of Florence's churches. Above, Prof. Kukenberger is pictured with students in Venice, Italy (2009), with the Basilica Cattedrale Patriarcale di San Marco (St. Mark's Cathedral) in the background. (Courtesy of Professor Christine Kukenberger)

A Haudenosaunee dancer performs in Storer Auditorium as part of the celebration of Native American Heritage Month, November 2003.

STUDENT AUTHORS, ARTISTS, PHOTOGRAPHERS AND JOURNALISTS

In 2004, the first edition of a student literary magazine called *Parnassas* was published with English Professors Yvonne Fish-Kalland, Kristen Brumfield and Paul Aviles serving as editors. By 2006, a growth in student involvement led to the formation of The Literary Society as a student club to oversee the editing and publication of a literary magazine called *Textuality*.

In May 2010, Editor-in-Chief Chris Huntley, along with student writers and editors, were proud to have the student newspaper, *The Overview*, recognized with several awards by the Syracuse Press Club. The recognition was quite a turn around for the student newspaper, which folded most recently in 2003 and had only been sporadically produced since that time.

COMMUNITY ENGAGEMENT

Community engagement has always been an integral part of the Onondaga identity. President Sydow served on the inaugural Executive Committee of New York Campus Compact, the statewide service learning organization. She encouraged service learning on campus through President's Incentive grants, which enabled participating faculty to infuse service learning into their courses. Prof. Nina Tamrowski (Political Science) and Prof. Emmanuel Awuah (Sociology) created the Service-Learning Committee in fall 2002 to share best practices, raise awareness and train other OCC faculty in this learner-centered pedagogy that stresses civic engagement. Since 2004, the College has sponsored four regional service-learning workshops in collaboration with the OCC Teaching Center and

POORHOUSE CAMPUS

As County Executive Nicholas J. Pirro was preparing to leave office in 2007, President Sydow made one final appeal. With enrollment booming and physical capacity increasingly limited, Sydow proposed College utilization of the remaining, long abandoned County Poorhouse (established 1827) property north of Route 173 across from the main campus. With Pirro's support, Sydow appealed to the Onondaga County legislature to transfer the 48-acre parcel and its two structures to the College, and County Resolution #210 made the transfer official on December 4, 2007.

The Board of Trustees supported utilization of H-1, the second hospital building, to house all community-based programs, including the Regional Higher Education Center (RHEC). Established during the 2004-2005 academic year in response to community demand for baccalaureate and graduate degree options on the OCC campus, the RHEC and all Continuing and Extended Learning operations moved in spring semester 2011 to their new location.

RHEC is made up of both public and private four-year colleges that make their senior-level degree programs available on the Onondaga campus. "The creation of the Regional Higher Education Center is unique in Central New York," said Sydow, in announcing the new facility. "By offering a convenient location and a variety of undergraduate and graduate degree options, RHEC allows local students to work toward their educational goals while remaining close to home on the Onondaga campus and saving on transportation costs."

"This is hallowed ground," said Sydow as she toured the property set aside for the poor and indigent in the late 19th and early 20th centuries. She spoke eloquently about the care of the property and two unmarked burial grounds now covered with brush. "We want to honor these people who were relegated to the Poorhouse without money or hope" by devoting the building and land to education. "To take a place that was once used for people who were homeless or indigent or infirm, to take it and turn it around into a place of hope, a spot that students can use as a launching pad for a start on their own mobility, seems almost beautifully poetic," said Sydow.

President Debbie Sydow and SUNY Chancellor Nancy L. Zimpher tour the former County Poorhouse Hospital building in August 2009, prior to renovations.

H-1 building under renovation in March 2010.

In 2000, then-First Lady Hillary Rodham Clinton made a stop at OCC as part of her New York senatorial campaign. She was welcomed by OCC's first female president (Sydow) and spoke in the College's Founders' Room (later converted to the Academic Computing Center) in Coulter Library.

"I am so grateful for my Marsellus Family Scholarship, which made it possible for me to attend OCC after being laid off. OCC is just what I needed at one of the most trying times of my life."

– Dianne
(Business Administration, 2004)

Phi Theta Kappa Honor Society students participate in the 2007 Literacy Festival.

Director of the Educational Opportunity Program (EOP) Corey Hudson (right) and Program Associate Kiersten King (center) work with students during a study session, March 2008.

the New York Chapter of Campus Compact. By 2009-2010, the service-learning program at OCC had grown to include 720 students engaged in service-learning opportunities that contributed over 4,500 hours of service back to the community.

One of the President's Incentive grant supported service-learning projects during the 2003-2004 academic year involved Electronic Media Communications students working with the Syracuse Alternative Media Network to mentor at-risk teens participating in the Youth ACTION Program of Eastside Neighbors in Partnership (ENIP). OCC students served as coordinating producers of a documentary produced by the youth on violence in the neighborhood as part of ENIP's Anti-Violence Organizing Campaign. The project culminated in a special screening and poster exhibit at the Onondaga Historical Society in May 2004. In April, along with Prof. Linda Herbert (Electronic Media Communications) and Prof. Awuah, the students presented at the Northeast Regional Campus Compact Conference on Service-Learning in Worcester, Massachusetts. Five of

the youth, most of whom had never left Syracuse before, also attended to share their story of collaboration.

In 2008, Onondaga Community College partnered with the Onondaga County Board of Elections to recruit new poll workers from among students enrolled at Onondaga Community College in order to help prevent an anticipated shortage of qualified poll workers for the November 2008 election. With grant support from the US Election Assistance Commission, approximately 190 students completed the training to become poll workers, and approximately 135 students served as poll workers, or in alternative roles assisting the Onondaga County Board of Elections. Election commissioner Ed Ryan remarked, "The idea that we could have a continued infusion of capable, computer-literate poll workers is a huge plus for us in our striving to continually improve our roster of poll workers." The project supported the Board of Elections and had a strong impact on students, with 98 percent of student respondents reporting that they "felt a commitment to voting in the future."

ENGAGEMENT IN THE ARTS

JAZZ FEST

Out of a flurry of new on-campus programming designed to re-engage the community in the early 2000s, one very special arts activity at OCC created a community buzz, and drew mega-crowds. At the invitation of President Sydow, in June 2001, Frank Malfitano (Jazz Fest Founder and Director; Humanities and Social Sciences, 1967) and Jazz Fest Productions brought the internationally renowned, largest free jazz festival in the Northeast to the OCC campus. For nearly 20 years, the Syracuse Jazz Fest, a weekend of jazz by world-famous artists, had been hosted at a number of different sites, including Longbranch Park and Clinton Square. Headline artists have included Natalie Cole, Aretha Franklin, The Dave Brubeck Quartet, Dr. John, Smokey Robinson and Diane Schuur. In 2010, the College marked its 10th anniversary as host of Syracuse Jazz Fest.

Sydow and Malfitano agreed at the beginning that the educational component of the Syracuse Jazz Fest would become even more prominent with the festival's move to campus. Each year, over 300 students are invited to participate in the Jazz Fest Education Program directed by Steve Frank (Director of OCC's Jazz Band and a band director in the West Genesee School District). Students are given the experience of performing on a professional sound stage and attend clinics, master classes, workshops and meet-the-artists sessions presented by some of the greatest jazz musicians in the business. The expansion of the Education Program received support from corporate sponsors and local foundations over the years, including the Allyn Foundation, Central New York Community Foundation, Gifford Foundation, John Ben Snow Foundation, Rockefeller Philanthropy Advisors, Triad Foundation and Verizon Foundation. As examples of the more than 70 educational sessions that Jazz Fest has provided for the community, in 2004, banjo great Tony Trischka hosted

an open rehearsal, explaining to students how his group puts a chart together and how the group works. Saxophonist James Carter concluded his workshop and wandered over to the workshop being offered by Gerard Gibbs on the Hammond B-3 organ to have an impromptu "after-hours" jam session. And trumpeter and Grammy award winner Randy Brecker returned several times to offer workshops and clinics, as did Wynton Marsalis. "A life-changing, magical experience" is how one Music student described the educational programming, and the festival itself.

STUDENT EXHIBITS

In 2000, the campus hosted the Scholastic Art Competition for the first time, providing a location for art students in grades 7-12 from across Central New York to display their work for judging. During the several months each spring when the student art work is displayed, corridors of the Whitney Applied Technology Center transform into a gallery, exhibiting paintings, drawings, photography and sculptures. Also, each May since 2001, the campus has welcomed Feats of Clay, which spotlights the varied and creative ceramics art education programs in high schools throughout Onondaga County and Central New York.

ARTS ACROSS CAMPUS

To put a spotlight on Onondaga's music, art, photography and other signature programs—and convinced that community arts organizations eager to bolster audiences would be ready

In 2001, the College hosted the Syracuse Jazz Fest for the first time. Director Frank Malfitano makes the announcement from the podium in December 2000. Behind him are (from left) President Debbie L. Sydow, U.S. Congressman James Walsh, County Executive Nick Pirro, President of M&T Bank Matt Schiro and Senior Vice President for M&T Bank Chris Papayanakos.

Each year, Jazz Fest draws 60,000-80,000 visitors to the campus. Above is the

partners—President Sydow established the Arts Across Campus (AAC) initiative in 2003. She charged a task force headed by Art Professor Andy Schuster to submit recommendations on physical space, budgets and programming. From 2003 to the time of this publication, AAC has partnered with nearly every local arts organization (Everson Museum, SSO, Syracuse Stage, Sculpture Space, etc.) to present an annual schedule of concerts, drama, films, art exhibits and public art.

New gallery space in the atrium of the Whitney Applied Technology Center, renovation of Storer Auditorium and its entrance area, renovation of the Ann Felton Multicultural Center and creation of The Gallery under Storer Auditorium were all part of AAC. The performances, films, exhibits and public art featured through Arts Across Campus each year enhanced the overall learning experience available to students and expanded access to the arts for the Central New York community. "The performances were amazing, and the rehearsals were some of the most beneficial learning experiences I have ever had," proclaimed one enthusiastic Music student who attended every AAC program in 2008-2009.

By 2011, there were 12 monument-sized sculptures on campus, including *Herculeum* and *Maiden Syracuse* by the late Rodger Mack. A self-guided map makes it easy for employees, students and visitors to enjoy a Public Art Walking Tour right on the OCC campus. Through such programs, OCC is building a cadre of artists and arts patrons for the future.

A WISE INVESTMENT

In half a century, OCC's impact on the community has met and even exceeded the dreams of its early founders. From recent high school graduates to career changers to returning veterans, OCC remains the gateway to college and to new opportunities for individuals throughout the Central New York community. OCC alumni sustain and lead local businesses, making up a significant segment of the local workforce. Civic and educational leaders with OCC on their résumé are now headline makers.

Cited in a December 2007 issue of *Community College Week* as one of the fastest-growing community colleges in the United States, OCC remains in every way the community's college. The College earned regional, state and national recognition for academic excellence, services for student-veterans, and commitment to sustainability and civic engagement. *University Business* magazine recognized Onondaga Community College as a "2010 Model of Efficiency." In 2011, *G.I. Jobs* magazine named Onondaga Community College as one of its 2012 Military Friendly Schools. The Aspen Institute College Excellence Program recognized Onondaga as among the top ten percent of community colleges nationwide, and *The Chronicle of Higher Education* recognized Onondaga as a top producer of Fulbright scholars.

In 2011, Onondaga Community College's vision is that "Students will discover an inclusive and welcoming environment that supports achievement of the highest potential. By nurturing lifelong learning, academic excellence, community engagement and service, global perspectives and open minds, Onondaga will enrich and enhance the quality of life in Central New York and beyond." By achieving that vision, the College enables individuals of all backgrounds and social circumstances to *explore*, *discover* and *transform* their lives through higher education.

The Honorable Joseph E. Fahey, Onondaga County Court Judge and 1969 OCC General Studies graduate, said it best: "This college is one of the best investments this community has ever made."

view of the audience from the Main Stage in June 2008.

Student art work from Central New York secondary schools on display in the Atrium of the Whitney Applied Technology Center during the 2003 Scholastic Art Competition.

Afterword
By Debbie L. Sydow, Ph.D.

On July 1, 2000, just two weeks shy of my 39th birthday, I arrived for my first day of work as Onondaga Community College's new president, the seventh permanent president in its history. However, as I was frequently reminded at the time, I was the fifth president in five years, and number thirteen if all acting and interim presidents were included in the total. Mindful of the College's proud but tempestuous history, I unpacked my few boxes and quickly set out to gain a working understanding of OCC—its culture, values and aspirations—and most of all, its people. By the end of December, I had filled a dozen legal pads with handwritten notes from more than 100 individual and small group meetings with students, alumni, board members, employees, retirees and corporate and community leaders. With the goal of synthesizing disparate interests into a shared vision, I posed only two questions: What is it that makes you proud of OCC? What changes are required to make the College even more effective in fulfilling its mission?

What I learned from those early meetings, and what has been reinforced over the course of more than a decade of service as president, is this: Onondaga Community College is one of the most reputable and successful community colleges in the nation, and it is unquestionably one of our region's most valuable resources. As the 50-year history shows, from the early 1960s to the present day, highly motivated and extraordinarily capable, creative and passionate individuals have—like fine artisans—painstakingly crafted an institution of higher education that has earned its reputation for academic excellence. There is not always agreement on the means, but everyone is aligned on the end goal, and that is student success and the success of our Central New York community. Despite the peripheral din of OCC's storied quarrels and commotion, at the heart of the institution is a calm, intense dedication to students.

At age 50, the College is vibrant, energetic and dynamic, a reflection perhaps of its magnificently diverse student body. Likely as a result of OCC's emergence in the social upheaval of 1960s America, the notion that education is the great "equalizer" has become a central philosophical feature and a defining characteristic of the College. By safeguarding the quality of its academic programs and by keeping those programs affordable and accessible for local families, Onondaga contributes to social justice, providing life-changing opportunities for individuals of all ages, backgrounds, ethnicities and socio-economic circumstances. In this way, Onondaga's history and core values reflect the history and values of the community college movement in the United States, a movement that in less than a century created for millions a gateway to mainstream America.

OCC's success as a gateway to a better life is evidenced by the accomplishments and contributions of alumni who are represented in virtually every industry in Central New York and beyond. They are architects, lawyers, artists, CEOs, media professionals and engineers. They are first responders, law enforcement officers and firefighters protecting the safety of local citizens. They are counselors, teachers and administrators in regional schools and colleges. They are accountants, computer programmers, telecommunications professionals, caterers, automotive technicians and small business owners. They are registered nurses, licensed technicians and physicians in area hospitals. Onondaga Community College's value to the community since 1961 can best be measured by the significant contributions that its more than 40,000 alumni—the vast majority of whom are local residents—have made to area businesses, non-profit organizations, the regional economy, and to the quality of life in Central New York.

For all those visionary civic leaders, board members and community advocates who have contributed their time, talent and resources, and for all those professionals who have dedicated their careers to OCC, it is enormously gratifying that community colleges have risen to become the dominant force in American higher education. In 2011, community colleges enroll more than half of the nation's college students, a trend that will likely continue. The stigma of "colleges of last resort" that lingered throughout the 20th century faded as individuals and families choosing colleges became increasingly less concerned about the prestige factor, and more concerned about earning a solid and lasting return on their educational investment.

By 2011, a postsecondary credential was required for most jobs, and as the knowledge-economy continues to expand, so will the need for lifelong learning. Community colleges are particularly well positioned to respond to these needs, as evidenced by the fact that President Barack Obama's administration and major private foundations, including the Lumina Foundation and the Bill and Melinda Gates Foundation, are presently directing funding to community colleges as a way to significantly increase the number of U.S. workers who attain degrees, certificates and other industry-recognized credentials by 2020. The goal is to improve the nation's economic competitiveness. With community colleges in the national spotlight as the single best solution for addressing workforce readiness, and with enrollment at an all-time high of over 12,000 students, Onondaga Community College is poised for continued success.

But what will success look like in 2012 and beyond? By the end of 2010, with the economy in disarray and government revenues tumbling, many colleges in New York and across the country had cut programs, laid off employees and raised student tuition to balance budgets. Although the financial picture at Onondaga Community College has been stable due, in part, to disciplined fiscal management and an increasingly favorable public perception, a disturbing shift in public policy threatens the integrity and stability of public higher education. To honor our commitment to open enrollment into the future will require that public colleges find new ways to inspire greater public interest and support. Long-term financial sustainability will likely be guided by increasingly entrepreneurial public college leaders, individuals who are vigilant and disciplined in aligning academic offerings with community demand, aggressive in containing costs, and creative in tapping opportunities to generate new revenues.

The challenges are many, but the opportunities are infinite. New programming in response to shifting industry demands, new students emerging from dramatic demographic shifts, new technologies and new delivery systems will quickly transform the Onondaga Community College of 2012. Likewise, a changing Central New York economy and an aggressive agenda for the development of Syracuse and the region at large will present new opportunities as the College aligns its programs and services in support of local economic goals. Even as it evolves, the core values that established and shaped OCC—and have served it so well for 50 years—will endure.

Over the course of five decades, Onondaga has matured and grown to become one of the largest colleges in the State University of New York, second in size only to Syracuse University in the Central New York region. Still, OCC hasn't lost the feistiness and what some have described as the "grit" that emerged as institutional character traits even in its infancy. In a 2003 study, students transferring to Onondaga noted that they often felt pressure at their previous institutions to fit a certain stereotype of how a typical college student should appear and act. By contrast, OCC provided an educational environment in which returning veterans, recent high school graduates, adults training for a new career and, indeed, every individual felt accepted, supported, free to be themselves, and free to re-create themselves. No different from its students, or the indomitable Greater Syracuse community, Onondaga Community College refuses to be bound by a mold or to be limited by expectations. Evolving in direct relation to the community it serves, in its first 50 years, OCC has indelibly carved its own unique niche in the higher education landscape of the region.

Looking back has a way of sharpening the focus in looking forward. In the same way that I began my presidency, in conversation with those who knew the College best and were most invested in advancing its mission, in 2011 I am once again immersed in discussions with students, alumni, board members, employees, retirees, and corporate and community leaders about OCC's future. As we work to collectively chart Onondaga's course for the next five years in an updated strategic plan—*A Framework for Success 2016*—it is certain that the "community's college" will continue to deliver on its promise to provide all students the opportunity to explore their interests, discover their talents and transform their lives, a promise that is, has been, and will always be Onondaga's hallmark.

Francis E. Almstead

Dr. Marvin A. Rapp

Dr. Roger J. Manges

FRANCIS E. ALMSTEAD
President • February 1962 to December 1965
B.S. and M.S. from St. Lawrence University; science teacher Coeymans, Clinton and Bellmore (all NY) High Schools; NYS Education Dept. Supervisor of Secondary Education; U.S. Navy 1942 to 1946; U.S. Office of Education 1946; SUNY Executive Dean for Institutes and Community Colleges, developed state-wide ETV network for NYS Education Dept. After OCC, Mr. Almstead became Director of Technical Services and Research at St. Lawrence University 1966 to 1981. He died December 13, 1985, in Schenectady, NY.

DR. KARL D. LARSEN
Acting President • January 1966 to June 1966
B.A. and M.A. from University of Maine; Ph.D. from Penn State University; Chair of Physics Dept., LaFayette College, PA; Onondaga Community College Dean of Faculty. After OCC, Dr. Larsen went to the University of Bridgeport (CT) Physics Dept. He died February 23, 1990, in Bridgeport, CT.

DR. MARVIN A. RAPP
President • June 1966 to August 1973
B.A. from Colgate University, Magna Cum Laude and Phi Beta Kappa; Master's and Ph.D. from Duke University; U. S. Army Air Corps Intelligence (World War II); Vice President and Executive Dean of Nassau Community College, Mitchell Field, Long Island, NY 1961 to 1966. After OCC, Dr. Rapp was appointed Special Assistant to the Council on County Colleges in Trenton, NJ; continued his publications on the history of New York State with a particular interest in the Erie Canal and in Ontario County; served on the Board of Trustees for Finger Lakes Community College; and received the New York State Outstanding Community College Educator award. He died July 9, 1999, in Canandaigua, NY.

DR. ROY A. PRICE
Interim President • August 1973 to May 1975
B.A. in Philosophy from University of Chicago; Ed.M. and Ed.D. from Harvard; retired as Chair of Doctoral Programs in Social Science at Syracuse University. After serving as Interim President, he continued at OCC as a consultant. He died May 25, 1992, in DeWitt, NY.

DR. ROGER J. MANGES
President • May 1975 to May 1977
B.S., M.S. and Ph.D. from Purdue University; on the faculty of the School of Education at Purdue 1966 to 1974; Dean and Director of Fort Wayne Campus of Purdue University 1971 to 1974. After OCC, Dr. Manges became Vice President of Ball State University in Muncie, IN.

DR. ALBERT T. SKINNER
Interim President • July 1977 to October 1977
B.S. in Mathematics and Physics, Alfred University; M.A. Secondary School Administration, Columbia University; Ph.D. Higher Education, Syracuse University; taught at Patchogue and Smithtown (NY) High Schools; Sampson College (Geneva, NY); retired after 22 years as Dean and President of Cayuga Community College (Auburn, NY) 1958 to 1977. He died November 27, 1992, in Auburn, NY.

DR. ANDREAS A. PALOUMPIS
President • November 1977 to October 1983
B.S. in Biological and Physical Science from Illinois State; M.S. in Aquatic Biology and Ph.D. in Fisheries Biology from Iowa State University; U.S. Army Air Corps 1943 to 1946; first President of Winston Churchill College, Pontiac, IL; Vice President Academic Affairs at Illinois Central College, Peoria, IL. After OCC, Dr. Paloumpis became President of Hillsborough Community College, Tampa, FL, 1983 to 1997, and Interim President of Luzerne (PA) Community College, 2000 to 2002. He died January 6, 2006, in Tampa.

Dr. Andreas A. Paloumpis

Dr. Bruce H. Leslie

Dr. Neal A. Raisman

Dr. Debbie L. Sydow

DR. THOMAS D. SHELDON
Interim President • October 1983 to February 1984

B.A., M.A. and Ph.D. from Syracuse University; Principal and coach Minoa (NY) High School; Army service in World War II; 174th Tactical Fighter Group 1961 and 1962; Colonel US Air Force (retired) and Brigadier General NY Air National Guard; Deputy Commissioner of Elementary, Secondary and Continuing Education NYS Education Dept.; President Utica College of Syracuse University 1977 to 1982; Professor of Educational Administration at Syracuse University 1983; Interim President Mohawk Valley Community College (Utica, NY) 1983. After OCC, Dr. Sheldon became affiliated with the Baltimore (MD) School System and was a trustee of the National Aerospace Education Foundation. He died August 14, 2006, in Bridgeport, NY.

DR. BRUCE H. LESLIE
President • February 1984 to July 1996

B.A. Baldwin-Wallace College; M.A. Sam Houston State University; Ph.D. University of Austin, TX; Vice President Prairie State College (Chicago Heights, IL). After OCC, Dr. Leslie became Chancellor of the Community-Technical Colleges of Connecticut; Chancellor of Houston Community College 2001 to 2006; and since 2007, Chancellor of the Alamo Colleges in San Antonio, TX.

BARRETT L. JONES
Interim President • July 1996 to July 1997

Retired CEO and President of Key Bank of Central New York; OCC Board of Trustees 1987 to 1992 and Board Chair 1991 to 1992. In 2002, Mr. Jones established the Juanita Jones Crumrine Endowed Scholarship Fund at OCC to honor his mother.

DR. NEAL A. RAISMAN
President • August 1997 to June 1999

B.A. University of Massachusetts; M.A. and Ph.D. in English, University of Massachusetts; Assistant to President of University of Cincinnati; Dean of Arts and Sciences at Lansing (MI) Community College; President Rockland Community College, Suffern (NY) 1993 to 1997. After OCC, Dr. Raisman started a consulting firm; became affiliated with Colleges of Baltimore (MD) Council; and in 2009 was an educational consultant in the Columbus, OH area.

DR. JOSEPH J. BULMER
Acting President • July 1999 to June 2000

B.S. in Chemical Engineering from Rensselaer Polytechnic Institute; M.S. in Chemical Engineering and Nuclear Engineering from University of Michigan; Ph.D. in Nuclear Engineering from Rensselaer Polytechnic Institute; 24 years as manager and nuclear engineer at Knolls Atomic Power Laboratory; President Hudson Valley Community College (Troy, NY) 1979 to 1996; Interim President Sullivan County (NY) Community College. After OCC, Dr. Bulmer became Interim President Fulton-Montgomery (NY) Community College. He died October 6, 2006, in Saratoga Springs, NY.

DR. DEBBIE L. SYDOW
President • July 2000 to Present

B.S. in English, University of Virginia College at Wise; M.A. in English, Marquette University; Ph.D. in English, Indiana University of Pennsylvania; Vice President of Academic and Student Services at Mountain Empire (VA) Community College 1995 to 2000; Acting President in 1998 at Mountain Empire; Dean of Humanities and Social Sciences Division SW Virginia Community College at Richlands.

JOHN H. MULROY

John H. Mulroy, Onondaga County Executive from 1962 to 1987, always regarded Onondaga Community College as his greatest accomplishment. Some people called him "The Father of OCC." Whatever his title, John Mulroy clearly understood the need for both the liberal arts and technical education that OCC offered to County residents at all stages of life.

John Mulroy knew from experience the benefits that formal education could offer. After serving overseas as an Army Air Corps pilot in World War II, he returned to work on his family's dairy farm. He attended Syracuse University on a part-time basis and received his degree in History in 1953.

John Mulroy promoted OCC throughout his career in County government, beginning in 1958 when he joined the Onondaga County Board of Supervisors as the Supervisor from the Town of Marcellus. He chaired the Board's committee that investigated the feasibility of a community college. When he became Chair of the Board of Supervisors, he led them to approve the legislation that created and funded OCC in 1961. As the County's first Executive, he supplied firm guidance for 28 years to build a permanent campus and expand the range of courses offered. The College was just one of Mr. Mulroy's many pioneering achievements.

In recognition of his dedicated work on behalf of the institution, Mr. Mulroy received OCC's Distinguished Citizen Award in 1988 and the College's first honorary associate's degree in 2008, posthumously. His pivotal role in establishing Onondaga Community College and his passion for its mission are gratefully remembered.

John H. Mulroy

NICHOLAS J. PIRRO

During his 42 years in County government, Nicholas J. Pirro contributed significantly to the development of Onondaga Community College. In 1965, he joined the Onondaga County Board of Supervisors, representing the Northside of the City of Syracuse. Although his constituents opposed moving the College out of Downtown Syracuse, Mr. Pirro decided that once Onondaga Hill was chosen as the site, it was up to everyone to make OCC "the best community college possible."

As a member of the County Legislature and later its Chair from 1980 to 1988, Mr. Pirro said he was frustrated by the years of bickering about College affairs. As the working relationship between the College and the County matured, the tensions and conflicts, so prevalent in the early years, eased. In 1988 Mr. Pirro became County Executive, succeeding John H. Mulroy. As County Executive, Mr. Pirro was nearly always a speaker at OCC Commencement exercises, and on one such occasion his own son, Nick, Jr., was among the graduates. "This location [Onondaga Hill] has turned out well," he said in 2007 as he prepared to retire after 20 years as Onondaga County Executive. Through his years on the Board of Supervisors, in the County Legislature, and as County Executive, he had witnessed all seven OCC presidents deal with a wide range of College issues. In 2008, he received an honorary associate's degree in recognition of his work on behalf of the College. In 2009, Mr. Pirro accepted President Sydow's invitation to serve as Honorary Chair of the College's 50th Anniversary Committee.

Nicholas J. Pirro

JOANNE M. MAHONEY

Joanne "Joanie" M. Mahoney was elected in November 2007 and re-elected in 2011, and is the first woman to serve as County Executive for Onondaga County. She became Onondaga County's third County Executive on January 1, 2008, and chose to hold her swearing-in ceremony in the Great Room of OCC's Gordon Student Center, the first County Executive to be inaugurated on the campus.

Ms. Mahoney was raised in Syracuse and graduated from Corcoran High School, Syracuse University's Whitman School of Management and SU's College of Law. After spending time in private practice, she accepted a position with the Onondaga County District Attorney's Office and spent five years as a criminal prosecutor. Prior to becoming County Executive, she was elected Councilor-at-Large in the City of Syracuse (1999), where she served a four-year term.

Joanne M. Mahoney

2011 CAMPUS MAP

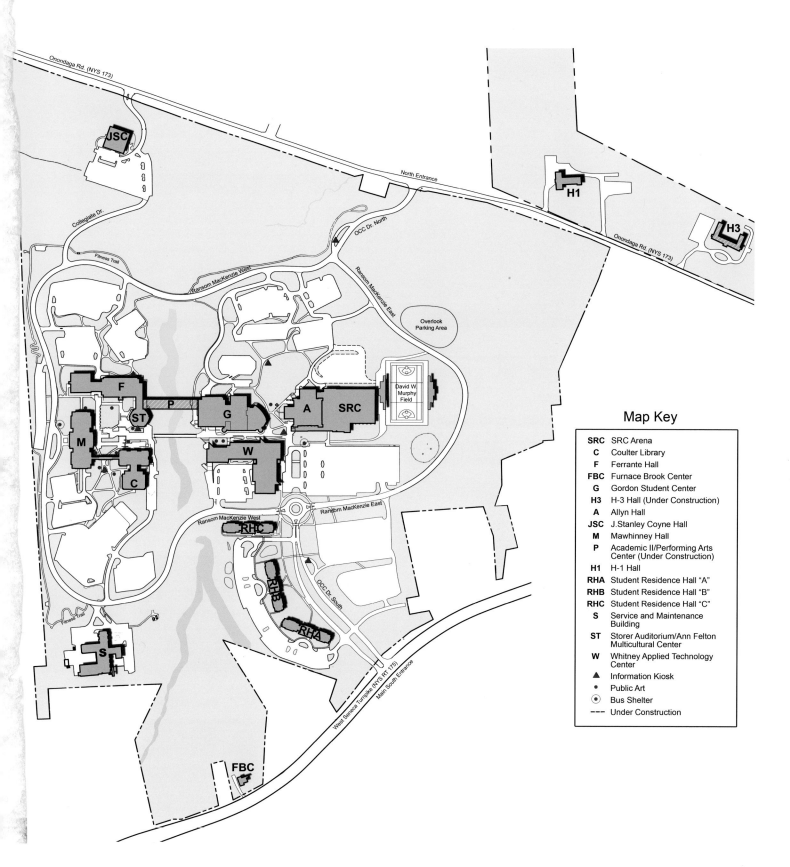

Map Key

SRC	SRC Arena
C	Coulter Library
F	Ferrante Hall
FBC	Furnace Brook Center
G	Gordon Student Center
H3	H-3 Hall (Under Construction)
A	Allyn Hall
JSC	J. Stanley Coyne Hall
M	Mawhinney Hall
P	Academic II/Performing Arts Center (Under Construction)
H1	H-1 Hall
RHA	Student Residence Hall "A"
RHB	Student Residence Hall "B"
RHC	Student Residence Hall "C"
S	Service and Maintenance Building
ST	Storer Auditorium/Ann Felton Multicultural Center
W	Whitney Applied Technology Center
▲	Information Kiosk
•	Public Art
⊙	Bus Shelter
- - -	Under Construction

Service and Maintenance Building

Occupied: **February 1970**
Architect: **Clark, Clark, Millis and Gilson**
Dedicated: **April 21, 1970**
Renovated: **1981 wing added; significant
renovation in 2005**

Sidney B. Coulter Library

Occupied: **January 1972**
Architect: **Clark, Clark, Millis and Gilson**
Dedicated: **June 24, 1973**
Renovated: **No major renovations**

The Library is named after attorney Sidney B. Coulter, a founding member of the OCC Board of Trustees (1961-1968). Spring 1976, the connecting bridge to Academic One [Mawhinney Hall] opened. (A feasibility study for the renovation of Coulter Library was included in the 2008-2013 Facilities Master Plan.)

Albert J. Gordon Student Center

Occupied: **January 1973**
Architect: **Clark, Clark, Millis and Gilson**
Dedicated: **June 24, 1973**
Renovated: **2005-2006; 2007**
Architect: **King + King Architects**

The Student Center is named after Albert Gordon, President of Penfield Manufacturing Co. and a founding member of the OCC Board of Trustees (1961-1966).

Nicholas Ferrante Hall
(Technology/Science/Paramedical Building)

Occupied: **September 1974**
Architect: **Clark, Clark, Millis and Gilson**
Contractor: **J.G.A. Construction Co.**
Dedicated: **December 9, 1974**
Renovated: **Phased renovations 2008-2010**

Ferrante Hall is named after Nicholas Ferrante, a local labor leader and founding member of the OCC Board of Trustees (1961-1971).

Storer Auditorium

Located in Ferrante Hall, Storer Auditorium is named after Simon B. Storer, an electrical engineer, who was a charter member of the local Technology Club. He willed his 200-acre sheep farm on Onondaga Hill to the Club, which later sold 24.72 acres to OCC, providing campus access from Route 175.

Donald M. Mawhinney, Jr. Hall
(Academic One)

Occupied: **January 1976 (except North Wing)**
Architect: **Clark, Clark, Millis and Gilson**
Contractor: **Kossoff & Sons**
Renovated: **Phased renovations 2007-2010**

In 2006, the building was renamed after attorney Donald M. Mawhinney, Jr., the longest serving member of the OCC Board of Trustees (1961 to present). (Spring 1976, the connecting bridge to the Library opened.)

Allyn Hall

Occupied: **Spring 1977**
Architect: **Clark, Clark, Millis and Gilson**
Contractor: **Visconti Construction**
Renovated: **2010–2011**

The Health and Physical Education Building was dedicated as Allyn Hall in December 2011 in honor of Bill and Penny Allyn, who contributed to the success of the College and its students through their generous philanthropic contributions, advocacy and volunteer service.

J. Stanley Coyne Hall

(formerly Unity Mutual Insurance; original construction 1973)
Occupied: **Unity Mutual, 1973-1991; OCC, 1991**
Renovated: **1991**

OCC originally named this building the EXCELL Center (Extension for Community Education and Life Long Learning). In 1997, it was renamed Coyne Hall in honor of J. Stanley Coyne in recognition of his philanthropic support of Onondaga and its students.

North Site

(rented space in Seneca Mall)
Occupied: **September 1999**

Ralph & Fay Whitney
Applied Technology Center

Occupied: **August 1999**
Architect: **Mitchell/Giurgola Architects**
Contractor: **Murnane Building Contractors, Inc.**
Dedicated: **November 1999**
Renovated: **2009 (relocation President's Office)**

The Whitney Applied Technology Center is named in honor of Ralph and Fay Whitney, recognizing their remarkable support of the College and its students. Mr. Whitney was a member of the Board of Trustees (1967-1983, including two terms as Chair) and of the Foundation Board of Directors (1980-2005).

Residence Halls
(Buildings A, B & C)

Occupied: **September 2006**
Architect: **Kideny Architects**
Contractor: **Hueber Breuer Construction Corp.**
Dedicated: **August 9, 2006, capacity 500 residents**
Renovated: **Reconfiguration (2007 & 2009) for additional 85 residents**

David W. Murphy Field

Occupied: **October 2008 (Phase I)**
Completed: **September 2009 (Phase II)**
Architect: **Bell & Spina Architects, P.C.**
Contractor: **Smith Site Development**
Dedicated: **April 17, 2009**

The stadium was named after David W. Murphy, member of the Board of Trustees (1998 to 2010) and Chair (2004 to 2010). Mr. Murphy was then Vice Chair of the Board and President of the Pioneer Companies.

H-1 Hall

(formerly County Poorhouse Building H-1: Second Hospital Building; original construction 1928-1929; Katherine Jackson Wing added 1968; acquired by OCC December 2007)

Occupied: **June 2011**
Renovated: **OCC conversion 2010 - 2011**

SRC Arena and Events Center

Occupied: **December 2011**
Architect: **Cannon Design**
Contractor: **LeChase Construction**

The Arena was named in recognition of SRC, an independent, not-for-profit research and development organization and its sub-sidiary, SRCTec, which pledged a $1.525 million gift in support of the Presidential Scholarship Program at OCC.

H-3

(formerly County Poorhouse Building H-3: Nurses' Building; original construction 1949-1950 acquired by OCC December 2007)

Occupied: **Scheduled for fall 2012**
Renovated: **2011-2012**
Projected Use: **Residence Halls**

Furnace Brook Retreat Center

(formerly Unity Church Retreat Center; original construction 1945; addition 1978; acquired by OCC August 2006)

Occupied: **Private Residence, pre-1996**
 Unity Church, 1996-2006
 OCC, 2012
Projected Use: **Future conference/retreat center; nature trails; access to residence halls via a walking path through the gorge**

Academic II
(Performing Arts Center)

Occupied: **Projected spring 2013**
Architect: **C&S Design**
Contractor: **Hueber-Breuer Construction Co.**

ACADEMIC PROGRAMS 1962 vs 2011

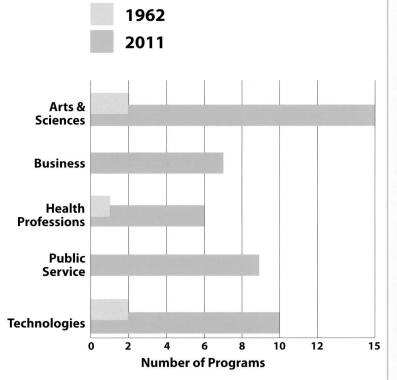

- 1962
- 2011

Arts & Sciences
1962: Humanities & Social Sciences, Mathematics & Sciences
2011: Architectural Tech, Art, Electronic Media Communications, Interior Design, Music, Photography, Adolescence Education, Childhood Education, Computer Science, Engineering Science, Environmental Tech, General Studies, Humanities & Social Sciences, Math & Science

Business
1962: None
2011: Accounting, Business Administration, Business Tech, Health Information Tech, Hospitality Management, Professional Communication, Professional Cooking

Health Professions
1962: Dental Hygiene
2011: Nursing, Physical Education & Exercise Science, Physical Therapist Assistant, Recreation Leadership, Respiratory Care, Surgical Tech

Public Service
1962: None
2011: Criminal Justice, Early Child Care, Fire Protection, Homeland Security, Human Services, Law Enforcement

Technologies
1962: Electrical Technology, Mechanical Technology
2011: Automotive Tech, Computer Engineering Technology, Computer Forensics, Computer Information Systems, Electrical Engineering, Line Mechanic-Utility Worker, Mechanical Tech, Microcomputer, Telecommunications, Web Tech

Chart categories (x-axis: Number of Programs, 0–15):
- Arts & Sciences
- Business
- Health Professions
- Public Service
- Technologies

ENROLLMENT

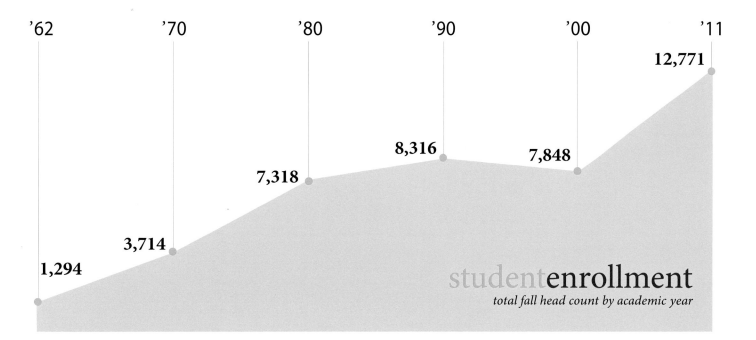

'62 — 1,294
'70 — 3,714
'80 — 7,318
'90 — 8,316
'00 — 7,848
'11 — 12,771

*student*enrollment
total fall head count by academic year

REGIONAL FINANCIAL IMPACT OF AN OCC EDUCATION

Since Onondaga Community College first opened its doors to students in 1962, the College has been serving the local community by creating jobs and income, providing area residents with easy access to higher education opportunities and preparing students for careers in the College's five-county service area.

Enrollment has grown from the College's original entering class to more than 18,000 credit-bearing students in 2008-09. The cumulative credit production of students has steadily increased over time, beginning with an estimated 4,000 credit hour equivalents (CHEs) in the College's first year to more than 5.8 million CHEs achieved by students since the College first opened its doors. Each of these CHEs achieved by students means added skills brought to the region once the student enters the local workforce. As thousands of former OCC students join or re-join the workforce year after year, the newly acquired skills attained by students have steadily accumulated in the workforce, leading to increased worker productivity and a more robust regional economy.

As the skills embodied by OCC's past students stockpile, a chain reaction occurs in which higher student earnings generate additional rounds of consumer spending. New skills and training also mean increased business output and higher property

OCC's service area embodies an estimated **2.3 million credit hour equivalents** that have accumulated in the workforce since the College first opened in 1962.

earnings is well documented and forms the basis for determining the benefits of education. As shown in Table 1, mean income levels at the midpoint of the average-aged worker's career increase for individuals who have attained higher levels of education. Adding direct and indirect effects of student productivity together (Table 2) yields a grand total of $384.1 million in added income. The $384.1 million omits the effect of educated workers on innovation and technical progress, which is generally labeled as "external" because it spills beyond businesses employing skilled workers. OCC's contribution to the local economy has been steadily accumulating since the College first opened 50 years ago, adding to the region's human capital as thousands of students enter the workforce year afer year. Former students who continue to live and work in the region today promote economic growth through their added skills, higher incomes and associated multiplier effects.

Former OCC students who have studied at the College over the past 50 years and who continue to work in the region today contributed **$384.1 million in added income** to OCC's five-county region in the analysis year.

Table 1: Expected income in OCC service area at midpoint of individual working career by education level

Education level	Income	Difference
Less than high school	$19,700	n/a
High school or equivalent	$30,600	$10,900
Associate's degree	$41,400	$10,800
Bachelor's degree	$59,400	$18,000
Master's degree	$71,700	$12,300

Source: Derived from data supplied by EMSI industry data and the U.S. Census Bureau. Figures are adjusted to reflect average earnings per worker in the five-county region.

income (i.e., earnings and value), causing still more consumer purchases and regional multiplier spending. The sum of all of these direct and indirect effects comprises the total impact of past student productivity on labor and non-labor income in the economy of the region. The correlation between education and

Table 2: OCC student productivity effect, 2008-09 ($ thousands)

	Labor Income	Non-labor Income	Total	% of Total
Total income in service region	$19,758,165	$10,087,559	$29,845,725	
Direct effect	$197,278	$99,504	$296,782	1.0%
Indirect effect	$59,606	$27,717	$87,324	0.3%
Total	$256,885	$127,221	$384,106	$1.3%

Source: EMSI impact model. This EMSI Report is based on data compiled in 2008-2009.

ACKNOWLEDGEMENTS

Celebrating the Promise: The First Fifty Years of Onondaga Community College (1961-2011) is the first written commemoration of Onondaga Community College. In 2002, President Debbie L. Sydow formed a steering committee to develop a "formal document chronicling the planning, establishment and evolution of the College" to "ensure that the content and spirit of Onondaga Community College's rich and eventful history [would be] accurately captured and properly preserved." Original members of the steering committee, which was charged to produce a readable, historically accurate account of OCC's history, included Dr. Joseph Agonito, Janet Agostini, Tom Burton, Dick Case, Dr. Barbara Davis, Frank Doble, David Feldman, Karen Hopkins, Marty Lewis, Nancy Licata, Anita Murphy, Rob O'Boyle, Melissa Reider, Dan Rizzo, Gail Rizzo, Connie Saldicco, Anthony Vadala and Yvonne Fish-Kalland. The History Steering Committee, which Dr. Sydow chaired, actively oversaw every phase of the project from 2002 to 2012 when the project was completed, and the College is deeply indebted to each of these individuals for their indefatigable enthusiasm, energy and effort.

Appreciation goes to the first researcher, interviewer and chronicler, Dr. Julian Vernet, a native of Kingston, Ontario, who conducted research for OCC in 2002, completed his Ph.D. in history at Syracuse University the same year, and taught at both SU and SUNY Cortland before becoming an Assistant Professor of History at Northern Michigan University.

Celebrating the Promise: The First Fifty Years of Onondaga Community College (1961-2011) is based largely upon the research, interviews and writings of Barbara Rivette. Rivette is a highly respected Onondaga County historian, journalist, author and editor. She has written many books on local history, as well as the history of printing and weekly newspapers in New York State, and her 50-year career in the daily and weekly newspaper business includes 14 years as executive editor of seven weekly newspapers in Onondaga and Madison Counties. In 2007, Rivette received the award for Excellence in Public History Projects and Publications from the state's Municipal Historians, and in 2004 she was recognized by the Onondaga Historical Association with its highest honor, the OHA Medal. OCC is forever indebted to Barbara Rivette for so ably capturing and telling the history of its first 50 years.

Co-Editors Kathleen L. Eisele, D.A. (English Department) and Timothy D. Stedman (Computer Studies Department) are commended for their outstanding work in the final stage of the project. Primarily responsible for final revision, editing, fact checking, and preliminary graphic design and layout, Eisele and Stedman contributed significantly to the final version of *Celebrating the Promise: The First Fifty Years of Onondaga Community College (1961-2011).*

Many others assisted along the way. In particular, the College thanks Onondaga Historical Association Curator of History Dennis Connors; Onondaga Town Historian L. Jane Tracy; the OCC Archives team of Prof. Rob O'Boyle, Viola Marcy and Barbara Roach; Dr. Agatha Awuah, Alex Cole, Kate Hill, Amy Kremenek, Nancy Martone, Nicole Schlater and Susan Tormey; and the many, many people who shared their memories and memorabilia.

Nicholas J. Pirro served as Honorary Chair of the 50th Anniversary Committee and in that capacity assisted greatly in promoting *Celebrating the Promise: The First Fifty Years of Onondaga Community College (1961-2011)* in the local community, which is deeply appreciated, as is the involvement of 50th Anniversary Community Advisory Committee members Tom Burton, Richard J. Calagiovanni ('68), Dick Case, Virginia Carmody, Dennis Connors, Dr. Kathy Eisele, Karin Franklin-King ('69), Terry Griffin, Amy Kremenek, Martha E. Mulroy, Jim Reith ('84), Barbara Rivette, Nancy Skahen, Tim Stedman, Sue Tormey, and Maureen McCarthy Tracy; and 50th Anniversary Special Events and Observances Planning Group members Philip Andon-McLane, Dr. Rob Bridge, Tina Brown, Michele Collins, Russ Corbin, Kim Court, Anne DeLand, Michele Ferguson, Nancy Gabriel, Shawn Gillen-Caryl, Kiersten King, Amy Kremenek, Sue Lamanna, Vi Marcy, Mike McMullen, Mike Mulholland, Anita Murphy, Rob O'Boyle, Shannon Patrie, Stephen Pierson, Vicki Powers, Tara Ross, Marguerite St. Claire, Elaine Taggart, Wendy Tarby and Eunice Williams.

In addition to images from OCC collections, the College wishes to acknowledge the use of such materials from the Onondaga Historical Association Museum & Research Center; the Town of Onondaga Historical Society; *The Post-Standard*; Cornell University; Onondaga County Executive's Office; Nicholas J. Pirro; and OCC employees and retirees. Historical background information came from *SUNY at Sixty—The Promise of the State University of New York* edited by John B. Clark, W. Bruce Leslie and Kenneth P. O'Brien, 2010, published by State University of New York Press, Albany.

The College expresses its sincere gratitude to Judy C. Flanagan, Carole Jesiolowski and the entire Data Key Communications team for their generous support of this publication. The expertise, guidance and support Data Key Communications provided to produce and publish *Celebrating the Promise: The First Fifty Years of Onondaga Community College (1961-2011)* was instrumental in bringing this project to fruition.

SPECIAL THANKS

OCC would like to thank the following companies for helping to make this 50th Anniversary book possible.

A-1 Trophy Co.
Alberta Crowe Letter Services
American Food & Vending Corp.
Architecteam
Ber-National Controls, Inc.
C&S Companies
CH Insurance, Inc.
Citizens Bank
CNY Laser Services
Community Bank N.A.
Coyne Textile Services
Delta Stratagem
EBSCO Subscription Services
Excellus BlueCross BlueShield
Haylor, Freyer & Coon, Inc.
Hiscock & Barclay, LLP
Hueber-Breuer Construction
   Company, Inc.
IKON Office Solutions, Inc.

Inficon
Keuka College
Latorra, Paul & McCann Advertising
Le Moyne College
Lockheed Martin Corporation
M&T Bank
MACNY
M/E Engineering, P.C.
Mohawk Valley Community College
Morrisville State College
Morse Manufacturing Company, Inc.
MVP Health Care
National Audio, Inc.
National Grid
Pasco
Pen & Trophy Center
Pioneer Companies
PRO-TEL People

Purcell's Paint & Wallpaper Co., Inc.
Riccelli Enterprises
Safety Council of Upstate New York
   Chapter of National Safety Council
SECNY Federal Credit Union
Seneca Data
Song Mountain Resort
SUNY College of Environmental
   Science & Forestry
SUNY Cortland
SUNY Empire State College
SUNY Upstate Medical University
Syracuse University
Sysco Syracuse
Thompson & Johnson Equipment Co.,
   Inc./Bobcat of Central New York
Utica College
Visiting Nurse Association of Central
   New York, Inc.